Secrecy

Secrecy

SILENCE, POWER, AND RELIGION

Hugh B. Urban

The University of Chicago Press   CHICAGO AND LONDON

The University of Chicago Press, Chicago 60637
The University of Chicago Press, Ltd., London
© 2021 by The University of Chicago
All rights reserved. No part of this book may be used or reproduced in any
manner whatsoever without written permission, except in the case of brief
quotations in critical articles and reviews. For more information, contact
the University of Chicago Press, 1427 E. 60th St., Chicago, IL 60637.
Published 2021

29 28 27 26 25 24 23 22 21 20   1 2 3 4 5

ISBN-13: 978-0-226-74650-0 (cloth)
ISBN-13: 978-0-226-74664-7 (paper)
ISBN-13: 978-0-226-74678-4 (e-book)
DOI: https://doi.org/10.7208/chicago/9780226746784.001.0001

Library of Congress Cataloging-in-Publication Data

Names: Urban, Hugh B., author.
Title: Secrecy : silence, power, and religion / Hugh B. Urban.
Description: Chicago ; London : The University of Chicago Press, 2020. |
Includes bibliographical references and index.
Identifiers: LCCN 2020027441 | ISBN 9780226746500 (cloth) |
ISBN 9780226746647 (paperback) | ISBN 9780226746784 (ebook)
Subjects: LCSH: Secrecy—Religious aspects. |
Secret societies—Religious aspects.
Classification: LCC BL65.S37 U73 2020 | DDC 299—dc23
LC record available at https://lccn.loc.gov/2020027441

Contents

Preface: Secrecy, the Human Dress ∗ vii

Introduction ∗ 1
The Vestment of Power

CHAPTER 1
The Adornment of Silence ∗ 23
*Secrecy and Symbolic Power in
American Freemasonry*

CHAPTER 2
The Secret Doctrine ∗ 51
*The Advertisement of the Secret in the Theosophical
Society and the Esoteric Section*

CHAPTER 3
The Seduction of the Secret ∗ 79
Eros and Magic in Twentieth-Century Europe

CHAPTER 4
Secrecy and Social Resistance ∗ 103
The Five-Percenters and the Arts of Subversive Bricolage

CHAPTER 5
The Terror of Secrecy ∗ 137
Racism, Masculinity, and Violence in the Late Brüder Schweigen

CHAPTER 6
The Third Wall of Fire ∗ 165
Scientology and the Study of Religious Secrecy in the Twenty-First Century

Conclusions ∗ 187
*The Science of the Hidden: Secrecy and the Critical Study
of Religion in an Age of Surveillance*

Acknowledgments ∗ 207
Notes ∗ 209 *Index* ∗ 255

Preface

SECRECY, THE HUMAN DRESS

> *Terror, the Human Form Divine*
> *And Secrecy, the Human Dress*
>
> WILLIAM BLAKE, "A Divine Image"[1]

Secrecy is a topic that has fascinated, preoccupied, and frustrated me throughout my academic career, since at least my early years as a graduate student in the 1990s and continuing to the present day. Indeed, it is perhaps the only consistent theme that runs through my otherwise eclectic body of work, from my research on Hindu Tantra in northeast India to my study of the Church of Scientology in Cold War America, from my work on sexual magic in modern esotericism to my attempts to understand the dual obsessions with religion and concealment in American politics.[2] While much of my research focuses on South Asian religions, I also firmly believe in the value of comparison as a methodological tool and write extensively about modern American and European traditions, which are the primary focus in this book.

Following William Blake in the passage quoted above, I have long regarded secrecy as a phenomenon that is an intimate part of human behavior—as the "human dress"—and also one closely tied to human conceptions of the divine—though in ever-varied, historically specific, and sometimes violent or even terrifying forms. This book thus attempts to tie some of the many threads of secrecy that have preoccupied me for the last two decades.

✳ INTRODUCTION ✳

The Vestment of Power

The sacred and the secret have been linked from earliest times.
Both elicit feelings of . . . the "numinous consciousness" that combines
the daunting and the fascinating, dread and allure. Both are defined
as being set apart and seen as needing protection.

SISELLA BOK, *Secrets*[1]

Secrecy dominates this world, and first and foremost as the secret of domination.

GUY DEBORD, *Comments on the Society of the Spectacle*[2]

In the early decades of the twenty-first century, Guy Debord's observation about secrecy seems uncomfortably relevant and resonant. Debord published his *Comments on the Society of the Spectacle* in 1988 as a critical commentary on the strange dynamics of consumer culture, advertising, and politics during the latter days of the Cold War. From my perspective today—writing in the US amidst seemingly endless wars against terrorism, a highly secretive executive branch, and an ever-expanding national security apparatus with the power to surveil ever more aspects of our private lives—the role of secrecy as the "power of domination" seems at once ubiquitous, inescapable, and oddly normalized.[3]

Following the collapse of the Soviet Union and the end of the Cold War, many observers had optimistically hoped that questions of secrecy and surveillance would become less and less relevant to citizens of modern democracies. Today, such optimism seems not only overly optimistic but grossly naïve. As Gilbert Herdt observes, the problem of secrecy has resurfaced in an even more intense way in our post–Cold War generation, above all in the wake of the attacks of September 11, 2001, and other recent terrorist events. We are perhaps now entering a "new Cold War" era, with an even more intense concern with secrecy, surveillance, and concealment. As the US and other governments have assumed unprecedented new levels of secrecy to wage often clandestine wars against elusive terrorist enemies, we are left wondering what the fate of civil liberties and rights to privacy might be:

> [J]ust as we thought secrecy was about to disappear from the national consciousness, at least as a signifier of state security and patriotic nationalism, the events of September 11, 2001, shattered the present. Amidst the worldwide hunt for those terrorists responsible for the attack ... the US government deployed new and virtually unprecedented measures of secrecy.... Secrecy refuses to go away and may become even more contested than ever in the life of civil societies.[4]

We now inhabit a world in which terrorism—both foreign and home-grown—manifests daily and modern security states use mechanisms of surveillance that George Orwell could never have imagined. In the words of James Bamford, the widely read historian of the National Security Agency, we now live under the gaze of a kind of "big, big Brother" that far outstrips anything described in *1984*, raising profound questions of individual privacy and civil liberties.[5]

Meanwhile, with the advent of the presidency of Donald J. Trump, the powers of political secrecy and social spectacle have been taken to even more unexpected, often quite surreal extremes. As presidents refuse to disclose their financial records and dealings with foreign powers, the private data of ordinary citizens is marketed and/or stolen to manipulate everything from consumer preferences to voting outcomes.[6] We have perhaps have entered an era of "generalized secrecy" and "unanswerable lies" that Debord could not have imagined.[7] As philosopher Charles Barbour suggests, issues of secrecy, privacy, security, and surveillance have emerged as "arguably the central element of our contemporary political experience."[8]

Yet political domination is only one of many possible ends to which secrecy may be put. As I argue in the pages of this book, secrecy also ties very closely—perhaps intimately and inherently—to *religion* and to the unique sort of power that religious claims to transcendent authority can wield. Religion and secrecy intersect in this way not only in extreme phenomena such as clandestine religious terrorist groups (both foreign and homegrown) or in the concealment of sexual abuse by the Catholic Church and other institutions; rather, secrecy lies much closer to the heart of religion in its most mundane forms, as well. Even the great early scholars of religion had made this observation. As Rudolph Otto puts it in his seminal work, *Das Heilige*, the very idea of the sacred or *mysterium* essentially refers to "that which is hidden or esoteric, that which is beyond conception or understanding."[9] More recently, the anthropologist Michael Taussig has suggested that religion is in many ways the very embodiment and epitome of secrecy. For, among other things, religion involves the claim that there exists a *hidden or unseen reality*, a power or presence that lies beyond ordinary perception and yet holds a tremendous, even ultimate kind of authority. It is, in short, "the sensation that behind the appearance of things there is a deeper, mysterious reality that we may here call the sacred, if not religion."[10] One might even say that secrecy lies at the foundation of religion, not simply as an unseen *mysterium* but as the claim to hidden power that is the underlying architecture of both the institutional and sociological structure of most religions. "Without secrets, religion becomes unimaginable," as Paul C. Johnson eloquently puts it, "for religion is in its cultural sense a technology of periodic human access to extraordinary powers, which generally remain concealed, and in its social sense a group of people who share such a technology."[11]

A growing body of fine scholarship on religious secrecy is now available. Included in it is the classic sociological work of scholars such as Georg Simmel and Stanton Tefft;[12] many important anthropological and ethnographic studies of secrecy in specific cultural contexts, such as Beryl Bellman's work on West African secret societies, Gilbert Herdt's work on Papua New Guinea, Paul C. Johnson's work on Brazilian Candomblé, Ian Keen's work on Australian aboriginal traditions;[13] and titles in the burgeoning field of Western esotericism pioneered by Antoine Faivre, Nicholas Goodrick-Clarke, Wouter Hanegraaff, and others.[14]

And yet, despite the importance of the topic, surprisingly little scholarship attempts to theorize secrecy as a broader, cross-cultural, and comparative phenomenon in the history of religions. Apart from a handful of critical studies,[15] much literature on religious secrecy has been disappointingly vague, general, and theoretically undeveloped. As Kees Bolle puts it in his volume on *Secrecy in Religions*, secrecy is the "mystery at the heart of all religions," whether it is the "Way of the Tao that cannot be named" or the "secret rebirth of Christian mystics."[16] Yet what Bolle and others have failed to examine are the complex ways in which secrecy also ties to the mysterious workings of *power* and to the more *this-worldly, historical*, and *material* aspects of claims to hidden knowledge.

A Critical History of Religious Concealment:
Secrecy, Authority, and Symbolic Power

In the chapters that follow, I argue that secrecy is indeed a central and even defining aspect of that particular form of human activity called religion[17]; but it is so in ways that are more complex, more problematic, and also more interesting than most earlier scholars have supposed. Rather than simply "the mystery at the heart of all religion," secrecy is better understood as a crucial part of the construction of religious authority itself and a fundamental element in both the maintenance and the dismantling of religious power in relation to broader social, political, and historical interests.

My approach in this book is at once narrowly historical—tracing one specific genealogy[18] of religious secrecy—and broadly comparative—raising much larger theoretical and cross-cultural questions. First, on the historical level, I examine the rapid growth of religious secrecy, secret societies, and occultism in Europe and the US from the mid-nineteenth century to the present. Although we often think of this period as one of rapid industrialization, scientific development, and technological progress, it was also a period of intense interest in the hidden realms of esoteric knowledge, with a wild proliferation of secret brotherhoods and esoteric orders. In addition to myriad forms of Freemasonry and related fraternal organizations, the late nineteenth and early twentieth centuries also gave birth to a vast number of new esoteric groups such as the Theosophical Society; magical orders such as the Golden Dawn, Ordo Templi Orientis, and Wicca; various modern forms of Gnosticism; new religious movements such as Nation of Islam and Scientology; and countless others.[19]

On the broader comparative and theoretical level, I approach secrecy as a historian of religions, understood in Bruce Lincoln's more critical definition of the phrase. As Lincoln defines it, the history of religions is essentially a method that examines the more mundane, worldly, and human aspects of phenomena that are claimed to be transcendent, otherworldly, or supra-human: "To practice history of religions ... is to insist on discussing the temporal, contextual, situated, interested, human, and material dimensions of those discourses, practices, and institutions that characteristically represent themselves as eternal, transcendent, spiritual, and divine."[20] In the case of religious secrecy, we also need to examine the material, historical, social, and political aspects of claims to hidden knowledge—in short, to analyze the human and temporal "vestments" with which divine secrets are clothed.

Secrecy and Modernity: The Myth of Transparency

One common, persistent, and, I think, mistaken narrative found in both popular and academic discourse is that modern Western history represents the progressive decline of secrecy and the rise of a new ideology of transparency. In post-Enlightenment democratic societies, we are often told, the power of secrecy has gradually receded in the face of a more open, democratic, and rational society. As the historian Daniel Jütte has recently argued, the true "Age of Secrecy" developed in Europe from the fifteenth to the eighteenth centuries, at a time when arcane knowledge circulated widely in a complex "economy of secrets."[21] Yet by the late eighteenth and nineteenth centuries, Jütte suggests, this economy of secrets was increasingly eroded by a new emphasis on transparency and an "ideology of openness," which in turn accompanied a broader disenchantment and demystification of the world. In the wake of the Enlightenment and the Scientific Revolution, he writes, "there was a massive acceleration of 'de-secretization' in the Western world over the course of the nineteenth century. The secret lost its cosmological status. This also had to do with the gradual 'disenchantment of the world' to use Max Weber's famous words."[22]

A number of recent scholars, however, have profoundly challenged this narrative of disenchantment and demystification. As Jason Josephson-Storm persuasively argues, modern European and American societies are in many ways far from disenchanted but have in fact witnessed an explosion of interest in the realms of the occult, the paranormal, and the mystical since the mid-nineteenth century. Josephson-Storm identifies a whole series of new revivals of spiritual and occult movements throughout these decades, beginning with "the 1840s with the birth of spiritualism, the 1850s with its globalization, the 1870s with birth of theosophy ..., the 1890s with a host of the fin-de siècle occult movement, and so on, into the twentieth century.... [D]ebates over the reality of spirits and the supernatural have preoccupied Euro-American thinkers over the *longue durée* ... [E]ven at its high point, 'modernity' was itself enchanted."[23]

Similarly, I argue in this book, the period of the nineteenth and twentieth centuries was by no means primarily one of de-esotericization or a shift from a culture of secrecy to one of transparency (though that may have been the case in some spheres). Rather, it was also one of a tremendous new interest in secrecy, in the proliferation of secret societies, esoteric brotherhoods, occult movements, and in the mysteries of the exotic Orient. Far from a decline of the "economy of secrets," this period witnessed the rapid growth of an even more lively, diverse, and competitive esoteric economy. As Wouter Hanegraaff notes in his monumental study of Western esotericism, the nineteenth century was a thriving "occult marketplace," inspired in no small part by the media revolution of the modern period, which spawned an "unprecedented wave of literature" in the domains of "superstition, magic and the occult sciences."[24] This was in many ways the very *opposite* of a disenchantment but instead a widespread and aggressive attempt to "enchant" the modern world: "Much of occultism was driven by a conscious rejection of what Max Weber has influentially identified as the 'disenchantment of the world.' ... The occult [was] a discourse that primarily addressed the search for a more meaningful place for human existence within a society increasingly experiencing their surroundings as alienating."[25]

In this sense, the growth of secrecy in the modern period was a key part of the rapidly expanding religious economy of the nineteenth century. As the historian R. Lawrence Moore suggests in his classic work *Selling God*, nineteenth-century American culture was a kind of thriving, competitive spiritual marketplace, in which religious groups were increasingly forced to advertise themselves and compete with countless other cultural goods in a rapidly industrialized and commercialized society: "By degrees, religion itself took on the shape of a commodity ... religion looked for ways to appeal to all consumers, using the techniques of advertising and publicity employed by other merchants."[26] Secret societies, spiritualist groups, magical orders, and other forms of esoteric religion quickly emerged as an important new niche within this broader economy of spiritual goods. In just the last two decades of the nineteenth century, more than 150 fraternal organizations were formed in the US alone (most of them part of or modeled on Freemasonry), while countless new esoteric orders emerged across England, Europe, and North America.[27] At the same time, the late nineteenth century also produced the first academic scholarship on "secret societies," beginning with Giovanni De Castro's *Il Mondo Secreto* (1864) and Charles Heckethorn's *Secret Societies of All Ages and Countries* (1875). The latter warns that such groups, "both religious and political, are again springing up all sides," ranging from the Carbonari in Italy to the Thugs in India.[28] Far from declining in the nineteenth and twentieth centuries amidst a new age of transparency, the "economy of secrets" that Jütte describes expanded and proliferated rapidly, giving birth to a stunning array of new brotherhoods, neo-Gnostic revivals, and all manner of other esoteric communities.[29]

Meanwhile, if we look beyond the sphere of religion to the broader domains of politics, economics, and technology, it seems very difficult to describe the modern period as one of increasing transparency or a declining interest in secrecy. If anything, the contemporary political and economic spheres are saturated by an intense obsession with secrecy and the systematic mining, refining, and marketing of valued bits of knowledge. Particularly in the US, the concern with secrecy escalated rapidly in the twentieth century, above all in the wake of World War II and the onset of the Cold War. As Angus MacKenzie observes in his study of secrecy and the Central Intelligence Agency (CIA), the economic and ideological struggle between the US and Soviet Union led to a massive acceleration of government secrecy—and conversely, a rapid erosion of privacy and civil liberties: "The cold war provided the foreign threat to justify the pervasive Washington belief that secrecy should have the greatest possible latitude and openness should be restricted as much as possible—constitutional liberties be damned."[30] Alongside the rapid growth of the military-industrial nexus also grew an immense "secrecy-industrial complex," in which knowledge became perhaps as important a resource as bombs and satellites.[31] By the late twentieth century, the US had elaborated a massive national security apparatus consisting of dozens of different agencies that mined, collected, stored, and manipulated literally billions of pieces of secret information. Philip Melanson describes the national security state at the end of the last millennium:

> Our secrecy system is vast and complex. It affects virtually every facet of politics and public policy—and of our lives. The U.S. government creates an estimated six million secrets a year.... The super-secret National Security Agency [NSA] stores its hard copies of satellite-intercepted messages in a half million cubic feet of building space. Military records starting at World War II consume twenty-seven acres of underground storage at a site in Maryland.... In vaults at the CIA, State Department, Justice Department, pentagon and other agencies, there are a staggering four to five *billion* secrets.[32]

Meanwhile, in the wake of 9/11 and the new "state of exception" invoked amidst the war on terror, the already massive secrecy-industrial complex has expanded exponentially.[33] From the NSA's vast networks of surveillance, to Wikileaks' calculated dissemination of confidential information, to the mass marketing of private data via Facebook and other social media platforms, secrecy has hardly receded or declined but has arguably emerged as *the* defining issue of twenty-first-century life.[34] In the current situation, which some observers have called the state of "surveillance society" or "surveillance capitalism," governmental and corporate powers of information gathering have grown massively, even as individual rights to privacy have dwindled to the point of near nonexistence. As legal scholar David Cole concludes, "Today, it is the citizenry that is increasingly transparent while government operations are shrouded in secrecy."[35] It seems perhaps premature to label any single historical period "*the* age of secrecy"; but the contemporary period is arguably anything but an "age of transparency."

Theorizing Religious Secrecy:
The Adornment and the Vestment of Power

One of the first obstacles in the attempt to make sense of religious secrecy is that it is so closely related to and confused with a variety of other similar terms. These include mysticism, esotericism, occultism, and various related "isms" (the related non-ism but important category of privacy is treated in this book's conclusion[36]). While I do not pretend to offer the final definitions of any of these terms, I do think we can usefully analyze them as largely distinct but partially overlapping conceptual categories—that is, as something like circles in a Venn diagram, with secrecy as perhaps the central space in which all of them intersect in one way or another.[37]

The category of mysticism has a long, complex genealogy of its own, and it has been defined in many different ways in relation to many different interests.[38] However, as Louis Dupré suggests, mysticism typically refers to experiences that are at once personal and in some profound sense *ineffable* or *incommunicable*. Derived from the Greek verb *muein*, "to close" (one's eyes or mouth), mysticism is generally characterized by the "private, or at least incommunicable, quality of the experience," which may be written about but never fully captured by human language.[39] Though it may claim a divine source and transcendent authority, the content of the mystery can never be transmitted—at least not directly or completely—to any but the one who has achieved such an experience.[40]

The terms "esoteric" and "esotericism," meanwhile, were first used in German and French literature of the late eighteenth and early nineteenth centuries to refer to traditions that were conceived as the "inner" or hidden teaching beneath outer, mainstream religious institutions.[41] In contemporary scholarship, the phrase "Western esotericism" usually refers to a complex body of literature that developed out of Hermetic, Gnostic, and Neoplatonic sources of late Antiquity and reached its height during the European Renaissance and early modern period. These include esoteric practices such as alchemy, magic, and astrology, as well as esoteric communities such as the Rosicrucian Fraternity, Freemasonry, and modern orders such as the Golden Dawn and Theosophy. While claiming to contain deeper "inner" knowledge, esoteric literature may or may not be "secret" in a sociological sense.[42]

"Occultism," then, refers primarily to a more recent current within Western esoteric traditions that developed during the nineteenth and twentieth centuries in response to major transformations in modern European and American society, politics, and economics. While the term "occult" had appeared in texts since at least the twelfth century, occultism as a modern movement really emerged amidst the secularizing trends of modern science, technology, and the ravages of the industrialization; it was, in short, a search for a deeper, hidden spiritual reality beneath the increasing materialism and rationality of modern life.[43] As Antoine Faivre puts it, "The industrial revolution naturally gave rise to an increasingly marked interest in the 'miracles' of science. . . . Along smoking factory chimneys came the literature of the fantastic and the new phenomenon of spiritualism."[44]

Finally, secrecy as understood in this book overlaps significantly with each of these categories of the mystical, the esoteric, and the occult. However, what is unique about secrecy is specifically its *social dimension*, the fact that a secret is paradoxically meant to be *communicated* to others and thereby establishes a relationship between individuals and groups who share in or are excluded from certain valued information. Derived from the Latin *secernere*, secrecy is by definition what "separates" or "divides" the one who knows from the one who does not, distinguishing those who possesses hidden knowledge from those from whom it is withheld. Thus, what is secret is neither simply a matter of information that one chooses to keep to oneself nor simply an ineffable mystical experience that one has alone with God in one's solitude; rather, as sociologist Georg Simmel long ago pointed out, secrecy is an inherently *triadic* relationship. That is, at a minimum, it defines relations between one who possesses a secret, another to whom it is revealed, and one or more others from whom it remains concealed.[45] Unlike an ineffable mystical experience, and unlike silence pure and simple, a secret by its very structure is *intended* to be disclosed. Paradoxically, secrecy is a "sociological form . . . constituted by the very procedures whereby secrets are communicated."[46] The prolific and wide-ranging philosopher, Jacques Derrida, eloquently captures this enigma at the heart of the secret, which negates itself by its very internal structure, insofar as it is designed to be revealed to another:

The secret as such, *as secret*, separates and already institutes a negativity; it is a negation that denies itself. It de-negates itself. This denegation does not happen to it by accident; it is essential and originary. And in the *as such* of the secret that denies itself because it appears to itself in order to be what it is, this de-negation gives no chance to dialectic. The enigma of which I am speaking here ... is the *sharing of the secret.* ... There is no secret *as such*; I deny it. And this is what I confide in secret to whomever allies himself to me.[47]

As a social relationship, secrecy is inextricably tied to questions of power. As I define it in this book, secrecy is not primarily about claims to ineffable mystical experience or the contents of arcane esoteric texts. Rather, it is best understood as a kind of *strategy*—specifically, a strategy for *acquiring, enhancing, preserving, and/ or protecting power*. Even more so than mysticism or esotericism—which are also often tied to struggles over authority and power[48]—secrecy is inherently a matter of valued knowledge and contestations over who does and not have access to that information. If Foucault is correct that power and knowledge are best understood as a joint sort of "Power/Knowledge" construction, inherently bound to one another in complex relations of domination and resistance,[49] then secrecy is perhaps the very *slash or hyphen* that conjoins the two. Access to and exclusion from valued knowledge are always closely tied to power, and never more so than in highly literate, technological, and information-based societies such as our own.[50] Moreover, to the degree that a particular kind of knowledge is claimed to be supra-human, transcendent, or eternal, specifically *religious* forms of secrecy tend to be invested with a unique and often very potent kind of authority.[51]

Yet the kind of power we are dealing with here is not exactly physical or even economic power; rather, it is the subtle, invisible, and often misrecognized form that Pierre Bourdieu calls "symbolic power." This is the power to impose one's view of the world and to define the taken-for-granted understanding of reality, not through physical force but through the status and authority with which one is *vested* by others: "Symbolic power is a power which the person submitting to *grants* to the person who exercises it, a credit with which he credits him, a *fides*, an *auctoritas*, with which he entrusts him by placing his trust in him. It is a power which exists because the person who submits to it believes that it exists."[52]

Secrecy, we will see, is intimately tied to symbolic power. For secrecy at once *enhances* the status and authority of the one who possesses the secret, even as it *conceals or obscures* their full identity. Thus, as a strategy for maintaining symbolic power, secrecy has two primary faces or aspects, which are the two sides of the dialectic of revelation and concealment—what we might call *secrecy as adornment*, which enhances, accentuates, and often exaggerates the power of the one who holds it, and *secrecy as vestment*, which hides, masks, or dissembles that power.

One of the central paradoxes of religious secrecy is that it often *displays* or *publicizes* every bit as much as it *conceals*. The public reputation that one possesses rare, precious, profound information can be an extremely valuable social resource, and it is often advantageous to have it widely understood *that* one holds esoteric knowledge while ensuring that few know exactly *what* that knowledge may be. Secrecy in this sense can be a very effective sort of "adorning possession," to borrow Simmel's brilliant phrase. Like fine clothing, jewelry, or regalia, secrecy can paradoxically serve to enhance the status and authority of the individual precisely by virtue of what it conceals: "The secret operates as an adorning possession," as Simmel puts it. "This involves the paradox that what recedes before the consciousness of others and is hidden from them is emphasized in their consciousness; that one should appear as a noteworthy person through what one conceals."[53]

Paul C. Johnson has coined the useful term "secretism" to describe this sort of public display of hidden knowledge. As he explains in his study of Candomblé in Brazil, secretism does not merely conceal but cultivates a *claim* to the possession of deep, foundational knowledge, accompanied by the "active milling, polishing and promotion of the reputation of secrets."[54] Indeed, "the divulgence of a reputation of secret knowledge is desirable. Paradoxically, the force of that reputation depends on the containment, the lack of divulgence, of secret knowledge."[55]

As a kind of adorning possession, secrecy can therefore serve as a valuable source of "capital," in Bourdieu's sense. As Bourdieu understands the term, capital refers not simply to material or economic wealth but to "all the goods, material and symbolic . . . that present themselves as *rare* and worthy of being sought after in a particular social formation."[56] This includes a variety of nonmaterial forms of wealth, such as "academic capital" (educational qualifications, measured by degrees and diplomas), "linguistic capital" (competence in dominant linguistic codes), "cultural capital" (valued cultural knowledge and dispositions), and "symbolic capital" (prestige, honor, status).[57] Each of these forms of capital is, in a sense, a "masked" or "disguised" form of wealth. For its symbolic nature conceals the material power that lies behind it—just as, for example, the distinction of good taste in fine wine or clothing at once conceals and yet legitimates the economic resources required to purchase such goods: "Symbolic capital is 'denied capital'; it disguises the underlying 'interest' of relations to which it is related, giving them legitimation. Symbolic capital is a form of power that is not perceived as power but as legitimate demands for recognition."[58]

Secrecy and esoteric discourse often act as a special kind of capital, as well as a powerful source of status and prestige. By advertising the value of a given piece of esoteric knowledge while restricting access to it, secrecy effectively transforms a given piece of information into a good that is "rare and worthy of being sought after"; and the possession of that knowledge can, in turn, become a powerful source of symbolic capital, in the form of prestige, authority, or status in a given social formation or religious hierarchy. As Tanya Luhrmann puts it in her seminal essay on the "Magic of Secrecy," "secrecy elevates the value of the thing concealed. That which is hidden grows desirable and seems powerful. All knowledge is a form of property in that it can be possessed. . . . Secret knowledge evokes the sense of possession most clearly."[59]

Yet like most forms of capital, secrets are not meant to be hoarded; rather, they are meant to be *exchanged*, and they typically circulate in complex economies of information.[60] As the anthropologist Lamont Lindstrom suggests in his work on the Tanna peoples of the South Pacific, secrecy is a central part of the larger "conversational economy" that constitutes more or less every social order. Secrecy converts information into something that can be owned, exchange, and accumulated—in short, a "commodity that can be bought and sold."[61] Thus, what is important about a secret is not simply the hidden meaning it professes to contain but also the value that it has as a good in a given market of information: "Secrets turn knowledge into property that can be exchanged. People swap or sell their secrets for money or other goods. . . . By preserving patterns of ignorance in the information market, secrecy fuels talk between people who do not know and those who do."[62]

Not all secrets, however, are intended to be displayed as an adornment. Many secrets, including many religious secrets, derive their power not so much from their display as from their concealment. Power in this sense is not the promise of secret knowledge that one advertises to an envious audience, but what one hides from a suspicious outsider. Hence, the second side of the dialectic of secrecy is what we may call the "vestment of power"—that is, the dissimulation rather than the display of symbolic power. In this sense, secrecy can play both a protective role—preserving the power of the one who conceals—and an obfuscating role—hiding, masking, or mystifying the true nature of what is concealed.

In some cases, after all, a religious secret may actually be a serious *liability* for its owner. One need only think of the massive cover-ups within the Catholic Church and more recently the Southern Baptist Convention, as church leaders have systematically concealed a shocking number of child sexual abuse cases.[63] Another example is the Church of Scientology, which has worked for decades to deny allegations of both fraud and physical abuse within the organization.[64] In each of these cases, secrecy has been an attempt to preserve and protect the power—both symbolic and material—that is "vested" in the church itself.

In other cases, however, secrecy as vestment can be a powerful *weapon* and part of a larger strategy of symbolic and/or physical violence. As the sociologist Elias Canetti famously observed, secrecy is one of the most basic tactics adopted by aggressive and predatory species; it is the art of masking and camouflage that helps the hunter pursue its prey and so is perhaps the essence of power:

> Secrecy lies at the very core of power. The act of lying in wait for prey is essentially secret. Hiding, or taking on the color of its surroundings and betraying itself by no movement, the lurking creature disappears entirely, covering itself with secrecy as with a second skin.[65]

Many centuries before Canetti, the classic Chinese handbook of military strategy, *The Art of War* attributed to Sun Tzu, made a similar point, calling secrecy nothing less than a "divine art" and the key to defeating one's opponents: "O divine art of subtlety and secrecy! Through you we learn to be invisible, through you inaudible; and hence we can hold the enemy's fate in our hands."[66]

Secrecy in this sense is among the most effective weapons deployed by religious movements that adopt a stance of resistance, rebellion, revolution, and/or terrorism against the dominant and political order. The most spectacular and devastating example of this use of secrecy in recent memory was probably the series of attacks by al-Qaeda and its affiliates from the early 1990s to 2001. Not only did the al-Qaeda hijackers very effectively use religious ideology and discipline in the period before and on September 11, 2001, to inspire acts that seemed to demand a supra-human source of authority and motivation;[67] they also made sophisticated use of secrecy in the planning, financing, and execution of the attacks. Indeed, it was largely their combination of intense religious devotion and highly disciplined methods of concealment that allowed a handful of men armed with nothing more than box cutters to strike a blow to the most powerful military and economic force on earth.[68]

Yet Islamic extremism of the sort embodied in al-Qaeda and its various affiliates (such as ISIS, al-Shabaab, and many others) is by no means the only or even most alarming example of this use of secrecy by violent terrorist groups. As chapter 5 discusses, an equally if not more disturbing trend in the twenty-first century is the rapid metastasis of white supremacist terrorist groups in the US and across Europe. Combining many of the same tactics of secrecy with a virulently nationalist, racist, and xenophobic ideology, radical white supremacists have proliferated rapidly in the decades since 9/11 and especially in the wake of the election of Donald J. Trump. In this case, the power they seek to preserve is primarily that of white males, many of whom perceive their own status and position to be "falling" and threatened by an increasingly heterogenous and globalized society. White supremacist and nationalist groups often have their own forms of religious ideology—frequently drawn from esoteric traditions—which include the hooded brotherhood of the Ku Klux Klan as well as more occult movements such as Odinists and other forms of far-right, racist paganism. One of the most influential white supremacists of the last few decades is David Lane, a former member of the terrorist group the *Brüder Schweigen* or Silent Brotherhood. Lane's racist philosophy combines elements of Theosophy and Freemasonry with Norse mythology, creating a powerful form of racist occultism that has been hugely influential throughout far-right movements in the US and Europe.[69]

How to Study Secrets (or Should You)?
The Ethical and Epistemological Double Bind of Secrecy

Anyone who seriously begins to study the topic of religious secrecy quickly encounters a fundamental and troubling dilemma: namely, how can one really study something that is supposed to be "secret?" And, still more basically, *should* one even attempt to probe the esoteric knowledge of another culture or tradition? As I discovered in my own early research on Hindu Tantric traditions in northeast India, the study of religious secrecy involves a basic and inescapable sort of *ethical and epistemological* double bind:[70] namely, how can one ever claim with any certainty to know the real content of a secret? And, even supposing one could know the content, how could one then in good conscience reveal it to an audience of uninitiated outsiders? How can one ever know that one has really reached the final degree, the highest level, the ultimate secret, rather than simply another receding veil that conceals yet a new layer of mystery? As Johnson aptly observes, "the final meaning of secrecy is unspeakable and indescribable, either because in many cases there finally is no mystery at all or because it is endlessly deferred. . . . The idea of the secret is that of hidden power itself, always shimmering on the horizon or glinting below heavy historical sediments."[71] Some critics have wondered whether there can *ever* be a claim to genuine access to the hidden content at all, since the very structure of the secret implies that it can always only be a partial revelation, always leading to still further partial revelation and general concealment. As the novelist and literary critic, Umberto Eco, famously put it,

> There can be no final secret. The ultimate secret of Hermetic initiation is that everything is secret. Hence the Hermetic secret must be an empty one, because anyone who pretends to reveal any sort of secret is not himself initiated and has stopped at a superficial level of the knowledge of cosmic mystery.[72]

But perhaps even more important and difficult than this epistemological question is the central ethical dilemma inherent in the study of secrecy: is the very attempt to penetrate the secrets of another tradition itself a kind of violation, perhaps even a form of intellectual imperialism or a kind of cultural theft (or, in the contemporary context, could it also be seen as a breach of intellectual property laws[73])? The history of anthropology offers ample evidence of the ways in which scholars have looted and pillaged the esoteric knowledge of other cultures, often working hand in hand with the looting and pillaging practices of the colonial powers who typically employed them.[74]

In this sense, the study of secrecy is really a kind of microcosm or acute example of the profound moral and hermeneutical problems in the study of religion as a whole, problems that strike to the heart of any attempt to understand other cultures or religious traditions. Namely, how can we responsibly study the sacred knowledge of others in a critical yet respectful way, without continuing the troubling legacies of colonialism and imperialism by invading and territorializing the sacred knowledge of others?[75]

While I do not believe there is any easy way out of this double bind, my approach in this book is basically twofold. First, following the advice of Jonathan Z. Smith, I believe that the historian of religion needs to remain "relentlessly self-conscious" in the study of all religious phenomena, and perhaps most especially the study of religious secrecy.[76] Here I follow Bourdieu's "reflexive" approach, which always strives to subject the practice of the researcher to the same critical eye as the practice of the researched and so "constantly turns back onto itself . . . the weapons it produces."[77]

Second and perhaps more important, I think we need to make a basic epistemological shift in our approach to religious secrecy. Specifically, I suggest that we shift our gaze from the ever-elusive "hidden content" of secrecy to the more visible *forms* through which secrets are concealed, revealed, and exchanged. This epistemological shift is similar to the one that Foucault suggests in his well-known analyses of power. As Foucault realized, power is best understood not simply as a monolithic form of domination operating in top-down fashion through state institutions but as a complex web of techniques and relations extending in something more like "capillary circulations" throughout the entire social body. "A theoretical shift had ... been required in order to analyze what is often described as the manifestations of 'power'; it led me to examine, rather, the manifold relations, the open strategies, and the rational techniques that articulate the exercise of powers."[78]

Similarly, I regard secrecy as neither a monolithic nor singular phenomenon; rather, it is better understood as a particular kind of *strategy*—or rather a complex of related strategies—for the calculated control of knowledge, which in turn can be deployed for a wide array of different social and political purposes. As such, it functions much like a "linchpin," similar to how Foucault sees sexuality as a kind of linchpin in social relations: "It appears rather as an especially dense transfer point for relations of power: between men and women, young people and old people ... priests and laity, an administration and a population," one that is "endowed with the greatest instrumentality: useful for the greatest number of maneuvers and capable of serving as a point of support, as a linchpin, for the most varied strategies."[79] As the key knot in the intersection between knowledge and power, secrecy acts as a kind of linchpin that can serve an equally varied number of strategies. Secrecy can protect the priest who sexually abuses children as much as it can empower the religious dissident who resists an oppressive political regime; it can aid the religious terrorist who plans a bomb attack as much as it can assist the abolitionist who hides fugitive slaves in the attic; it can buttress the authority of a religious teacher who claims possession of a rare body of esoteric knowledge even as it can empower the disaffected apostate who reveals "cult secrets."

Although religious secrecy might appear in a tremendous diversity of forms, certain common strategies and tactics recur across cultures and throughout historical periods.[80] And I understand these not as universal "archetypes" in a sort of Eliade-an or Jungian sense but as cross-cultural patterns that tend to crop up in many different social and historical locations. These strategies include:

1. *Hierarchization of truth and controlled access to information.* The creation of complex hierarchies of graded access to information is one of the most basic features found throughout most secret societies. The value of the concealed information is typically enhanced by its difficulty of access; and the further one ascends in the esoteric hierarchy, the greater the value of the knowledge. Like other forms of symbolic capital, secrecy thus becomes a self-reproducing form of wealth that increases in power as one advances in the organization.[81]

2. *Double-coding and writing between the lines.* Secrets are often transmitted through a deliberate strategy of coding or an "art of writing," to use Leo Strauss's phrase, which transmits a relatively ordinary or innocuous message to most readers and a deeper esoteric meaning to those who have "ears to hear."[82]

3. *The skillful use of obscurity.* Secret information is typically concealed through the use of intentionally vague, mysterious, and confusing language, or a kind of deliberate use of ambiguity in the control of religious ideology.[83] Obscurity is one of the most basic strategies that transforms ordinary language into something awesome, rare, and highly valued, even as it excludes the noninitiate who lacks the key to its interpretation.

4. *The dialectic of veiling and unveiling.* In contrast to silence plain and simple, secrets are structured in such as a way as to be disclosed. Often this involves a dynamic of lure and withdrawal—that is, the claim to possess rare, valuable information while keeping its content just beyond the reach of the uninitiated. Secrecy in this sense works much like *eroticism*, which, as Georges Bataille suggests, depends on a play of veiling and unveiling, of partial revelation and general concealment.[84]

5. *The inscription of the body.* Secrecy is very often a material and embodied practice expressed through clothing, masks, and jewelry, or literally incorporated into the body through a kind of esoteric anatomy. Classic examples of this occult physiology include the Indian yogic system of *chakras*, or energy centers of the subtle body (which were widely adopted by Theosophy and many other modern traditions), and esoteric understandings of gender and sexuality (which runs through the current of modern sexual magic).[85]

6. *Disinformation and counterespionage.* Secrecy is often not simply a source of symbolic power but also a means of protecting oneself from the scrutiny of outsiders. Esoteric groups frequently come under attack from government and other institutions and so resort to elaborate tactics of dissimulation to preserve themselves. In more extreme cases,

this may lead to forms of counterespionage in which the esoteric group takes aggressive action to infiltrate and subvert its opponents.[86]

These strategies are meant to be neither exhaustive nor comprehensive; readers will no doubt think of other techniques of concealment that could be added to this brief list. However, these will serve as sort of the internal threads of the chapters that follow, running like the fibers through the fabric of the historical examples that are narrated in the remainder of the book.

In Defense of Comparison: The Flawed but Inescapable Method of the Historian of Religions

While these six strategies are by no means intended to be universal archetypes found in all times and places, they do, I think, provide a useful basis for a more modest and pragmatic form of cross-cultural comparison. This book focuses primarily on a relatively brief historical period: from the late nineteenth to the early twenty-first century in the US and Europe. But it also draws extensively on insights from many other cultures and historical contexts. Moreover, my hope is that the strategies and modes of concealment outlined here will have much larger comparative implications for the study of secrecy and religion more broadly.

As many critics have observed, comparison as a method in the study of religion has often gone tragically astray, leading to all manner of problematic generalizations and oversimplifications. It has often, at best, fostered a kind of facile, naïve perennialism that sees all religions as reflections of some grand universal Truth; and, at worst, it has helped pave the way for imperialism and the colonization of other cultures within the all-consuming eye of Western scholarship.[87] And yet, as Bruce Lincoln persuasively argues, comparison remains not only important but in fact *inescapable*, insofar as acts of comparison are inherent in any attempt to find meaning or understand other cultures. Methods of comparison — such as the consideration of similarities, differences, and contrasts between objects, accompanied by the generation of larger theoretical connections — are inherent in all scholarship as well as in human thought itself: "Experience suggests that comparativists go wrong in many ways, and no principles or protocols guard against every pitfall. Nonetheless, we are obliged to continue, for even the most circumscribed inquiry has its comparative aspects."[88]

While noting the common failures of grand, large-scale universalistic approaches to comparison of the sort that Mircea Eliade, Claude Lévi-

Strauss, and others had attempted, Lincoln advocates a "weak" form of comparison. Rather than seeking universal archetypes or deep structural patterns common to all cultures, Lincoln suggests a more modest comparative approach that focuses on a small number of *comparanda*, emphasizing difference as well as likeness, and remaining especially attentive to social, historical, and political contexts.[89] This more modest style of comparison is similar to what Wendy Doniger calls a "ground up" as opposed to a "top-down" approach, one that does not begin with grand universal archetypes but with a set of specific historical examples and their concrete contexts before generating broader comparative connections.[90]

This book follows a similar kind of "weak" and "bottom-up" comparative approach by examining a small number of historically interconnected examples, placing each of them concretely in their social and political contexts. However, I hope to use these examples to generate some larger insights into the workings of secrecy, not as some kind of universal archetypes but as a set of strategies that are used widely across many cultures and time periods. To cite another of the great gurus of the comparative method, Jonathan Z. Smith, "Comparison does not necessarily tell us how things are.... [L]ike models and metaphors, comparison tells us how things might be conceived, how they might be 'redescribed.'"[91] Such redescription through the lens of comparison is a primary goal of this book.

Outline of the Book: A Brief History of Secrets in the Modern Age

This book is organized both historically and thematically, tracing six primary forms or modalities of secrecy through six historical periods stretching from the late nineteenth century to the present. The six modalities I call "the adornment of silence," "the advertisement of the secret," "the seduction of the secret," "secrecy as social resistance," "the terror of secrecy," and "secrecy as historical process." Each of these general forms of secrecy is illustrated by one primary example, tracing six different but historically interrelated esoteric movements that developed in the US and Europe over the last 150 years. I have chosen these examples not at random but primarily because they offer especially clear illustrations of the six modes of concealment that I want to highlight here, as well as six instructive periods in the history of modern secrecy. The various strategies of hierarchization, double-coding, and so on discussed above are woven as threads through each of these chapters, serving as sort of the "warp" for the "weft" of each of the six forms of secrecy that follow.

Thus chapter 1, "The Adornment of Silence," focuses on Scottish Rite Freemasonry—one of the most elaborate and densely symbolic Masonic orders—in late nineteenth-century America, closely examining the key role of secrecy as a kind of "adorning possession." For architects of the Scottish Rite such as Albert Pike, the secrecy of the Masonic Lodge was not simply a matter of arcane esoteric knowledge; it was also closely tied to the complex social and political dynamics of post–Civil War America, at a time when many white, native-born men were struggling to maintain their traditional status and privilege even as that status was increasingly challenged by the growing power of women, blacks, and immigrants. Here I pay special attention not only to the esoteric symbolism of the Scottish Rite but also to its more literal and material "adornments," such as the regalia, jewelry, crowns, and robes that accompany the higher degrees of the order.

In chapter 2, "The Secret Doctrine," I discuss the paradoxical fact that religious secrets are seldom if ever completely hidden; rather, they are very often "advertised" as part of a complex economy of knowledge. That is, the possession of highly valued pieces of esoteric sacred knowledge is often publicly announced and widely circulated, even as the contents of that knowledge are largely obscured. This advertisement of secrets was particularly evident in the late nineteenth century, amidst the increasingly diverse religious marketplace that spread across the US and Europe, with the rise of new occult, magical, and esoteric orders that often competed intensely with one another. To explore this theme, I focus on the Theosophical Society, perhaps the most influential esoteric movement of the modern period, founded in 1875 by the enigmatic Russian mystic, Helena Petrovna Blavatsky. In particular, I examine the widespread publication of esoteric knowledge in Theosophical texts—such as Blavatsky's massive tome entitled *The Secret Doctrine*—and in the formation of Theosophy's inner circle—the "Esoteric Section"—which emerged, in part, due to competition with rival esoteric movements such as the Golden Dawn.

Chapter 3, "The Seduction of the Secret," continues this focus on display and advertisement by looking specifically at the *erotic and sensual* nature of secrecy—that is, the dynamic of lure and withdrawal, concealment and striptease, that is integral to many esoteric traditions. Specifically, this chapter focuses on the practice of sexual magic, which spread rapidly throughout European and US esoteric circles of the late nineteenth and early twentieth centuries and achieved one of its most tantalizing articulations in the work of the Russian-born Parisian mystic, Maria de Naglowska. In Naglowska's system, secrecy acts as a powerful form of *eroticism* that leads the initiate ever deeper into the mysteries of sexual magic, through her tantalizing use of Satanic imagery, toward the most transgressive and potentially dangerous esoteric practices, such as erotic ritual hanging.

In chapter 4, "Secrecy and Social Resistance," I turn to the role of concealment as a means of evading, critiquing, and subverting the dominant order. Focusing on the Five Percenters—a more radical offshoot of the Nation of Islam that formed in the 1960s—I examine the role of secrecy as a means of both protecting marginalized groups and of creating a kind of "black market symbolic capital" that circulates outside of the dominant cultural markets. During the 1980s and 1990s, the movement's most powerful influence has been in the genre of hip-hop, where many rappers have used the Five Percenter's coded language in their lyrics, videos, and album art. Ironically, through the massive commercial success of hip-hop, the underground discourse of the Five Percenters quickly entered into a much more mainstream marketplace, where it helped to generate a great deal of economic capital as well.

Chapter 5, "The Terror of Secrecy," examines the role of secrecy as a tactic of religious violence, focusing primarily on white supremacist movements in modern America. While most of the scholarship on religious secrecy and terrorism has focused on radical Islam, white supremacist movements are arguably more widespread, pervasive, and potentially destructive in the US and much of Europe. To highlight this trend, I focus primarily on the *Brüder Schweigen* or "Silent Brotherhood," perhaps the most infamous white supremacist terrorist group to emerge in the US, which went on a brief but surprisingly successful spree of counterfeiting, bank robbery, and murder during the 1980s. This chapter also pays special attention to the role of both race and masculinity, arguing that the idea of a secret brotherhood offered these white, mostly working-class males a sense of power, significance, and sacred duty at a time when there was a general sense of "white man falling" in late twentieth-century America. All of this has obvious resonance in twenty-first-century America, with the rise of the alt-right, new forms of violent white supremacy, and the policies of the Trump administration.

In chapter 6, "The Third Wall of Fire," I then examine the role of secrecy as a more dynamic *historical process* that changes, adapts, and morphs over time. Focusing on the Church of Scientology, I first grapple with the complex methodological questions involved in the study of religious secrecy (the ethical-epistemological double bind described above). With its myriad layers of secrecy, espionage against government offices, and intense litigation against critics, Scientology is perhaps the ultimate test case for this double bind. Focusing on just one key aspect of Scientology's advanced esoteric teachings—known as the "Third Wall of

Fire"—I suggest that we probably never can claim to know with any certainty the "real secrets" of movements such as Scientology. However, we can still say quite a lot about the ways in which secret knowledge is advertised and concealed, how it changes over time in relation to changing social and political forces, how it becomes a key part of legal disputes, and how it sometimes becomes a source of intense scandal and embarrassment.

Finally, in the conclusion, "The Science of the Hidden," I reflect on the larger study of religious secrecy and its role both in academia and in contemporary society more broadly. Here I follow Bourdieu's suggestion that critical scholarship is inherently a "science of the hidden," in the sense of bringing to light relations of power that are normally unrecognized or obscured. This is among the most important roles for the critical study of religion today, one that pertains not only to esoteric currents of the nineteenth and twentieth centuries but also to the immense networks of secrecy, religion, and power that now dominate much of twenty-first-century life. This critical role is more than relevant; it is urgent, as we increasingly inhabit complex information economies and security states driven by mass surveillance, a vast expansion of government secrecy, and a profound erosion of individual privacy. Whereas the "vestment of power" of secrecy had once been held primarily in the hands of religious institutions—the church, the lodge, the secret society—that power has been increasingly transferred to secular entities such as the NSA, the CIA, and (more recently) private corporations. The all-seeing eye in the pyramid that once embodied One Nation Under God has today become the all-seeing eye of the NSA and other agencies that command what some call our "One Nation Under Surveillance."[92] And these government agencies now work in complex, interlocking ways with the all-seeing eyes of Facebook, Google, and other corporate entities that exercise far more diffuse, decentralized, but probably more powerful forms of surveillance. Therefore, the task of the critical historian of religions in the twenty-first century is at once more complicated and arguably more urgent than in previous generations—the task of critically interrogating not only religious claims to power but also the increasingly invasive claims of those governmental and corporate entities that wield ever more domination over our personal and public lives.

✳ CHAPTER 1 ✳

The Adornment of Silence

SECRECY AND SYMBOLIC POWER
IN AMERICAN FREEMASONRY

*Secrecy is indispensable in a Mason of whatever degree. It is the first
and almost only lesson taught to the Entered Apprentice. . . .
The secrets of our brother, when communicated to us, must be sacred.*

ALBERT PIKE, *The Morals and Dogma of the Ancient and
Accepted Scottish Rite of Freemasonry*[1]

*[A]lthough apparently the sociological counter-pole of secrecy,
adornment has, in fact, a societal significance with
a structure analogous to that of secrecy itself.*

GEORG SIMMEL, "The Sociology of Secrecy
and of Secret Societies"[2]

In 1871, the American adventurer, soldier, and scholar, Albert Pike (1809–91), published a massive compendium of Masonic lore and symbolism entitled *The Morals and Dogma of the Ancient and Accepted Scottish Rite of Freemasonry*. One of the most colorful characters of nineteenth-century America, Pike served as a brigadier general in the Confederate army but suffered a humiliating scandal during the Civil War and spent a period of exile in the wilderness. Yet he was also one of the leading Masonic scholars of his day, who served as the sovereign grand commander of the Scottish Rite's Southern Jurisdiction for thirty-two years and immersed himself in the world's ancient mystical systems, ranging from the Hindu Vedas to medieval alchemy and Kabbalah (fig. 1.1).[3] His monumental tome, *Morals and Dogma*, is both the most important work on Scottish Rite Freemasonry in the US and a major synthesis of esotericism, mysticism, and comparative religions collected up to the nineteenth century.

As the most elaborate of the many branches of Freemasonry,[4] the Scottish Rite first emerged in France in the early eighteenth century and then spread to the US a few decades later.[5] While most Masonic orders limit

FIGURE 1.1. Albert Pike. Photo from Library of Congress, Brady-Handy Collection.

themselves to three degrees of initiation, the Scottish Rite developed an additional twenty-nine increasingly esoteric and complex grades.[6] Moreover, as we see in figures 1.2, 1.3, and 1.5, the Scottish Rite also developed some of the most ornate regalia, with elaborate robes, crowns, scepters, jewels, and other paraphernalia to accompany the increasingly mysterious grades of the upper degrees. Secrecy in this tradition is very clearly a *literal* as well as a symbolic form of adornment—that is, not simply a kind of hidden knowledge that lends status and prestige but also a visible garment, jewel, or medal that at once embodies and displays that status.[7] In this sense, Scottish Rite Freemasonry is a particularly striking illustration of Simmel's insight into the role of secrecy as an "adorning possession," which paradoxically enhances one's status by virtue of what it conceals.

Indeed, if we can speak of "material religion" and "material Christianity," we can also speak of *"material esotericism"* — that is, the role of clothing, jewelry, and physical regalia in the practice of esoteric religious movements.[8] Like masks in African and other indigenous religions, Masonic regalia is an art that at once "reveals and conceals."[9]

Yet Pike's *Morals and Dogma* needs to be read not simply as an important text of occult symbolism and a key document in the history of modern esotericism (though it is surely that). Published as it was by a former Confederate general just six years after the end of the Civil War, the text also needs to be examined critically in its social, historical, and political contexts, in relation to larger cultural, demographic, gendered, and racial dynamics in late nineteenth-century America.

In this chapter, I examine the complex role of secrecy in the Scottish Rite, with special attention to its social, political, and racial implications in the context of post–Civil War America. Many authors have suggested different explanations for the striking rise and popularity of Freemasonry in the late nineteenth century, which was really "American fraternalism's golden age," as "membership grew exponentially, and every year saw the creation of at least one new order."[10] Some such as Lynn Dumenil suggest that Freemasonry played a key sociological role, providing a spiritual oasis in a rapidly changing, increasingly heterogeneous world, while reinforcing the traditional status of middle-class, white, Protestant males.[11] Others such as Mary Ann Clawson argue that fraternalism offered a form of unity among men of different social classes while providing an alternative to the female domestic sphere and so preserving male autonomy.[12] Some such as Mark Carnes focus more specifically on the role of gender and ritual, suggesting that the fraternal orders provided a kind of rite of passage for young men, helping to facilitate the transition from the domestic world of women into the masculine workplace.[13] And others such as Steven Bullock and David Hackett argue that Freemasonry both shaped and was shaped by other major developments of early America, such as the emerging ideals of democracy and individualism. As both a counter and a complement to the Protestant churches, Freemasonry was a key part of the American religious landscape and a template for a larger public sphere.[14]

While not denying any of these useful analyses, this chapter focuses on a distinct but closely related reason for the rapid growth of Freemasonry, and particularly of the more elaborate orders such as the Scottish Rite: namely, the power of secrecy itself, the role of concealed knowledge as a highly valued source of "adornment." This adornment was at once symbolic — in the form of the elaborate symbolism, arcana, and mysteries revealed in each of the higher degrees—and quite literal—in the form of the elaborate costumes, jewelry, and regalia that accompanied each of those degrees. Pike and other men of the late nineteenth century found in the mysteries of the Scottish Rite not simply a form of "symbolic power" in Bourdieu's sense but also one with a distinctly tangible, material presence.

This was, however, a kind of power that was fraught with deep tensions. Most important, Pike's Scottish Rite reflected a central tension between the Masonic ideals of equality and universality and an underlying current of classism and racism that ran through much of America in the late nineteenth century.[15] Even as African Americans and immigrants were entering both mainstream society and the Masonic world, many white Masons remained deeply conflicted about these trends.[16] The lodge was more than a new kind of social space; it was also often a contested space where many of these tensions were clearly highlighted. And Pike's work is perhaps the most striking example of these tensions within Freemasonry and throughout the US more broadly. Even as he celebrated the Masonic ideals of freedom and equality, he frequently made racist remarks and fiercely opposed the admission of black men into his Rite. In the highest degrees of the Scottish Rite, Pike articulated his own attempted resolution of these conflicts, worked out through the esoteric symbolism and adornments of the lodge. At least in Pike's system, Freemasonry offered a means of preserving the cherished ideals of democracy and freedom, while maintaining a clear form of elitism and exclusivism. At the same time that it constructed an elaborate hierarchy of advancements and symbolic adornments, ostensibly based on merit, it also served to mask and recode deeper differences of class, sex, and race.

"The Moses of American Freemasonry"

While Albert Pike was just one of many thousands of American men who joined the lodges in the nineteenth century, he was in many ways emblematic of several religious, social, and demographic trends in the decades after the Civil War. Famed in his youth as an adventurer and "one of the most remarkable characters in the annals of the Southwest," Pike was revered in his later years as perhaps the greatest authority on American Freemasonry and the foremost proponent of the Scottish Rite.[17] Born in Boston, the son of an irreligious, alcoholic cobbler and a pious, puritanical mother, he was from his youth a man of extremes and seeming contradictions. Although he attended Harvard in 1821, he was forced to leave when he was unable to pay the tuition. Thus, in 1824, he decided to ignore his mother's wish that he become a minister to live an adventurer's life in the Southwest, riding wagon trains, surviving snow storms, and fighting Indians. As Mark Carnes notes, he seems to have "longed to share in the unconstrained life of the noble savage."[18] He was known, moreover, for his wild parties, his skill in seducing women, and his tremendous physical and sexual appetites: "Torn by extremes represented by his irreverent father and pious mother, Pike initially pursued a quest ... reflected in frontier adventures, the pursuit of wealth and military glory, gastronomic and sexual excess."[19]

In 1831, Pike returned to the eastern US, where he studied law and was admitted to the bar in 1836. Famed for his heroism in the Southwest, Pike built a reputation among the wealthy society of Little Rock, Arkansas. However, the real turning point in his life was his entry into the Confederate army during the Civil War, where he held the rank of brigadier general, placed in command of the Indian regiments. Pike suddenly became the center of an enormous scandal when the Indians under his charge allegedly killed and mutilated the bodies of Union soldiers. At the war's end, Pike was blamed for the incident—by both Union and Confederate sides—and denounced as a malevolent rebel, charged with disobeying commands and inciting the Indians to revolt. His former wealth and property were confiscated, along with his former status and prestige. Fleeing civilized humanity, Pike withdrew into the hills of Arkansas and lived as a hermit in the wilderness. It was not until 1869 that he was publicly pardoned and returned to mainstream society.[20]

One of the most troubling questions in Pike's life is his possible relationship with another infamous secret brotherhood that also emerged in the South during the postwar years—the Ku Klux Klan. Many critics have charged that Pike was not only a member but even a founding father of the KKK.[21] As Walter Lee Brown has shown in his definitive biography, there is no concrete evidence that Pike was ever a member of or had close ties to the Klan; however, given his political views and his general hostility to the black suffrage movement, it is not difficult to imagine that he would have been sympathetic to such a group: "one might reasonably surmise that Pike, considering his strong aversion to the Negro suffrage and his frustration at his own political impotence, would not have stood back from the Klan."[22] In letters from the mid-1850s, Pike clearly defended slavery as a necessary part of God's divine plan for the "civilizing" of the negro, who is inherently incapable of civilizing himself.[23] Likewise, in numerous published editorials of the late 1860s, Pike lamented the "disenfranchisement of 80,000 white men and the abuse of the privilege by 50,000 ignorant negroes" after the war; but he also expressed his confidence that the South "will not always bear ... the disgrace of negroism."[24] He also compared newly enfranchised black voters to "South American monkeys"[25] and asserted quite flatly that "we mean that the white race, and that race alone, shall govern this country."[26] In his *Lectures on the Arya* (1873), Pike also praised the "Aryan race" as the original, conquering, dominant white race of mankind, in terms that foreshadow many later twentieth-century race theorists: "They were white men, as we are, the superior race in intellect, in manliness, the governing race of the world, the conquering race of all other races. They called themselves the Arya, the Aryans, the Warlike, or ... the Noble."[27]

As far as is known, Pike referred to the Klan only once in print. In an editorial in the *Memphis Daily Appeal* in 1868, Pike wrote not uncharitably about the Klan, suggesting that its main problems lay not in its aims but in its methods and leadership: "We do not know what the Ku Klux organization may become.... It is quite certain that it will never come to much on its original plan. It must become quite another thing to be efficient."[28] In fact, Pike went on to call for something even more ambitious than the Klan—a "great Order of Southern Brotherhood," that would unite all white men in the South in a secret fraternity to defend their traditional property and power and to work against "negro suffrage":

> The disenfranchised people of the South, robbed of all the guarantees of the Constitution ... can find no protection for property, liberty or life, except in secret association. Not in such association to commit follies and outrages; but for mutual, peaceful, lawful, self-defense. If it were in our power, if it could be effected, we would unite every white man in the South, who is opposed to Negro suffrage, into one great Order of Southern Brotherhood, with an organization complete, active, vigorous, in which a few should execute the concentrated will of all, and whose very existence would be concealed from all but its members. That has been the resort of the oppressed in all ages. To resort to it is a right given by *God*.[29]

It is not clear from this editorial whether Pike meant this "Order of Southern Brotherhood" to refer to something like a better organized Klan or something like his own Masonic order. Yet it seems not insignificant that he made this remark just three years before the publications of his monumental guide to the Scottish Rite.

After his return to civilization, Pike began to immerse himself even more deeply in the study of the most arcane secrets of the world's esoteric traditions—the Greek mysteries, Kabbalah, Gnosticism, alchemy, Templar traditions, as well as Indian religions and Zoroastrianism. While his military career had ended in shame and scandal, Pike appears to have found a new sense of meaning in the inner realm of mystery, secret ritual, and symbolism. As Carnes recounts,

> Pike's life was in ruins. He faced charges of inciting the Indians to revolt, and his property was confiscated by Union officers. He had squandered his fortune, and his marriage had disintegrated....
>
> Pike sought to refract his experiences through the wisdom of the ancients. To do so, he scoured the classic religious texts, translating form Latin and German Sources, the *Zend Avesta* and the Indian Vedas, studying the Cabala and the writings of the Gnostics.[30]

Much of Pike's knowledge of esotericism and ancient religions came to him through the work of the great French occultist, Éliphas Lévi, whose own massive tome, *Dogme et Rituel de la Haute Magie* (1854–56), was widely read throughout Europe and the US.[31] However, perhaps Pike's greatest contribution was to synthesize these many older esoteric currents within the system of modern Freemasonry. Commonly regarded as one of the most important figures in American Freemasonry, Pike has been called the "Moses and Second Creator" of the lodge, who "smote the rock of chaos and brought forth a system of morality more perfect than was ever built by human hands."[32]

Pike is thus a telling example of a much broader trend taking place in late nineteenth-century America. As Dumenil, Clawson, and others argue, the sudden popularity of Freemasonry during these decades related closely to the rapidly changing social and economic context of post–Civil War America: "The period from the 1870s to the 1890s was one of prolonged, intense, bitter class conflict.... Yet it also witnessed the growth of fraternal orders that attracted a membership of massive proportions."[33] This period saw rapid change on all levels—the growth of an increasingly heterogenous society, the breakup of small-town communities, enormous technological changes, and national corporations that undermined local businesses. At the same time, the homogeneity of white society was shattered by the influx of blacks and immigrants, who did not always appear to share the values of middle-class American culture. As we see throughout Masonic literature of the late nineteenth century, there were growing fears of "Pandemonium, confusion, strife" and the destruction of all stable values of traditional America.[34]

Many middle- and upper-class men also appear to have been seeking an alternative to the mainstream Protestant churches of the day. As Dumenil notes, the churches of the post–Civil War era began to worry increasingly about their lack of influence over the urban masses (particularly non-English-speaking immigrants), who constituted a large sector outside the pale of American Protestantism; there was thus a growing effort to attract and accommodate these groups. At the same time, the Protestant churches of the late nineteenth century were becoming increasingly dominated by women and "women's concerns." During a period in which two-thirds of all Protestants were female, the church came to be identified with the "woman's realm," the private sphere of domesticity, children, and morality. For many white middle- and upper-class males, all of this signified that the church had been "emasculated," "feminized," and robbed of its traditional "American" (i.e., white, native, male) values.[35]

Amidst this increasingly pluralistic world, Freemasonry offered a kind of "spiritual oasis"[36] and the model of a harmonious society free from the increasing chaos of the outside world, where white, native males still formed a homogenous and well-governed society. "The fraternal order was a model society," as Kenneth Ames suggests, "where the traits of male culture were enshrined and often exaggerated."[37] The brotherhood provided a vision of traditional values, as well as a form of respectability and prestige, for many men who may have felt deeply threatened by the changes taking place around them: "The importance of Masonry's commitment to morality and its promise of respectability can be understood in the context of late nineteenth century Americans' struggle to maintain their traditional ideology in the face of an increasingly disordered world."[38]

Pike's *Morals and Dogma* is not only one of the most important works of nineteenth-century American Freemasonry but also a powerful articulation of its social ideology. By no means simply a commentary on a set of arcane rituals, it is a *political* document that regularly reminds the Mason of the direct relevance of the Craft for a well-ordered society and just government. In fact, the first three chapters of the text discuss government and politics as much as they explicate Masonic symbolism; and the entire third degree of "Master" seems to be an exhortation to men of public office, warning against the dangers of political misrule and advocating the virtues of proper governance.[39] Pike's work makes it clear that Freemasonry is anything but a rebellious or subversive movement; rather, it claims to be the fullest embodiment of true "American" values.[40] The text is filled with strong criticisms of the social and political world around it, calling for good men to join the well-governed society of Freemasonry. Bemoaning the weakness of the society of his time, Pike observes that "there are certainly great evils of civilization at this day," that this nation is in "distress," that "fraud, falsehood, and deceit in national affairs are the signs of decadence," and that contemporary politics, both in America and in Europe, has become "selfish and driven by greed." The nation has become feminine, passive, and emasculated, as "the effete State floats on down the puddled stream of Time until ... the worm has consumed its strength, and it crumbles into oblivion."[41]

For Pike, Freemasonry is nothing other than the ideal society; the model of perfect, just government; and the true "Holy Empire." For it represents the wedding of the sovereignty and freedom of the individual with the communal ideal of fellowship and mutual respect for all:

> From the political point of view, there is but a single principle—the sovereignty of man over himself. The sovereignty of one's self over one's self is called LIBERTY.... The identity of concession which each makes to all is EQUALITY.... This protection of each by all is FRATERNITY.[42]

As we will see, however, this ideal of freedom and equality for all was in constant tension with Pike's outspoken views about gender, class, and especially race.[43]

The Lodge as a New Social Space: Egalitarianism, Elitism, and Meritocracy

Throughout Pike's writings on the Scottish Rite, we are confronted by a persistent ambivalence and a double-edged rhetoric, which carried over to much of nineteenth-century American Freemasonry as a whole. On the one hand, the lodges consistently proclaim the virtues of Freemasonry as an egalitarian, democratic institution, in which men of all classes and creeds join as equals. Yet on the other hand, the lodges were predominantly comprised of upper- and middle-class white males, and they often helped to reinforce the privilege of a small elite, while generally excluding other groups such as blacks, women, immigrants, and lower classes.[44] As Bullock notes, the lodge was always a complex tension between "social inclusiveness and exclusion," containing "theoretically contradictory but situationally complementary ideals and practices."[45] Part of the key to this double-edged logic is the claim that the lodge represents a form of "meritocracy"; that is to say, it is a system of progressive advancement and distinction that is based ostensibly on the acquisition of virtue and moral excellence but that also, in many cases, obscures deeper forms of elitism, classism, and racism.

Like most Masonic works, Pike's writings celebrate the ideals of equality and the brotherhood of all mankind. The lodge is hailed as the embodiment of the unity of all men and all religions, which is ultimately older than Christianity, Islam, and other world faiths: "Freemasonry is one faith, one common star around which men of all tongues assemble." Whereas other institutions such as the Catholic Church exclude and reject other faiths, the lodge opens its doors to all sects and creeds, recognizing that every man is free to choose his own religion: "It is the universal, eternal, immutable religion, such as God planted it in the heart of universal humanity."[46] As such, Pike suggests that Masonry is not only compatible with but is the true fulfillment of the ideals of democracy and freedom represented by the US system of government.

Yet despite this apparently liberating democratic ideal, Pike's Scottish Rite, like most lodges, was far from egalitarian. As Margaret Jacob and others have argued in the case of European Freemasonry, the rhetoric of egalitarianism was often rather superficial and frequently helped to obfuscate deeper asymmetries and social hierarchies. Even though "cosmopolitanism and natural equality are the obligatory themes of all the harangues of the lodges," the European lodges were usually far from democratic but were predominantly aristocratic and elitist organizations: "Fraternal binding also obscured the social divisions and inequities of rank endemic to the lives of men who embraced 'equality' and 'liberty.' In making social divisions less obvious, freemasonry ironically served to reinforce them.... They obfuscated the real divisions of wealth, education and social practice."[47]

A similar though perhaps even more extreme dynamic characterized the American lodges, particularly the more elaborate orders such as the Scottish Rite. As Dumenil and others note, the American Masons' rhetoric of universality and tolerance was generally belied by the fact that the nineteenth-century lodge was largely a white, middle-class, and Protestant community. Among other barriers, the various financial costs demanded of the Masons were generally far beyond the means of blue-collar men, meaning that few among the working classes could become members: "While Masonic membership was available to men of all classes, the dues, regalia costs and other fees placed it beyond the reach of most workers. And although members were not required to have education, mastery of the degree rituals required some measure of literacy, as well as leisure time."[48] Rather than opening their doors widely to men (much less women) of all races and classes or creating a truly egalitarian society, the lodges were typically highly exclusive spaces, which offered clear avenues to achieving status, distinction, and social connections to those who could afford them: "Preoccupied by issues of status in a rapidly changing society, these ambitious and politically active men did not intend to throw the doors of the lodges open to all comers, but rather conceived of the order as a means of validating their own attainments."[49]

Particularly in the case of Pike's work, we can see a significant amount of racism in many of the American lodges. If Freemasonry provided a kind of "male oasis" from the increasingly feminized church, it also provided for many men a kind of "white oasis" from an increasingly complicated and interracial American society (which is still quite true today in many southern lodges, many of which remain segregated and even refuse to recognize African American Masons[50]). Despite the number of black Masonic orders active in the late nineteenth century—the Prince Hall lodges[51]—many white Masons dismissed them as illegitimate.[52] Pike's own position on black Masonry is complex and ambivalent, reflecting the deep tensions surrounding the issue in the late nineteenth century. In a famous speech in Columbus, Ohio, in 1875, Pike did acknowledge that Prince Hall is as "regular lodge as any lodge created by competent authority"; but then just a few lines later, he forcefully declares: "I took my obligation to white men, not Negroes. When I have to accept Negroes as my brethren or leave Masonry, I shall leave it."[53] While there is no solid evidence that Pike was formally involved with the KKK, there are numerous indications that he and other Masons were sympathetic to the KKK cause. As Dumenil notes, the two secret brotherhoods shared at least a few things in common, including a suspicion of racial and ethnic groups (primarily Jews, blacks, and immigrants) who did not appear to share what group members regarded as essential American values:

> Although Masonry was less virulent in its American campaign than the Ku Klux Klan ... both organizations shared some of the same goals. Dismayed by all the factions disturbing America's harmony, both called for unity in American life. But this unity ... meant conformity to their vision of American ideals, which included political and social dominance of their own kind.[54]

While the nineteenth-century lodges were often idealized as harmonious oases that would transcend the tumult of mainstream society, in many ways they were fissured with deep tensions of their own. Foremost among these were the tensions between egalitarianism and privilege, between the ideal of a universal brotherhood and the reality of an exclusivist community that reinforced deep asymmetries of gender, class, and race. While ideally constructed a kind of "meritocracy," in which individuals would advance in status and rank through hard work and acquisition of virtue, the lodges also reinforced many deep relations of power. As Bourdieu incisively observes, systems that are presented as "meritocratic" can often serve to obscure and reproduce underlying "aristocratic" sorts of hierarchies.[55] Bourdieu describes a similar process at work, for example, in modern educational systems. Whereas education in most modern developed societies is usually imagined to be democratic and meritocratic, it frequently reinforces the power of the dominant classes, who are usually those who can afford to live in areas with good schools and send their children to expensive colleges. Providing the dominant classes with a kind of "theodicy" of their own privilege, it transforms their economic power into a form of cultural power — in the form of degrees, linguistic skills, and social connections — which in turn justifies their status in the social hierarchy, making it appear "legitimate" or "natural." "The academic meritocracy is a form of aristocracy. It is rooted in the notion of 'natural' rights and abilities of individuals, which masks inherited cultural advantages."[56]

In a similar but perhaps even more exaggerated way, the elaborate system of advancements in the Scottish Rite lodge served to bestow a kind of symbolic power on the initiate, a status and reputation as a virtuous, upstanding, respectable, and "distinguished" individual. Despite the rhetoric of meritocracy, hard work, and virtue, it often helped to legitimate and naturalize the status of white, middle-class, native-born men.

Symbolism and Secrecy: Scarce Resources of Knowledge and Power

As the most "the elite mystical branch of the craft,"[57] the Scottish Rite places tremendous emphasis on secrecy and on the importance of esoteric symbolism in the itinerary of the aspiring Mason. Pike states repeatedly that concealment is both the starting point and the end point of all Masonic practice: "It is for each individual Mason to discover the secret of Masonry, by reflection upon its symbols and wise consideration and analysis of what is said and done in the work. Masonry does not *inculcate* her truths. She *states* them, once and briefly; or hints them, perhaps darkly, or interposes a cloud between them and eyes that would be dazzled by them."[58] Like the mysteries of the Greeks or the occult symbols of the Egyptians, Masonic truths are too profound to be conveyed in plain literal language; rather they must be transmitted through obscure, often seemingly nonsensical symbols and enigmas. Moreover, secrecy has often been necessary to preserve the most precious teachings from corruption by institutional churches or tyrannical governments:

"When despotism and superstition ... reigned everywhere ... it invented, to avoid persecution, the mysteries, that is to say, the allegory, the symbol and the emblem, and transmitted its doctrines by the secret mode of initiation. Now ... it smiles at the puny efforts of kings and popes to crush it."[59] Pike also makes it clear that a primary function of secrecy is precisely to *mislead and confuse* the uninitiated, to lead the unworthy astray by means of obfuscation and confusing symbolism:

> Masonry, like all the Religions, all the Mysteries ... *conceals* its secrets from all except the Adepts and Sages, or the Elect, and uses false explanations and misinterpretations of its symbols to mislead those who deserve only to be misled....
>
> So Masonry jealously conceals its secrets, and intentionally leads conceited interpreters astray.[60]

Yet despite these repeated warnings, it would seem that most of the symbols of Masonry are not particularly shocking or remarkable; in fact, many are quite mundane and not particularly difficult to discover for non-Masons. "Many people who take the oath would be hard pressed to define what they are supposed to keep secret, unless it is simply the ritual steps, signs and passwords. These have long been accessible to any outsider who cares to do a little research in a good library."[61] So why is it that they need to be surrounded with such an enormous amount of secrecy and mystery? Perhaps because it is the very power of secrecy itself—the adornment of silence—that helps transform an otherwise unremarkable body of teachings into rare, scarce, highly valued pieces of knowledge. It creates a body of precious resources, a kind of esoteric currency, which in turn grows in value as one advances in the lodge.

A complete analysis of all the various symbols—not to mention the various levels of interpretation and hidden meaning—in Pike's Scottish Rite system would require a study at least as massive as the *Morals and Dogma* itself. Let it suffice here to mention just a few of the more important symbols. The lodge itself is imagined as a great temple full of symbols, patterned after the Temple of Solomon, which mirrors the great cosmic temple of God's universe. Its two main pillars, called by the biblical names Jachin and Boaz, symbolize the primordial balance of the positive and negative forces of creation—male and female, light and darkness, sun and moon. "Every lodge," Pike tells us, "is a Temple, and as a whole, and in its details, symbolic.... The arrangement of the Temple of Solomon, the symbolic ornaments which formed its decorations ... all had referents to the Order of the Universe."[62]

In each chapter of *Morals and Dogma*, Pike unveils a new set of symbols relating to each grade of the Rite, unfolding a kind of ever-expanding web of figures, meanings, and deeper interpretations. From his eclectic readings of the world's sacred texts and the occult writings of Éliphas Lévi, Pike weaves an elaborate symbolic tapestry, drawn from the imagery of Masonry as well as alchemical, Kabbalistic, and Templar lore.[63] In the first degree of Apprentice, for example, the initiate is instructed in the basic meanings of the gavel, the chisel, and the 24″ gauge, which represent the faculties of passion, analysis, and measured choice; in the second degree, he is taught the significance of the level, plumb-line, and square, which symbolize respectively the standards of justice, mercy and truth; and then in the third degree, he is taught the inner meaning of the compass, pencil and skirrett, representing the capacity for creativity, understanding, and balanced judgment. Beyond these initial, rudimentary symbols, as one passes into the higher grades of the Scottish Rite proper, the symbols multiply exponentially.

Yet even as he devotes hundreds of pages to elaborating their meaning, Pike repeatedly warns that the symbols of the lodge can never be reduced to any final interpretation. Indeed, their power lies precisely in the fact that they transcend the limits of ordinary human thought. Ultimately, the *content* of the symbols is not even the most important factor: what is important is the *effect* of the symbols on the initiate, their *affective power* in generating a sense of *awe, mystery, the hidden power of the Masonic tradition.* For "even if members fail to comprehend the nuances of the rituals, the symbols evoked an appropriate *feeling.*"[64] What is important about secrets in this case (and in many others, I would argue) is not primary the occult knowledge they process to contain; rather, it is the way in which secrets are exchanged, the mechanisms of power through which they are conferred, and the kind of status and symbolic power that the possession of secret information bestows on the individual. The content is not, of course, entirely arbitrary or meaningless; but its importance is secondary to its function as a source of symbolic power. Pike says as much when he describes the power of the "Grand Arcanum"—a secret so profound that it cannot be expressed in any form, so dangerous that it would destroy those who reveal it, and so precious because it is the source of both knowledge and power. Thus, the Grand Arcanum is

> that secret whose revelation would overturn Earth and Heaven. Let no one expect us to give them its explanation! He who passes behind the veil that hides this mystery, understands that it is in its very nature inexplicable, and that it is death to ... him who reveals it.

> This secret is the Royalty of the Sages, the Crown of the Initiate.... The Grand Arcanum makes him master of gold and the light....[65]

Not only are the numbers of symbols unlimited, but the levels of interpretation—which become progressively more mysterious—are equally endless. At each grade of initiation, the previous truths of the earlier grades are stripped away, shown to be limited teachings for the immature, while the deeper truth lies beyond. Pursuit of knowledge becomes like peeling the layers of an onion or exploring a set of Chinese boxes: information on one level is the deceitful cover that gives way to a deeper kind of meaning at another level. For truth, Pike explains, is so easily profaned that it must be intentionally obfuscated from low-level initiates and reserved solely for the better-prepared adepts:

> The Blue Degrees are but the outer court or portico of the Temple. Part of the symbols are displayed to the Initiate, but he is *intentionally misled by false interpretations*. It is not intended that he shall understand them; but is intended that he shall *imagine* he understands them. Their true explication is reserved for the Adepts.[66]

Even at the highest thirty-second degree of the Sublime Secret, the candidate is not actually told the innermost meaning of Masonic symbols; rather, he is informed that many symbols have still deeper meanings and ties to ancient mysteries of which he has merely "succeeded in obtaining but a few hints" and about which nothing more can be communicated to him.[67] As the great French occultist, Éliphas Lévi, put it in *The Great Secret*, "Freemasonry is only so powerful in the world because of its dread secret, so wonderfully kept that the initiates, even those who are in the highest degrees, do not know it."[68]

In short, this system of progressive unveiling, this peeling of the layers of secrecy, ensures that the power and value of the secret as a precious commodity remains intact. It remains a source of mystery and a scarce resource, precisely because the Mason can never know its final meaning but must continue ascending grades of initiation, uncovering ever deeper levels of truth. As Pike explains, "Symbolism tended continually to become more complicated; all the powers of Heaven were reproduced on earth, until a web of fiction and allegory was woven ... which the wit of man ... will never unravel."[69] Like all capital, then, the symbolic capital produced by the possession of esoteric knowledge continues to grow and reproduce as one ascends in rank and status.

38 CHAPTER 1

Material Esotericism:
Clothing, Regalia, and Physical Adornment

In many esoteric traditions, the acquisition of deep levels of knowledge is accompanied by the acquisition of various kinds of material regalia to mark, encode, and render that knowledge visible, at least to those who know how read it. As Colleen McDannell notes in her study of Mormon garments, clothing and other forms of religious dress are often at once a mark of prestige and a kind of "language" that communicates particular sorts of information through both nonverbal and non-iconographic means: "clothing draws attention to the individual and projects an air of religious and social confidence.... [C]lothing is used as a language to convey religious meanings and intentions without the use of traditional ... iconography."[70] As such, clothing is often closely tied to secrecy, insofar as both are forms of concealment that also mark status and difference: "secrecy empowers and emboldens the holder. Secrets provide special knowledge and protection. Secrets tell believers that 'you are one of us.' At the same time, the set-apartness serves as a constant reminder of difference."[71]

Freemasonry in general and the Scottish Rite in particular arguably represent the epitome of this sort of physical adornment, adding a specific set of aprons, jewels, collars, swords, and other regalia to each of the higher degrees. In a very concrete way, "Freemasonry requires material culture to function at its full potential as an organisation whose ceremonies are 'veiled in allegory and illustrated by symbols.'"[72] And yet, these esoteric adornments not only bear deep symbolic meaning but also visibly mark prestige and distinction: "For many American men," Hackett notes, "the Masonic square and compass on one's watch chain was a recognizable sign of middle-class respectability."[73] The Masonic adornment was therefore not simply an outward marker of esoteric knowledge but, perhaps most important, a powerful key that opened doors to critical social connections, business opportunities, and status in the broader world outside the lodge: "Belonging to the Craft almost became a prerequisite for politicians and businessmen in the period between 1890 and 1930, as the Masonic ring or lapel pin proved the wearer to be a dependable and upstanding man."[74]

As the lodges grew in numbers and ornate complexity, the production of fraternal regalia developed into a huge commercial industry during the late nineteenth and early twentieth centuries. For much of the early days of American masonry in the eighteenth century, as John Hamilton notes in his study of Masonic material culture, "the sewing and decorating of Masonic articles remained the domain of a Mason's female relatives," a task for wives and daughters in the home. However, by the early 1800s, an increasing number of professional artists had begun to fashion masonic aprons, uniforms, and jewelry. During the Civil War, the industry for regalia quickly "boomed" with the need for new uniforms and other accoutrements; and then, after the war, Masonic regalia began to be aggressively advertised and marketed as part of the larger economy of fraternal organizations that expanded rapidly during the 1870s through the 1890s: "Advertisements for fraternal regalia began to appear almost as soon as the war ended. Regalia manufactures issued attractive goods catalogs that catered to an expanding variety of organisations."[75] These included not just Masonic aprons and jewels, but also an array of other theatrical outfits worn by various actors — such as costumed priests, roman centurians, shepherds, kings, scholars, scribes, craftsmen, knights, and monks — who performed a number of ritual scripts during initiations to "heighten the impact upon candidates of the moral lesson."[76]

In addition to proliferating the most elaborate degrees, the Scottish Rite also developed the most elaborate regalia to mark the Mason's progress through the grades, which became increasingly impressive and ornate. Thus, the twenty-eighth degree Mason received a pentacle as a jewel and on his apron, along with a collar bearing an eye; the thirtieth degree is marked by a cross-shaped jewel bearing the double-headed eagle, along with a sword and dagger; at the thirty-second degree, one received a cap bearing the double-headed eagle and an apron adorned with a nonagon (fig. 1.5), and so on. But perhaps the more intricate of these many adornments is the thirty-third degree jewel marking the highest "official grade" of inspector general (fig. 1.2). The jewel condenses multiple layers of symbolism in a single adornment: a double-headed eagle is flanked by the Masonic square and compass and by the Latin phrases *Ordo ab Chao* ("order out of chaos") and *Deus Meumque Jus* ("God and my right"), and letters spelling out *Sapientia* ("Wisdom"). All of this is surrounded by a cross, a nine-pointed star, two crossed swords, and finally the Ouroboros or serpent devouring its own tail. As Pike explains, the serpent consuming its tail is an ancient "symbol of eternity" and the cycles of time drawn from Egyptian, Gnostic, and alchemical traditions,[77] while the cross is the symbol of "universal nature, pointing to the four quarters of the world."[78] Similarly, the double-headed eagle is said to be another ancient symbol that has been used from the ancient Chaldees and Egyptians through the Middle Ages to symbolize the profound mystery of duality resolved into

FIGURE 1.2. 33rd Degree Scottish Rite jewel. Photo by author.

unity—for example, the mystery that man is both eternal and temporal, composed of both spirit and body, that both faith and reason are necessary, and so on.[79] Here we see secrecy and adornment literally fused into one; the adorning jewel itself is a tightly woven network of esoteric symbols, each with multiple layers of meaning to be discovered by the initiate as he progresses through the degrees.

As the anthropologist Victor Turner has famously shown, religious symbols in most cultures tend to be complex knots comprised of many levels of significance. The efficacy of a deeply meaningful symbol lies precisely in its powers of "condensation," "multivocality," and "polyvalence"—that is, in its ability to contain several layers of meaning and multiple overlapping dimensions of interpretation simultaneously.[80] The regalia of the Scottish rite—and esoteric symbolism more generally—is a particularly striking example of this sort of condensation and polyvalence. The entire point of such symbols is to serve as the outermost, visible covering or veil that is to be peeled away, only to reveal ever deeper layers of interpretation as the initiate penetrates further into inner recesses of the tradition.

By the early 1900s, the elaborate costumes and jewelry of the Rite were accompanied by still more impressive lodges, with increasingly sophisticated props and stages for the dramatic performance of initiations and degrees. As Kenneth Ames suggests, this incredibly ornate material and visual culture was perhaps the single greatest reason for the explosion of interest in the Scottish Rite during the first decades of the twentieth century.[81]

As such, the elaborate regalia and ornamentation of the Scottish Rite is a particularly explicit and striking illustration of Simmel's key insight into the adorning power of secrecy. As a kind of accentuation of the personality, adornment expresses one's status and the means by which that status appears legitimate and recognizable: "Adornment thus appears as the means by which his social power or dignity is transformed into visible, personal excellence."[82] Like the mystery and awe that surrounds the secret, adornment is thus a kind of aura of power that emanates from the individual, enhancing his status and prestige, precisely by virtue of what it conceals:

> Adornment intensifies or enlarges the impression of the personality by operating as a sort of radiation emanating from it. . . . The radiations of adornment, the sensuous attention it provokes, supply the personality with such an enlargement of its sphere: the personality, so to speak, *is* more when it is adorned.[83]

Particularly in the ornate regalia of the Scottish Rite, with its crowns, robes, and scepters all modeled on European royalty, the adorning power of secrecy is designed to enlarge the personality quite significantly indeed. One may become not just a Secret Master, but a "Knight Rose Cross," a "Grand Pontiff," a "Prussian Knight," or a "Prince of the Tabernacle," among other impressive titles (fig. 1.3). As Mark Carnes puts it, "On lodge nights, men who had climbed the corporate ladder . . . exulted in the explicit challenges and confrontations . . . the swords, the crowns, and the mitres of authority. When the lights blazed forth and the men strode across the stage, they wielded power."[84] Yet here we also see the deep tension between the ideals of egalitarianism and the elitist hierarchy of the lodge: while theoretically open to all men irrespective of class, the lodge exaggerated social hierarchy and its own kind of esoteric aristocracy, embodied in the equally exaggerated costumes of European royalty.

42 CHAPTER 1

FIGURE 1.3. Costumed Scottish Rite degree team, ca. 1917. Reproduced in William L. Fox, *Lodge of the Double-Headed Eagle* (Fayetteville: University of Arkansas Press, 1997).

Initiation, Hierarchy, and Status: Ascending Grades of Distinction

Secrecy in the Scottish Rite is closely tied to hierarchy and to a complex, graded system of concealment and revelation (fig. 1.4). "Power in our Rite *descends* from the summit," as Pike put it in a letter of 1866.[85] Yet at the same time, hierarchy also serves as a kind of "ladder of symbolic power," a means to upward mobility that confers increasing status and power on the Mason. Again, the centrality of hierarchy to the Masonic system seems to be in clear tension with its stated ideals of democracy and egalitarianism, revealing that the latter is typically much more complicated than it at first appears. As Bruce Lincoln aptly puts it, "Egali-

FIGURE 1.4. The Steps of Freemasonry. Print based on a 1956 painting by Everett Henry.

tarianism ... is never a simple matter, there being a multitude of ways in which hierarchy may be reasserted, the most egalitarian of claims and intentions notwithstanding."[86]

As the most elaborate and complex of all the many fraternal traditions, the Scottish Rite builds on the usual three Masonic grades of Entered Apprentice, Fellowcraft, and Master Mason, adding an additional twenty-nine increasingly ornate levels of initiation. The first three or "blue" grades, as described above, contain the basic teachings of morality, loyalty and obedience, as the novice is instructed in the meaning of key Masonic principles and the symbolism of architecture. The third degree involves the important initiatory process of death and rebirth, in which the Mason dies to his old identity in the exoteric world and is reborn into a new identity within the lodge. The brothers reenact the legendary narrative of Hiram Abiff, the architect who was believed to be assassinated for his knowledge of the secrets of Solomon's temple. In the process, the initiate undergoes a symbolic death and rebirth, now grafted as a limb onto the hierarchical body of the lodge.[87]

Passing beyond the lower three degrees, the Scottish Rite Mason enters into the upper grades, which expand as a kind of intricate architectonic structure or pyramid of increasingly esoteric ranks with ever more impressive aristocratic, military, and royal titles. In the narrow confines of this chapter, we need not analyze all twenty-nine—which begin with the fourth degree of Secret Master and extend to the highest grade of Sublime Prince of the Royal Secret, followed by a thirty-third "official grade" of Grand Inspector General. Importantly, these progressively esoteric grades create a complex "map" of the ideal social order, one based on ever more complicated degrees of esoteric knowledge.

Jonathan Blanchard's classic work, *Scottish Rite Masonry Illustrated* (1882), provides a particularly detailed account of the upper degrees. On entry into the thirty-second degree of the Sublime Prince of the Royal Secret, the candidate is led to the west end of the lodge, where a series of complex geometric figures is drawn on the floor. First is a nonagon, around which the other members stand, which is said to symbolize "an encampment of the Masonic army."[88] The candidate is told that he will now learn the most esoteric meaning of the Scottish Rite and then circumambulates the nonagon twice. Surrounding the nonagon is a series of flags, and as the candidate passes by them, the commander explains the meaning of the first eighteen degrees. Within the nonagon, there lie a septagon, a pentagon, and finally a triangle. The septagon, he is told, represents the nineteenth through twenty-sixth degrees, the pentagon the twenty-seventh through thirtieth degrees, and the triangle the highest three.[89] In this way, the entire hierarchy of the lodge is imaginatively constructed as a great pyramid or series of concentric geometric figures, mirroring the architectonic structure of God's universe.[90] Just as the cosmos ascends as a hierarchical structure, rising from its base in the material world toward the supreme point of Divinity Unity, so too the lodge ascends from its base in lower grades rising to its highest point of Masonic virtues of the uppermost degrees. (This same series of concentric geometric figures is reproduced in the regalia of the thirty-second degree, appearing on the Mason's apron; fig. 1.5.)

As Bourdieu, Lincoln, and others have shown, symbolic maps and hierarchical schemes of this sort very often also map social space. That is, they provide structural blueprints for a particular social and political arrangement, making that arrangement appear to be "natural," as though inscribed into the very fabric of creation. In short, "symbolic space (e.g., house, temple) is a model of social space (social, economic and political hierarchies)."[91] In fact, these kinds of religious and symbolic hierarchies often mask and recode social hierarchies, making them appear not arbitrary or accidental but essential and "legitimate." By providing a kind of "ideological mystification for sociopolitical realities," "arbitrary social hierarchies are thus represented as if given by nature."[92]

At the same time, the elaborate grades of this initiatory hierarchy serve not only as a social map but also as a kind of "ladder" of symbolic power.

FIGURE 1.5. 32nd degree apron. Photo by author.

As Dumenil suggests, one of the primary reasons for the enormous popularity of Freemasonry in the nineteenth century was that it offered young men a clearly-marked and exclusive pathway to ascending positions of status and distinction. By creating an elite group and offering advancements through degrees, it served to both "confer status on a small number" and offer access to networks of "financial aid, business, and political connections and sociability."[93] The elaborate ranks and promotions of the Scottish Rite were especially attractive to many American men in an era of rapid economic change, allowing them at once to climb to new levels of status and to adorn that status with an aura of legitimacy, validation, and royal adornment:

> The fraternal order was a model society, where the traits of male culture were enshrined and often exaggerated. Hierarchy, a key feature of most patriarchal organization, was ... vital to the Masonic system: Initiates with enough time and money could advance through twenty-nine stages to become thirty-second-degree Masons. The fixed, immutable, hierarchy of the Masonic orders offered a security and stability missing in the larger society.[94]

Ultimately, at the highest levels of initiation, the Scottish Rite Mason comes to learn the most profound secrets that lie not just at the heart of

XXXII.

SUBLIME PRINCE OF THE ROYAL SECRET.

[Master of Royal Secret.]

FIGURE 1.6. Rebis or Androgyne. Reproduced in Albert Pike, *Morals and Dogma of the Ancient and Accepted Scottish Rite of Freemasonry* (Charleston, SC: Supreme Council of the Ancient and Accepted Scottish Rite, 1871), 839.

the lodge but also at the heart of human nature and of the social order itself. Drawing heavily on older esoteric traditions such as Kabbalah and alchemy, Pike calls this the "Mystery of Balance" or complementary and union of opposites. In fact, the frontispiece of chapter 32 of *Morals and Dogma* is a famous alchemical engraving of the Rebis or Androgyne, the key symbol of the great work of alchemical transformation (fig. 1.6). As Pike explains, all contrary forces ultimately emanate from God: male and female, sun and moon, light and dark, all come from the same source, and all reunite in the highest initiation. This mystery of duality in unity is found throughout Masonic symbolism, from the basic square and compass, to the two pillars Jachin and Boaz, to the double-headed eagle that is the key emblem of the Scottish Rite. Diving still further down into the esoteric weeds, Pike suggests that this profound mystery can be discovered by using the Kabbalistic technique of letter combination and analysis, by taking apart and reforming the letters of the Tetragrammaton, the most holy name of God, YHWH. If the Tetragrammaton is divided and then reversed, it becomes a male-female binary that embodies the divine mystery of duality in unity that is the ultimate secret of all religious traditions and the key to Creation itself:

> Reversing the letters of the Ineffable Name, and dividing it, it becomes bisexual, as the word *Yud-He* or *JAH* is, and discloses the meaning of much of the obscure language of the Kabalah, and is The Highest of which the Columns Jachin and Boaz are the symbol. "In the image of Deity," we are told, "God created the Man: Male and Female created He *them*."[95]

In his study of Freemasonry and masculinity, Mark Carnes interprets this passage largely in terms of the psychology and gender. In his analysis, it affirms the secret that men too have a feminine side, something that few Victorian American males could admit publicly.[96] Yet, beyond the gender dynamic, there also appears to be a profound social and political dimension to this mystery. Pike suggests that the true meaning of this union of opposites is the harmonious balance of individual freedom and hierarchical authority, the wedding of self-will and obedience to law, which is the basis of the ideal social order. It is the subordination of individual appetite—the human in us—to reason and moral judgement—the divine in us. This hierarchical union is the foundation of Freemasonry and the means to achieving the true "Empire," of which the lodge is the model: "FREEMASONRY *is the subjugation of the Human that is in man by the Divine....* That victory, when it has been achieved ... is the true HOLY EMPIRE."[97] On social and political levels, this is also the union of individual free will and obedience to hierarchical power, which is the foundation of just government. Inscribed in the very motions of the planets, it is

> that Equilibrium between Authority and Individual Action which constitutes Free Government, by settling on immutable foundations of Liberty with Obedience to Law, Equality with Subjection to Authority, Fraternity with Subordination to the Wisest and Best.[98]

Here perhaps we find the resolution (or at least attempted resolution) to the deep tension running throughout American Masonry noted above: namely, the tension between ideals of freedom and equality, on one hand, and the reality of hierarchy and elitism, on the other.

Ultimately, Pike suggests, this is the natural law at work in all of creation — the subordination of the lesser to the great, the weak to the strong, the poor to the wealthy — which God has ordained in both nature and the just society. Class hierarchies, labor relations, even racial domination and slavery, all of these are established by God's will, and the Mason's duty is to freely obey them. As Pike explains in one particularly telling passage,

> The law of Justice is as universal [a] one as the law of Attraction.... Among the bees, one rules, while the others obey — some work, while others are idle. With the small ants, the soldiers feed on the proceeds of the workmen's labor. The lion lies in wait for and devours the antelope that has apparently as good a right to life as he. Among men, some govern and others serve, capital commands and labor obeys, and one race, superior in intellect, avails itself of the strong muscles of another that is inferior; and yet, for all this, no one impeaches the justice of God.
>
> No doubt all these varied phenomena are consistent with one great law of justice.... It is very easy for some dreaming and visionary theorist to say that it is most evidently unjust for the lion to devour the deer, and for the eagle to tear and eat the wren; but the trouble is, that we know of no other way, according to the frame, the constitution, and the organs which God has given them, in which the lion and the eagle could manage to live at all. Our little measure of justice is not God's measure. His justice does not require us to relieve the hard-working millions of all labor, to emancipate the serf or slave, unfitted to be free, from all control.[99]

Thus, the secret of the highest degrees is also the secret to reconciling the Masonic ideal of egalitarianism with the preservation of hierarchy and status. This secret offers a means of harmonizing democracy with the accumulation of power, rank, and privilege — including the privileges of class, wealth, race, and even slavery. Or, to put a sharper edge on it, the rhetoric of the former serves not only to obscure but also to mask and recode the reality of the latter. At the same time, Pike's account of the highest degrees remains consistent with his political writings of the 1850s and 1860s, in which he defended slavery, condemned Negro suffrage, fiercely rejected the idea of allowing blacks into his lodge, and even championed the idea of a white "Order of Southern Brotherhood."

Conclusions: The Superficiality of the Secret and the Decline of American Freemasonry

No less surprising than the dramatic rise of Freemasonry in nineteenth-century America was its rapid decline in the twentieth century. For a time, at least, the lodges had provided a kind of oasis, an ideal realm in which white, middle-class, male values could be preserved and even reinforced. For men like Pike, the secret symbols, initiations, elaborate robes, and ornate regalia offered a means of acquiring and preserving status amidst an increasingly heterogeneous world and multiracial society. But more important, the layers of secrecy also served to legitimate that status, making it appear to be based not on arbitrary birth, wealth, or skin color but on merit, character, and moral goodness.

By the second quarter of the twentieth century, however, the lodges had lost much of the dominant role they once enjoyed. From their peak of popularity at the turn of the century, they declined rapidly in the years between 1925 and 1940; by midcentury, few Americans still took the elaborate ceremony of the lodges very seriously. According to some scholars such as Dumenil, this decline was due to the increasingly secular character of modern American culture, which made the mystical regalia seem outdated, archaic, and "out of step with modern times."[100] Others suggest that Freemasonry became a victim of the increasing commercialization of the lodges during the early twentieth century, as they began to function less as repositories of ancient esoteric wisdom and more as part of the "business of brotherhood" and aggressive tactics of growth that drove lodges to compete for members and to strive to increase their size.[101] As Kenneth Ames argues, the lodges ironically became a victim of their own commercial success, as superficial profit seemed to overtake the ideal of deep esoteric content or fraternal bonding:

> The radical changes in Freemasonry ... reflected the impact of the market mentality ... and the predominance of the profit motive. The great transformation of the Scottish Rite was yet another example of the ubiquitous market principle at work: The fraternity emphasized the most marketable aspect of its activity, and its dues-paying membership soared.... As growth became the major goal of the organization ... initiate involvement in the ritual became increasingly depersonalized and remote. Appearance overtook substance.[102]

In Simmel's terms, the "adorning" function of secrecy had begun to displace whatever deeper mystery it might have concealed, leaving only a variety of empty ornaments, jewels, and costumes—hollow signifiers no longer pointing to any profound realities. Adornment having become an end in itself, the aura of deeper mystery was largely forgotten by the mid-twentieth century.

At the same time, as we will see in chapter 2, the American spiritual marketplace was being flooded by a growing number of movements that promised secret knowledge. These included a wide array of fraternal orders derived from Masonry and new esoteric movements such as the Theosophical Society, many neo-Gnostic orders, modern magical groups such as the Golden Dawn, and exotic imports from South Asia such as Yoga and Tantra, among myriad others. Increasingly, the secret knowledge of Freemasonry was only one among many competing systems in a vast and rapidly expanding occult marketplace. As the esoteric wisdom of the world's traditions became increasingly accessible through new purveyors, the elaborate initiations and regalia of the Masonic lodges became perhaps more of an obstacle than an attraction. And yet, the hierarchical structure and adorning power of Masonic symbolism would serve as the quintessential template for most later esoteric traditions, reappearing not only in obvious places such as the Golden Dawn and other initiatory groups but even in unexpected spaces such as the Nation of Islam, the Five Percenters, and the Church of Scientology.

Freemasonry has not disappeared completely from the American cultural landscape; it retains a significant presence in the twenty-first century, though now more as a social and charitable organization than as a repository of arcane esoteric knowledge.[103] Moreover, the deep racial tensions within the Scottish Rite and many American lodges have also continued to this day. Particularly in the southern US, most of the lodges remain racially segregated, and the Grand Lodges of twelve southern states still refuse to even *acknowledge* the black Prince Hall Masons as legitimate brethren.[104] Meanwhile, the Supreme Council Southern Jurisdiction of the Scottish Rite recognized black Freemasonry as a legitimate tradition only in 2013 (while itself remaining segregated).[105] In short, the profound slippage between the ideal of equality and the stark reality of exclusion and racism has remained a central problem for American Masons from Pike's time to the present day.

✳ CHAPTER 2 ✳

The Secret Doctrine

THE ADVERTISEMENT OF THE SECRET
IN THE THEOSOPHICAL SOCIETY AND
THE ESOTERIC SECTION

*[T]he outline of a few fundamental truths from the Secret Doctrine of the
Archaic ages is now permitted to see the light, after long millenniums of the most
profound silence and secrecy. I say "a few truths," advisedly, because that which
must remain unsaid could not be contained in a hundred such volumes, nor could
it be imparted to the present generation of Sadducees. But, even the little that
is now given is better than complete silence upon those vital truths.*

HELENA PETROVNA BLAVATSKY, *The Secret Doctrine*[1]

*To hide and unveil, to contain and release—
this is the rhythm of secrets and also of the sacred.*

PAUL C. JOHNSON, *Secrets, Gossip, and Gods*[2]

One of the fundamental paradoxes at the heart of most esoteric religions,
as noted in the introduction, is that secret knowledge is rarely entirely
"secret." In contrast to silence pure and simple, secrets are typically structured to be transmitted and communicated, at least to a chosen few. But
more than simply communicated, secrets are often *advertised*—at least in
partial form—to a public audience and offered with the tantalizing promise of deeper mysteries to come. For a secret is significant only if someone
knows *that* one has a secret; but it retains its power only so long as not
everyone knows what the secret is really about.

In his study of Jewish mysticism, Elliot Wolfson eloquently describes
this paradoxical advertisement of the secret—this back-and-forth dialectic of partial revelation and general obfuscation that is a common feature
of religious concealment. Secrecy, he writes,

> does not simply involve the hiding of information from others. Quite the
> contrary, an important aspect of secrecy is clearly the investiture of power
> to those who seek to disseminate the secret they possess, but in such a way

that the hidden nature of the secret is preserved.... What empowers me as the keeper of a secret is not only that I transmit it to some and not to others but that in the very transmission I maintain the secret by holding back in my advancing forward.... [T]he secret is a secret only to the extent that it is concealed in its disclosure.[3]

The secret, in other words, is crafted in such a way as to publicize its existence, while also concealing its content, employing the former to carefully but only partially reveal the latter.[4] As we saw above, Paul Johnson captures this paradoxical nature of concealment very nicely in his concept of "*secretism*," which involves both the "active milling, polishing and promotion of the reputation of secrets" *and* the "promiscuous circulation of a secret's inaccessibility."[5]

Perhaps the clearest illustration of this sort of advertisement of the secret in the modern era is the eclectic, controversial, but hugely influential movement known as the Theosophical Society. Founded in New York City in 1875 by the enigmatic Russian mystic, Helena Petrovna Blavatsky (1831–91), and her American cohort, Henry Steel Olcott (1832–1907), the Theosophical Society was a key part of the broader proliferation of new religions, sects, and alternative spiritualities in nineteenth-century America. Other rapidly growing new movements included the popular wave of Spiritualism, which spread like wildfire after the 1840s, Mormonism, which had its own esoteric and Masonic elements, and various neo-Gnostic orders, among many others.[6] As discussed in the introduction, nineteenth-century America was a teeming spiritual marketplace, in which religion increasingly assumed the "shape of a commodity." As a result, religious leaders resorted to many of the same techniques of advertising used by other merchants: "Ministers needed to learn the techniques of self-promotion and rely, like other people who had ... products to sell, upon handbills, newspapers and the telegraph. Advertising created expectations. How the preacher spoke, not what he said, became a marketable commodity."[7]

The modern occult revival was a key part of this lively marketplace. Particularly through the new power of mass publishing, authors such as Éliphas Lévi offered a wide array of esoteric texts to huge public audiences, even while warning that this profound knowledge was intended for only the chosen few.[8] If Jütte is correct that the fifteenth to eighteenth centuries saw the rise of a kind of "economy of secrets,"[9] this economy surely did not end in the nineteenth century but proliferated wildly. The occult revival offered a critical new niche market that continued but also crucially transformed many older currents of premodern Europe.[10]

A remarkable mixture of esoteric traditions drawn from both European and Asian traditions, Theosophy offered an attractive alternative amidst this new economy of secrets. Throughout her vast writings, Blavatsky freely mingled elements of Kabbalah and Hermeticism with Hindu Yoga, Vedanta, and Vajrayana Buddhism, weaving them around the ideal of a single esoteric teaching transmitted throughout the ages by a group of secret Masters. Theosophy promised to hold the innermost key that unites all these systems, revealing "the wisdom-religion esoteric in all ages" that was "preserved among Initiates of every country."[11] As such, Blavatsky is arguably the single most important figure in the development of modern esotericism, forging an ambitious synthesis of "Western" and "Oriental" mysteries that helped spark the rise of many new religions in the twentieth century.[12]

Much of the literature on Theosophy has focused either on Blavatsky's unique character or the details of the elaborate metaphysical and religious synthesis that she created.[13] In this chapter, I take a rather different approach by focusing instead on the role of secrecy in the movement. Here I mean secrecy not simply in the sense of a complex esoteric cosmology but as a more strategic *advertisement* that helped create the aura of mystery, awe, romance, and exotic allure that surrounded the early Theosophical Society. This included both the elaboration of a vast "occult rhetoric"[14] and the cultivation of an entire occult personality or *"occult habitus"* in the person of Blavatsky.[15] With her aristocratic background, her travels to the distant Orient, and her flamboyantly exotic appearance, Blavatsky presented an image that was ideally suited to the context of nineteenth-century America and Europe, at the height of the Orientalist fascination with the mystical East and fin de siècle occultism.[16] Indeed, her own life story is itself a kind of "advertised secret." Her claims to communication with a lineage of hidden Masters is a remarkable advertisement of esoteric authority that at once legitimated her position as the voice of ancient wisdom while skillfully concealing its actual sources.[17] And her two most important works—*Isis Unveiled* and *The Secret Doctrine*—are striking examples of secretism as the "promotion of the reputation of secrets," promising to uncover the deepest truths contained in all the world's sacred traditions. Finally and perhaps most important, Blavatsky formed two new confidential groups within the Theosophical Society: the Esoteric Section and the Inner Group. These were designed, as least in part, to compete with other new rivals in the occult marketplace of the nineteenth century, such as the Hermetic Order of the Golden Dawn.[18]

The early growth of Theosophy was thus in many ways a process of *ever-increasing secretism*. It might be described as a complex set of "Russian dolls," a progressive layering of concealment comprised of secret Masters, secret doctrines, secret orders, and finally an occult understanding of the human body itself, containing its own multiple layers of hidden truth.

HPB: Fashioning the Image of the Quintessential Occultist

Helena Petrovna van Hahn was born in Ekaterinoslav (modern Ukraine) of combined Russian, French, Huguenot, and German heritage and was the daughter of an army colonel from minor German nobility. From her earliest childhood, she was said to have displayed psychic powers, including the ability to perceive supernatural presences. She also developed an early interest in esotericism, immersing herself in the occult library of Prince Pavel Dolgorukov, her grandmother's father, who had been initiated into Rosicrucian Freemasonry in the 1770s.[19]

In 1849, at the age of seventeen, she married Nikifor Blavatsky, vice governor of Erivan province in Armenia. Having no apparent interest in marriage, however, she deserted him on their honeymoon and left her family to roam the world. For the next twenty-five years, Blavatsky traveled extensively, though her exact itinerary is uncertain and her own accounts are largely uncorroborated and conflicting in their details. She later claimed to have journeyed widely over the world, "contacting shamans and masters of arcane lore in places as far apart as Egypt, Mexico, Canada and inner Asia," and finally to have reached her ultimate goal of Tibet.[20] However, many skeptics today find it difficult to imagine that Blavatsky—an aristocratic woman traveling on her own—could have made the difficult trek into Tibet, a feat that few outsiders had accomplished in the mid-nineteenth century.[21]

Regardless of whether she actually visited all of these regions in the flesh or solely in her imagination, Blavatsky was a key figure in the larger imagining of India and Tibet in nineteenth-century Orientalist discourse. As Chris Goto-Jones notes, Blavatsky and other "new occultists" imagined these Eastern lands as the last repository of "secret magical knowledge," which was no longer available in the "rational, scientific and post-spiritual" world of the modern West.[22] Above all, like many others of her day, Blavatsky romanticized Tibet as the ultimate source of esoteric wisdom, the most ancient, remote, and exotic realm where pure access to the innermost recesses of spiritual knowledge is still available in the modern world. Blavatsky both imbibed and helped promulgate the image of Tibet as a mystical Shangri-La, a realm of hidden knowledge, indeed, the *most secret* of all the secret locations within the mystic Orient itself. In the words of her disciple, A. P. Sinnett, "From time immemorial there has been a certain secret region in Tibet, which to this day is quite inaccessible to and unapproachable by any but initiated persons ... in which adepts have always congregated."[23] As Donald Lopez observes, this exoticized image of "secret Tibet"—of which Blavatsky was a chief architect—has continued to this day.[24]

In 1873, Blavatsky returned to the US and arrived in New York City, just as the country was witnessing the height of popularity of Spiritualism, mediumship, and contacts with unseen worlds. The Spiritualist movement had begun in the 1840s in the "burned over district" of western New York State and was reaching a vast popular audience in the parlors and domestic spaces of many American homes.[25] As Blavatsky wrote of her move to the US, her mission was largely a matter of unveiling and exposure, of revealing what is true and unmasking what is false: "I am here in this country sent by my Lodge, on behalf of *Truth* in modern Spiritualism, and it is my most sacred duty to *unveil what is,* and expose *what is not.*"[26]

Blavatsky's personality, appearance, and self-presentation left an impression on all those who met her (fig. 2.1). In her physical features, her clothing, her accent, and her mannerisms, she radiated an aura of mystery, concealed knowledge, and contact with unseen power: "she was laden with the exotic aura of a lady of Russian aristocratic background. She seemed an exile from a world of monarchical splendor. Moreover, she told tales of long intervening years of fabulous travel and initiations by members of a secret occult order in Greece, Egypt and Tibet."[27]

One of the more colorful early descriptions of Blavatsky in America was provided by Elizabeth Holt, a young schoolteacher who stayed in the same tenement house occupied by her in 1874. As Holt recalled many years after the encounter, Blavatsky was outlandish in her dress and personal habits, wearing strange garish clothing and constantly smoking hand-rolled cigarettes; but she was also a person of undeniable charisma and even "Stalin-esque" power:

> [S]he was like a magnet, powerful enough to draw round her everyone who could possibly come. I saw her, day by day, sitting there rolling her cigarettes and smoking incessantly; she had a conspicuous tobacco pouch, the head of some fur-bearing animal which she wore round the neck. . . . [S]he had a broad face and broad shoulders, her hair was lightish brown and crinkled like that of some Negroes. Her whole appearance conveyed the idea of power. I read somewhere lately an account of an interview with

Stalin; the writer said that when you entered the room you felt as if there was a powerful dynamo working. You felt something like that when you were near H. P. B.[28]

However, perhaps the most famous early description of Blavatsky was that of her future collaborator and cofounder of the Theosophical Society, Henry Steel Olcott. A successful New York lawyer who had served as a special commissioner in the War Department, Olcott wrote of his first

FIGURE 2.1. Helena Petrovna Blavatsky, London, 1889.

encounter with Blavatsky in 1874 while visiting the Eddy homestead in Chittendon, Vermont. As a site of Spiritualist phenomena, the Eddy farm had attracted a variety of curious viewers, including HPB. In Olcott's account, Blavatsky appears at once outlandish and fascinating, a character of otherworldly power behind her wild clothing and imposing features:

> My eye was first attracted by a scarlet Garibaldian shirt [she] wore, as being in vivid contrast with the dull colours around. Her hair was then a thick blond mop, worn shorter than the shoulders, and it stood out from her head, silken-soft and crinkled to the roots, like the fleece of a Cotswold ewe. This and the red shirt were what struck my attention before I took in her features. It was a massive Calmuck face, contrasting in its suggestion of power, culture, and imperiousness, as strangely with the commonplace visages about the room as her red garment did with the grey and white tones of walls and woodwork.... Pausing on the door-sill, I whispered ... "Good gracious! look at *that* specimen will you."[29]

Olcott's famous description of Blavatsky was a key part of her growing notoriety in the late nineteenth century. As he portrayed her in the *Daily Graphic* newspaper, HPB emerged as a fascinating mixture of a noble aristocrat, a fearless world traveler, an explorer of all the ancient spiritual mysteries, and a personality of tantalizing allure:

> The arrival of a Russian lady of distinguished birth and rare educational and natural endowments ... was an important event in the history of the Chittendon manifestations. This lady—Madame Helene P. de Blavatsky—has led a very eventful life, travelling in most of the lands of the Orient, searching for antiquities at the base of the Pyramids, witnessing the mysteries of Hindoo temples, and pushing with armed escort far into the interior of Africa.... In the whole course of my experience, I never met so interesting and ... eccentric a character.[30]

Inspired by Olcott's account, the editor of the *Daily Graphic* published a feature article on Blavatsky. In this description, she appears not only mysterious and noble but also surprisingly attractive: "handsome, with full voluptuous figure, large eyes, well-formed nose, and rich sensuous mouth and chin. She dresses with remarkable elegance, and her clothing is redolent of some subtle and delicious perfume which she has gathered in her wanderings in the Far East."[31]

Blavatsky's exotic appearance was matched by the exotic aura of her New York City apartment, which she occupied in the mid- to late 1870s while the Theosophical Society was established and her first major works were composed. Known as the "Lamasery," the apartment became a kind of "magnet for diverse intellectuals and bohemians drawn to the new revelation."[32] Thick with smoke, incense and the discussion of Oriental esoterica, her rooms became both the hub of the early Theosophical movement and the heart of an exciting avant-garde cultural scene:

> The room where H. P. B. held commerce with her Masters, wrote *Isis Unveiled,* and entertained Olcott and others with psychic "phenomena," was heavy with smoke from incense and her imported cigarettes.... The fantastic apartment in New York was the center of something at once dangerously *avant-garde* ... and full of whispers of ancient caves and tombs. Above all there was the presence of H. P. B., defiant of society, talking in exotic accent of mysteries far outside its purview.[33]

As such, Blavatsky was in many ways "secretism" embodied. From her remarkable biography, to her dress, language, and self-presentation, to the space in which she lived and worked, she was a striking advertisement for something hidden, powerful, potentially dangerous and deliciously outside the polite boundaries of nineteenth-century American society.

The Great Brotherhood of the Himalayas: The Complex Amalgam of the Secret Order of Masters

A key part of Blavatsky's display of secrecy was her claim to have unique contact with an ancient order of Masters, who served as the source of both her esoteric knowledge and her authority within the Theosophical Society. Blavatsky's knowledge of esoteric sciences came not from her insight alone, she claimed, but from her contact with this network of enlightened beings who were endowed with superhuman powers and had secretly transmitted the wisdom of antiquity through the ages of human history. Her first contact took place during her travels in August 1851, when she met a Master known as Morya, who informed her that she should prepare for an important mission that would require three years of study in Tibet. Morya was said to live in the remote Himalayas near the great monastery of Tashi Lhunpo, the seat of the Panchen Lama. There, Morya and his fellow Master, Koot Hoomi, ran a school for adepts adjacent to the monastery.[34] Eventually, Blavatsky would claim to be in contact with a number of other Masters, including Serapis Bey and Tuitet Bey, members of a secret community called the Brotherhood of Luxor.

Although Blavatsky's various accounts of the Masters were not systematic, the later Theosophical tradition would organize these enlightened beings into an elaborate metaphysical hierarchy that combined esoteric ideas drawn from both East and West, extending from the divine Logos down to the historical Buddha.[35]

Secrecy, Blavatsky explained, has always been the key to the survival and ongoing guidance of this brotherhood of Masters. The wisdom tradition carried by the Masters has continually been viewed with suspicion by mainstream society, and, today, in the face of modern materialism, their message has become even more inaccessible to the masses:

> Many and various are the nationalities to which belong the disciples of that mysterious school, and many the side-shoots of that one primitive stock. The secrecy preserved by these sub-lodges, as well as by the one and supreme great lodge, has ever been proportionate to the activity of religious persecutions; and now, in the face of the growing materialism, their very existence is becoming a mystery.[36]

Blavatsky's order of secret Masters has a number of precedents in earlier esoteric traditions. Perhaps most notably, it draws inspiration from the Rosicrucian Fraternity, which had its origins in seventeenth-century Germany and was imagined as an ancient order of enlightened teachers passing down secret wisdom through the ages. However, many authors have noted that at least part of Blavatsky's inspiration was likely derived from a fictional source: the British novelist Edward Bulwer-Lytton. Today most famous for penning the opening line "It was a dark and stormy night," Bulwer-Lytton also wrote one of the most influential works of occult fiction, the 1842 novel *Zanoni*. Claiming to be a translation of a mysterious manuscript "written in an unintelligible cipher,"[37] *Zanoni* is something of an "encyclopedia of ideas about the occult sciences."[38] And Bulwer-Lytton appears to have at least some direct involvement in the spiritual world of the nineteenth century, participating in magical works with the great occultist, Éliphas Lévi (who also inspired Pike, as discussed in chapter 1). One of the most important figures in the occult revival of the nineteenth century, Lévi had also taught the existence of a "secret doctrine" known to the hidden elites of all ages that unites all religious systems.[39] Bulwer-Lytton's novel fictionalized many of Lévi's ideas, including the belief in a secret order of Masters, which includes the Rosicrucians but extends much further back into the ancient past. So close is the resemblance between Blavatsky's order of secret Masters and Bulwer-Lytton's novel that some critics have concluded that much of Theosophy was "virtually manufactured from his pages."[40] Blavatsky even quotes from *Zanoni* as an epigraph on page one of the very first chapter of her first great tome, *Isis Unveiled*: "We commenced research where modern conjecture closes its faithless wings. And with us, those were the common elements of science which the sages of today disdain as wild chimeras, or despair of as unfathomable mysteries."[41]

In keeping with Blavatsky's dramatic personality and mysterious way of communicating, the Masters typically sent their messages in unusual forms — most commonly through "precipitation" or the sudden, miraculous appearance of a letter falling onto a table or found under a pillow. Thus, in 1875, when Olcott was first called to begin studying occultism with HPB, he received an impressive letter written in gold ink on thick green paper, signed by the Egyptian Master, Tuitit Bey.[42]

The letters from the Masters range in content from the sublime to the mundane. While many discuss the finer points of cosmology, spiritual practice, and metaphysics, others discuss the most crass aspects of business and finance. As Joscelyn Godwin notes, many of the letters from the Master Serapis Bey to Olcott seem less concerned with esoteric spiritual matters than with enmeshing the colonel in rickety business schemes with Blavatsky's then-husband:

> Serapis' letters to Olcott have little of the reverence and high moral tone one might expect of an adept, and virtually no indication of how the disciple might proceed on the quest to perfection.... They read more as the advice of a Machiavellian schemer than as the words of a "Master of Wisdom." Serapis ... seems mainly concerned to bind Olcott to his cause by way of occult promises and financial ties. He urges the credulous Colonel to involve his in-laws in dubious business ventures with Blavatsky's temporary husband, Michael Betanelly, for whom "there are millions in the future in store."[43]

Many skeptics have long assumed that the Masters were largely the product of Blavatsky's fertile imagination. However, there is also some evidence that they might have been based at least in part on real, earthbound individuals. Drawing on extensive evidence from Blavatsky's travels and correspondence, K. Paul Johnson has suggested the intriguing possibility that the Masters may have been more complex amalgams of real historical persons, combined with elements of Blavatsky's own fanciful elaboration. Thus, Johnson argues that Masters Morya and Koot

Hoomi were actually composite characters inspired by well-documented figures, such as Ranbir Singh, the Maharaja of Kashmir, who was interested in Vedanta philosophy; Thakar Singh, a Sikh activist who hoped to restore the throne of Punjab to his cousin, Maharaja Dalip Singh; and other prominent religious and political figures.[44] Other Masters, Johnson suggests, were amalgams of various individuals, such as Swami Dayananda Sarasvati and Ugyen Gyatso. The Masters, in other words, were neither entirely the product of Blavatsky's imagination nor exactly the beings she claimed them to be; rather, they were more like fictionalized versions of real people whose identities Blavatsky obscured with her own fanciful details: "The nature and extent of HPB's communication with the Masters remain mysterious. But it is reasonable to conclude that the Mahatma letters are more the work of HPB than believers care to accept, yet more inspired by real Masters than her critics have ever imagined."[45]

In this sense, we could say that the Masters themselves were also "advertised secrets." That is, the Masters were *presented and publicized* as representatives of a secret, ancient order of initiated teachers, whose existence was partially known through Blavatsky's published works but whose actual identities were carefully concealed beneath multiple layers of imaginative narration.

Isis Unveiled: The First Revelation of the Hidden Wisdom of the Orient

Blavatsky's two major works are both—even in their very titles—"advertised secrets," promising to divulge profound and ancient hidden truths to their readers. Both are really masterpieces of what Gunn calls "occult rhetoric" or the elaborate fashioning of language to create and advertise an aura of tremendous secret power, which became a central feature of modern esoteric literature. And both are also classic examples of nineteenth-century Orientalism—that is, the imagining of "the East" (here India, Tibet, Egypt, and almost everywhere else outside of Europe and America) as an exotic repository of secret knowledge and hidden mysteries.

Published in 1877, *Isis Unveiled* was presented as nothing less than a "Master Key to the Mysteries of Ancient and Modern Science and Technology." The work's composition embodied secretism; it was produced largely by unseen means through the work of various Masters, who inspired the "shell of her body" and held her pen with "invisible fingers."[46] Large sections materialized while Blavatsky slept, piles of pages waiting for her in the morning, while other sections were produced by automatic writing, as a Master would take over Blavatsky's body and write through her. Olcott provided a tantalizing account of the composition of *Isis*, which he describes as the product of trance states and occult vision of unseen texts:

> Her pen would be flying over the page, and I could see her every movement, when she would suddenly stop, look out into space with the vacant eye of the clairvoyant seer, shorten her vision as though to look at something held invisible in the air before her, and begin copying on her paper what she saw.[47]

Composed in two parts, *Isis Unveiled* begins with a critique of modern Western science and then delves into a long foray into comparative religion and an exposition of esoteric Buddhism as the ancient wisdom within which science and religion can be united. The first volume on science opens by discussing Darwin's *Origin of Species* and rejecting materialist science, while the second volume on theology critiques Christianity and discusses esoteric and Eastern religions. An instant success, the first printing of a thousand copies of *Isis Unveiled* sold out immediately and became the first example of nineteenth-century "occult rhetoric" to be consumed by a mass popular readership.[48]

Blavatsky presents the work as a distillation of the esoteric traditions that lie at the core of all religions and philosophies. These secret teachings have been largely lost to the modern world primarily due to "prejudice and bigotry," such that none of them "have reached Christendom in so unmutilated a form as to secure it a fair judgment."[49] Yet this ancient wisdom tradition is now being recovered in the modern world thanks to the archival and exegetical work of Blavatsky and her cohorts, who possess the key to interpreting these primordial traditions. As such, Theosophy is not only *the most ancient tradition* in the world but also *the religion of the future*, at once the foundation of all the religions of the past and the key to synthesizing these traditions for the modern age: "This ancient wisdom religion will become the religion of the future. In a few centuries, the world-religions of Buddhism, Hinduism, Christianity, and Islam will recede before the 'facts' and 'knowledge' of the ancient and universal doctrine."[50]

Yet Blavatsky also makes it clear that even in *Isis Unveiled*, this disclosure of secret knowledge is only partial and incomplete; even this profound text could reveal only hints and sketches of the deepest mysteries, which would only be revealed in still later works. In *Isis* itself, the explanations of a hundred mysteries lie but half-buried—they were altogether buried in earlier works on Occult philosophy—only waiting for the application of intelligence guided by a little Occult knowledge to come out into the light of day. When *Isis* was written ... the time was not ripe for the explicit declaration of a great many truths which they are now willing to impart in plain language. So the readers of that book were supplied rather with hints, sketches, and adumbrations of the philosophy....[51]

Passages like these make it clear that Blavatsky is a master of occult rhetoric and the skillful advertisement of the secret. Every secret revealed is always a partial revelation, at once a glimmer of hidden depths and a tantalizing reminder that more concealed mysteries remain to be uncovered, unfolding in an endless dance of attraction, allure, and withdrawal.

The Secret Doctrine: Rending the Veil of Hidden Knowledge

The culmination of Blavatsky's work—and arguably the single greatest example of nineteenth century "occult rhetoric"—is *The Secret Doctrine*. Begun in the mid-1880s after Blavatsky had settled in London and first published in 1888, the book was initially conceived as an expanded version of *Isis Unveiled*, running into two volumes and some 1,500 pages. This compendium of the world's mythology and religious traditions attempts to trace this ancient wisdom into the prehistoric and mythic past through various cosmological cycles. The two volumes are divided into Cosmogenesis, the explanation of how and why the universe came into being, and Anthropogenesis, the history of mankind and our descent from another planet who gradually took physical form through a series of "root races." The text is presented as a long commentary on a mysterious manuscript called the Stanzas of Dzyan, composed in the "Senzar language." No scholar has ever come across either a text by this name or even a language called Senzar (although a few intrepid authors have tried to relate the Stanzas of Dzyan to certain secret commentaries within the Tibetan Buddhist canon).[52] While the Sanskrit and Tibetan terminology throughout the text is taken from Buddhism and Hinduism, the underlying metaphysical system, as Goodrick-Clarke observes, is largely "a variant of Hermeticism" and based on Western esoteric traditions.[53]

The opening lines of *The Secret Doctrine* are perhaps the quintessential example of "secretism" and the advertisement of hidden knowledge. The author begins by making certain that the reader knows how ancient, profound, and mysterious this text truly is: "An archaic Manuscript—a collection of palm leaves made impermeable to water, fire and air, by some specific and unknown process—is before the writer's eye."[54] The introduction to the text goes on to explain that this manuscript is so complex and esoteric that even the writer could not understand all of it and so had to occlude the most secret parts of the document: "It is almost unnecessary to say that only portions of the Stanzas are here given. Were they published completely they would remain incomprehensible to all save the few higher occultists. Nor is there any need to assure the reader that, no more than most of the profane, does the writer, or rather the humble recorder, understand those forbidden passages."[55]

Readers of *Isis Unveiled*, however, would have been prepared already for the revelation of this mysterious ancient manuscript; for Blavatsky's previous work hinted at the existence of an archaic text that had served as the basis for the Hebrew Kabbalah: "There exists somewhere in this wide world an old Book—so very old that our modern antiquarians might ponder over its pages an indefinite time, and still not quite agree as to the nature of the fabric upon which it is written. . . . The most ancient Hebrew document on occult learning—the *Siphra Dzeniouta*—was compiled from it."[56] *The Secret Doctrine* then reveals the manuscript of the *Stanzas of Dzyan* to be precisely this ancient manuscript, which is the source of every esoteric tradition in the world. Thus, the "very old book" described in *Isis Unveiled*

> is the original work from which the many volumes of *Kiu-ti* [books that refer to the Tibetan Buddhist tantras] were compiled. Not only this latter and the *Siphrah Dzeniouta* but even the *Sepher Jezira*, the work attributed by the Hebrew Kabalists to their patriarch Abraham (!), the book of *Shu-king*, China's primitive Bible, the sacred volumes of Egyptian Thoth-Hermes, the Puranas in India, the Chaldean *Book of Numbers* and the *Pentateuch* itself, are all derived from that one small parent volume. Tradition says, that it was taken down in *Senzar*, the secret sacerdotal tongue, from the words of the Divine Beings, who dictated it to the Sons of Light in Central Asia.[57]

Like *Isis Unveiled*, *The Secret Doctrine* repeatedly uses the rhetorical trope of a progressive, ever deeper—and yet always *partial*—revelation of hidden mysteries. While *Isis* had revealed more hidden truths than any previous esoteric text, *The Secret Doctrine* reveals even greater mysteries, taking the reader still further down the path of initiatory knowledge:

Some fifteen years ago, the writer was the first to repeat, after the Kabalists, the wise Commandments in the Esoteric Catechism. "Close thy mouth, lest thou shouldst speak of *this* (the mystery), and thy heart, lest thou shouldst think aloud." ... A few years later, a corner of the Veil of Isis had to be lifted; and now another and a larger rent is made.[58]

The rhetoric of veiling and unveiling and the imagery of inner and outer levels of truth recurs throughout the text. For *The Secret Doctrine* is itself precisely the unveiling of the hidden unity of all traditions, which is by necessity concealed beneath the outer layers of exoteric religious dogmas: "Esoteric philosophy reconciles all religions, strips every one of its outward, human garments and shows the roots of each to be identical with that of every other great religion."[59]

Yet once again, Blavatsky warns that even this "greater rent" in the veil of secrecy is not complete. This translation of the Stanzas is only a tiny portion of the vast esoteric knowledge that awaits the adept who delves further into the secret doctrine. Even this text, "though giving out many fundamental tenets from the SECRET DOCTRINE of the EAST, raise[s] but a small corner of the dark veil."[60] Like pearls before swine, knowledge of this sort could be misunderstood only by the multitudes of ignorant skeptics: "For no one, not even the greatest living Adept, would be permitted or could—even if he would—give out promiscuously to a mocking, unbelieving world that which has been so effectually concealed from it for long aeons and ages."[61]

Gaining access to even the outer threshold of this secret wisdom requires initiation at the hands of trained Masters; and even then, what can be revealed is only a tiny fragment of the vast treasures of knowledge concealed within the depths of this secret doctrine:

> [N]o Theosophist, *not even as an accepted chela*—let alone lay students—could expect to have the secret teachings explained to him *thoroughly and completely*, before *he had irretrievably pledged himself to the Brotherhood and passed through at least one initiation*.... [W]hat was revealed was merely the esoteric lining of that which is contained in almost all the exoteric Scriptures of the world-religions.... It was a small portion of what is divulged far more fully now in the present volumes; and even this is very incomplete and fragmentary.[62]

The reason for this continued secrecy is not simply the ignorance of the uninitiated masses; rather, it is also because of the inherent *danger and power* of these teachings—a power that could be as destructive as an explosive device in the hands of the misguided or ill-intentioned. Indeed, *"there are secrets that kill* in the arcana of Occultism, and unless a man *lives the life* he cannot be entrusted with them"; therefore,

> [I]f purely material implements are capable of blowing up, from a few corners, the greatest cities of the globe, provided the murderous weapons are guided by expert hands—what terrible dangers might not arise from magical *occult* secrets being revealed, and allowed to fall into the possession of ill-meaning persons! A thousand times more dangerous and lethal are these, because neither the criminal hand, nor the *immaterial*, invisible weapon used, can ever be detected.[63]

Both *Isis Unveiled* and *The Secret Doctrine* thus deploy an occult rhetoric quite skillfully to construct the tremendous aura and tantalizing allure of the secret. The rhetorical strategies in these two texts include, at least, the following four tropes: (1) exoticism, Orientalism, and the claim to reveal the secrets of the mystic East (Egypt, India, Tibet); (2) esoteric transmission, or the claim to reveal this exotic knowledge through occult means, such as contact with secret Masters, automatic writing, invisible communication, and discovery of ancient manuscripts in unknown languages; (3) *veiling and unveiling,* or a complex dialectic of partial revelation and partial obfuscation of esoteric knowledge that can be disclosed in some fashion but must remain largely mysterious; and (4) the rhetoric of dangerous power and persecuted knowledge, or the assertion that the secret doctrine is both tremendously valuable but also potentially destructive, bringing untold spiritual wealth to those who are worthy and unimaginable sorrow to those who are not.

Together, these rhetorical strategies—combined with Blavatsky's own biography—helped to make Theosophy one of the most popular spiritual movements of the late nineteenth century. If the American religious landscape after the Civil War can be described as an expanding spiritual marketplace, then Theosophy was surely one of the fastest growing young businesses, offering a rare commodity that combined the mystique of the exotic Orient with insights from occult Masters and the secret key that unites all the world's religions. In this sense, Theosophy was not simply *a* religion for the late nineteenth century. It was arguably *the* religion for the late nineteenth century, combining the new global awareness of religious diversity provided by colonialism and imperialism with a new capitalist sense of an expanding global marketplace and a new occult desire for the reenchantment of a disenchanted industrial world.

The Scandal of the Secret: The Coulomb Affair

If the rhetoric of "unveiling" is a powerful one in the construction of the secret and in creating the reputation that surrounds a claim to possession of esoteric knowledge, it can also be a key metaphor for the *undermining* of that reputation. In addition to the power of secrecy as a source of symbolic capital, there is also a certain liability that can lead to critique, scandal, and exposé. Not only does the practice of secrecy often lead to all manner of conspiracy theories and speculations about immoral behavior (Freemasons are homosexuals, the Mau Mau are ready to revolt, etc.), but secrecy also brings the temptation for others to expose the esoteric community, to unveil real or imagined scandals and so rob it of symbolic power. As Simmel observes, the secret "is full of the consciousness that it *can* be betrayed.... The secret is surrounded by the possibility and temptation of betrayal.... The secret creates a barrier between men but, at the same time, it creates the tempting challenge to break through it, by gossip or confession."[64]

Simmel's comments provide a useful insight into the fate of the Theosophical Society in the late nineteenth century. In 1885, at the height of Theosophy's popularity in the US and Europe, Blavatsky became the center of an enormous controversy and "unveiling" that proved disastrous for her reputation and for the entire movement. The controversy began with a conflict between Blavatsky and a couple named Emma and Alex Coulomb, who first met her in Cairo in 1871 and had founded their own short-lived Spiritualist movement. In 1879, the couple contacted Blavatsky after running into financial problems and becoming stranded in Sri Lanka. They were then brought to India and given positions in the Theosophical Society in Adyar, placed in charge of cooking, gardening, and looking after her rooms while she was in Europe. However, a conflict emerged between Blavatsky and the Coulombs and quickly escalated, during which the couple tried to blackmail her and were dismissed. The Coulombs then published a devastating article in the *Madras Christian College Monthly* that denounced HPB as a fraud and the Masters' letters as the product of her own hand.[65] Amidst a series of charges and countercharges, the affair became well known throughout India and Europe. Indeed, the Society for Psychical Research was inspired to send Richard Hodgson, a specialist in paranormal phenomena, to India to investigate the incident and determine whether Blavatsky's communications with the Masters indicated genuine spiritual phenomena or mere chicanery. After examining the Mahatma letters and the physical spaces in which the psychic phenomena were observed, Hodgson issued a 200-page report concluding that the evidence did support the Coulombs' accusations. The shrine at the Adyar house, he determined, was elaborately built with hidden doors "with a view to the secret insertion of letters and other objects through a sliding panel at the back, and regularly used for this purpose by Madame Blavatsky or her agents." In sum, Hodgson concluded that Blavatsky was perhaps one of the most successful frauds the world had ever seen: "we regard her neither as the mouthpiece of hidden seers, nor as a mere vulgar adventuress; we think that she has achieved a title to permanent remembrance as one of the most accomplished, ingenious, and interesting impostors in history."[66]

It is worth noting, however, that this sort of exposure of the secret is by no means unique to Theosophy. As anthropologists such as Franz Boas long ago observed, it is a common phenomenon among the medicine men and so-called shamans in many cultures, where there is typically a complex mixture of belief and skepticism, credulity and fraud in the secret powers of the holy man. As he wrote of the Kwakiutl shamans, "It is perfectly well known by all concerned that a great part of the shamanistic procedure is based on fraud; still it is believed by the shaman as well as by patients and their friends. Exposures do not weaken the belief in the 'true' power of shamanism.... [T]he shaman himself is doubtful in regard to his powers and is always ready to bolster them up by fraud."[67] In a sense, the power of the shamanic figure is far more complex than a simple matter of "real" or "fraud"; rather it lies in the delicate play of secrecy, concealment, and exposure. As Michael Taussig suggests, it is this dense network of secrecy and revelation that helps generate the hope that the shaman's magic *could* be truly powerful:

> [A]lthough it is widely suspected that such magic is fraudulent, it is nevertheless believed to be efficacious or potentially so.... "[F]raud" and "belief" in "magic" are so many (inadequate) expressions not of skilled concealment but of skilled revelation of skilled concealment—this in atmospheres of expectation made dense by the see-sawing contradictions built into the labyrinth that is the public secret of knowing what not to "know" about the practices in question.[68]

Taussig's insights into the power of the shaman go a long way toward explaining the influence of Blavatsky—and of Spiritualism more broadly— even after the exposés of the late nineteenth century. While the Coulomb affair surely undermined the symbolic value of Blavatsky's teachings, it also highlighted a paradox inherent in much of nineteenth-century occultism: for surely part of the appeal of occult phenomena lay in the complex see-sawing between belief and skepticism, between the hope of being persuaded by the supernatural display and the anticipation that it might be a fraud. While it surely damaged her career, the Coulomb incident also added a new dimension to Blavatsky's occult *habitus*—another layer of mystery, intrigue, and the tantalizing hint of untold power coupled with a mischievous hint of sleight-of-hand.

The Esoteric Section and the Inner Group: Competition and Rivalry in the Marketplace of Secrets

In January 1887—just a few years after the infamous Hodgson report—Blavatsky first mentioned the idea of creating a new inner circle within the Theosophical Society, a kind of school for personalized instruction that would be "a nucleus of true Theosophists."[69] This new group was formally established as the "Esoteric Section" (E.S.) in October 1888 and then advertised prominently in an issue of *Lucifer* that same month[70] (significantly, the E.S. would later change its name to the E.S.T., or "Eastern School of Theosophy," highlighting the Eastern and yogic nature of many its inner teachings[71]). As the elite core of the most dedicated Theosophists, the E.S. was to be "a select group of brave souls, a handful of determined men and women hungry for genuine spiritual development and the acquirement of soul-wisdom," who could embody and help restore the original ideals of the Society, which had apparently been lost in recent years.[72] Most of the documents relating to the E.S. were surrounded with an even greater aura of secretism, each marked "STRICTLY PRIVATE AND CONFIDENTIAL," clearly signaling their status as powerful, valued pieces of knowledge.[73]

Members of the E.S. were asked to sign a special pledge and to follow a series of strict rules. Significantly, the pledge asked its members to combat the many accusations of fraud and chicanery that were then swirling around the Society: "I pledge myself never to listen without protest to any evil thing spoken about a brother Theosophist and to abstain from condemning others."[74] Meanwhile the rules of the E.S. demanded a vow to absolute secrecy and obedience in all matters relating to the Section, warning that one would be expelled for violating any of these provisions:

a) Obedience to the Head of the Section *in all Theosophical matters.*
b) The Secrecy of the Signs and Passwords;
c) The Secrecy of the Documents of the Section.[75]

There are several reasons why Blavatsky likely created the E.S. at this point in the development of Theosophy. One reason was clearly to solidify support among her most loyal disciples in the face of the charges of fraud leveled by the Coulombs and the Hodgson report. As Blavatsky put it, the E.S. was established in the wake of the Coulomb affair, after some disciples had abandoned her and, still worse, were disseminating their own version of the secret doctrine: "Since the explosion of the infamous Hodgson & Coulomb conspiracy against me some of my ex-pupils ill-grounded in the theosophical spirit, have, for various reasons deserted me, after posing for chelas.... Hence that time they have been giving out *travestied* versions of the esoteric philosophy."[76] Thus, the E.S. was designed for those loyal students who still had utmost confidence in her and in her genuine communication with the Masters, despite the slanderous conspiracy: "I was enabled and encouraged by the devotion of an ever-increasing number of members ... to establish an Esoteric Section, in which I can teach something of what I have learned to those who have confidence in me, and who prove this confidence by their disinterested work for Theosophy."[77] In fact, the members of the Inner Group of the E.S. even issued a formal "Declaration" in the May 1891 issue of *Lucifer*, defending their teacher in the strongest possible terms; the accusations made against Blavatsky, they asserted, were either "entirely false" or else "the grossest possible distortions of the simple facts."[78]

However, a second and perhaps more important reason for the formation of the E.S. lay in the growing competition among esoteric orders in the spiritual marketplace of the late nineteenth century. In her preliminary remarks on the instructions for the E.S., she took sharp aim at other so-called esoteric orders and "all those Societies whose pretensions are great, but whose names are simply masks—nay, even SHAMS."[79] One of the key rules of the E.S. explicitly forbade members from belonging to "any other organisation for the purpose of mystic study or occult training," making it clear that the E.S. demanded their exclusive commitment.[80]

As R. A. Gilbert suggests in his incisive study of the E.S., the Society faced a number of rivals among the many new occult, magical, and esoteric movements that emerged during the late nineteenth century—above all, the influential British group, the Hermetic Order of the Golden Dawn. The heavy emphasis that Theosophy placed on Eastern mysticism had begun to create dissatisfaction and dissension among some British members, who were seeking a form of esotericism more rooted in "Western" traditions.[81] Thus, Anna Kingsford and Edward Maitland both resigned in 1884, forming a short-lived Western-based group called the Hermetic Society. This was followed in 1887 by the formation of a far more successful order, the Golden Dawn, by William Wynn Westcott, William Robert Woodman, and Samuel L. Mathers. Inspired by Theosophy's Masters, the Golden Dawn had its own rival lineage of "Secret Chiefs," with Mathers calling himself the "Ambassador of those Secret and Unknown Magi"—a move that was a clear effort to challenge Blavatsky's monopoly on communications with the Masters.[82] The Golden Dawn, however, based its rituals not on Hindu and Buddhist cosmology but on the stages of the Kabbalistic Tree of Life.[83] Eventually attracting such prominent figures as poet William Butler Yeats and occultist Aleister Crowley, the Golden Dawn would become perhaps the best known and most prestigious esoteric order of the early twentieth century.[84]

The formation of Blavatsky's Esoteric Section, Gilbert suggests, was in no small part a response to the recent rise of the Golden Dawn and its emphasis on the "Western" mysteries. Offering her own, innermost confidential teachings, Blavatsky hoped to staunch the hemorrhaging of seekers from the Society toward these new rival orders:

> Aware now of both the existence and growing appeal of the Golden Dawn, Madame Blavatsky responded to its perceived threat by announcing the formation of a new body: The Esoteric Section.... [T]he Esoteric Section was created specifically to avert the loss of would-be practical occultists to the ranks of the Golden Dawn and to prevent a complete split between the followers of the Eastern and those of the Western Path.[85]

Despite the success of the E.S., however, Blavatsky apparently remained uneasy about rivals such as the Golden Dawn and began to order members of the E.S. not to belong to any other occult order. An exception to this rule was eventually made for Westcott, who joined the Esoteric Section as a sort of compromise but was unable to progress to the Inner Group because of its strict "conditions of abstinence and chastity that he was unwilling to accept."[86]

Ultimately, Gilbert suggests, the Golden Dawn and Theosophical Society came to coexist as rival, competing, but clearly distinct esoteric orders. The former attracted those interested in the Western mysteries and a more independent spiritual path, and the latter attracted those who were drawn to the exotic mysteries of the Orient and secret authority of the Mahatmas: "The Golden Dawn appealed primarily to the occultist who wished to be his own master and to explore the spiritual world in his own manner, while the Esoteric Section satisfied those who wanted the glamour of secrecy but coupled with occult dogmas revealed by hidden Masters."[87]

Finally, within the esoteric community of the E.S., Blavatsky created yet another, still *more* esoteric order in London in July–August 1890 called the Inner Group.[88] This consisted of just twelve members—six men and six women—handpicked by Blavatsky: Countess Constance Wachtmeister, Isabella Cooper-Oakley, Emily Kislingbury, Laura M. Cooper, Annie Besant, Alice Leighton Cleather, Archibald Keightley, Herbert Coryn, Claude Falls Wright, G. R. S. Mead, E. T. Sturdy, and Walter Old. As Alice Cleather later recalled, the meetings of the Inner Group took place in a special room built for it adjacent to Blavatsky's bed chamber, with the male students seated on her right side and the female on her left:

> The Inner Group was formed, and held its weekly meetings at 19 Avenue Road, in a room which had been built for it, leading out of HPB's bedroom; no one but herself and her twelve pupils ever entered. We each had our own place, and our own chair; and HPB sat with her six men pupils on her right and the six women on her left side, in semi-circular formation, during our instructions.[89]

Members of the Inner Group were required to take another, even more serious pledge, one that carried more dire consequences than the E.S. pledge:

> Warning: H. P. B. explained the extreme seriousness of this Pledge taken by members of the Inner Group. Occultism must be everything or nothing. This pledge once taken resignation avails nothing; its breach means the most terrible consequences in the present life and in future incarnations. It was a more serious pledge than the voluntary initial pledge given by the Chela to the Master.[90]

Before Blavatsky's death, plans been drawn to build yet another secret compartment adjacent to her own, a much smaller "Occult Room," where the most secret of secret teachings could be transmitted. Here, Blavatsky declared, she would *"teach to the elect that which I do not dare to entrust to the mails."*[91] Although never completed, the Occult Room was intended to be a uniquely designed geometric space with a glass roof and mirrored walls, all of which would concentrate the occult energies surrounding the pupil, who would be observed through a small window by Blavatsky. As C. Jinarajadasa later recalled:

[O]ne descended by four or five steps ... into a small heptagonal or octagonal room above eight feet in diameter. It had a glass roof. ... Each wall of the room was to be covered with a particular metal. The mirrors ... were intended for some purpose of concentrating both light and occult influence upon the esoteric student who was to be seated in the centre of the room for "development" ... [T]here was an opening, a window, from H. P. B.'s room into the Occult Room, so that she could keep the student in Yoga under observation.[92]

Secret Bodies: Occult Physiology in the Esoteric Instructions

Much of the content of Blavatsky's Esoteric Instructions to the E.S./E.S.T. focuses on the notion of the subtle body and on a kind of occult physiology.[93] This material draws heavily from Indian yogic traditions — particularly Raja Yoga, Hatha Yoga, and Hindu Tantra[94] — with some notable innovations by Blavatsky. Even as members of the E.S. were conducted into the inner sanctum of Theosophy and then still further into the Inner Group within the E.S., they were also being introduced to the deeper levels of the human corpus.

First, Blavatsky borrowed from Hindu Yoga and Vedanta to develop a complex doctrine of "subtle bodies" — that is, of progressively incorporeal bodies that lie beyond the gross physical body.[95] As John L. Crow explains, the Theosophical view of the human being is a "matrix of seven interpenetrating bodies, physical and subtle, composed of matter of varying degrees."[96] Using Sanskrit terminology, Blavatsky identifies seven such bodies or sheaths, which conceal one another like the layers of an onion, from the gross material to the transcendent spirit:

1. Rupa or Sthula Sharira (the physical body)
2. Prana, Life or Vital principle
3. Linga Sharira, Astral Body or Phantom Body
4. Kama-Rupa, seat of animal desires and passions
5. Manas, Mind or Intelligence
6. Buddhi, Universal Soul or Mind
7. Atma, Spirit[97]

Second, Blavatsky also borrowed from and expanded on the yogic idea of the chakras, the "centers" of vital energy, which are believed to lie throughout the subtle body and are imagined in the form of wheels, circles, or lotus flowers. Most Indian yogic systems identify a series of chakras — usually numbered at seven — that lie along the axis of the body, from the base of the spine to the crown of the head.[98] Blavatsky, however, describes these as the "lower" and inferior chakras (or "plexuses," to use her term), identified with seven specific organs or glands within the physical body: "the pharyngeal, laryngeal, cavernous, cardiac, epigastric, prostatic, and the sacral plexus."[99] In her view, most Indian yogic traditions—especially those associated with what she considers to be the more "debased" forms of yoga, such as Tantra—focus on these seven basic centers and particularly on the lowest of them, which she associated with the selfish pursuit of magic power:

> The Tantrists do not seem to go higher than the six visible and known plexuses ... and the great stress they lay on the chief of these, the Muladhara (the sacral plexus), shows the material and selfish bent of their efforts towards the acquisition of powers.[100]

In contrast to these lower chakras are seven higher or "Master Chakras" known only to Theosophy, according to Blavatsky, which exist entirely in the head. These higher and more secret centers are ruling chakras that govern all the others, despite being completely undetectable by modern science:

> Our seven Chakras are all situated in the head, and it is these Master Chakras which govern and rule the seven (for there are seven) principal plexuses in the body.... The fact that no microscope can detect such centres on the objective plane goes for nothing.[101]

As figure 2.2 shows, Blavatsky's Esoteric Instructions identified these seven higher chakras or governing centers within the seven layers of the subtle body discussed above. Thus, the Buddhi is identified with the right eye, the Manas with the left eye, the Kama Rupa with the left ear, the Prana or Life Principle with the right nostril, and so on.[102]

With this complex mapping of the traditional yogic chakras and her secret Master Chakras, Blavatsky engages in a common esoteric strategy that we could call the "inscription of the body."[103] The body here serves not simply as a "microcosm" that reflects the grand macrocosm of the universe; more crucially, it serves as a kind of *esoteric socio-cosm* that also reflects the hierarchy of the Theosophical Society and its inner core, the Esoteric Section. Just as the E.S. is revealed to be the secret inner core of Theosophy, so too, the initiate in the E.S. is instructed in the secret inner nature of the subtle body itself, discovering new, hidden chakras that lie even deeper than those of the traditional yoga system.

A. Sexless, Unmanifested Logos.
B. Potential Wisdom.
C. Universal Ideation.

a. Creative Logos.
b. Eternal Substance.
c. Spirit.

D. The Spiritual Forces acting in Matter.

A. B. C. The Unknowable.

a.b.c. This is Pradhâna, undifferentiated matter in Sankhya philosophy, or Good, Evil and Chaotic Darkness (Sattva, Rajas, and Tamas) neutralizing each other. When differentiated, they become the Seven Creative Potencies: Spirit, Substance and Fire stimulating matter to form itself.

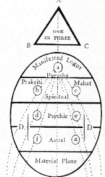

2ND.—MICROCOSM (THE INNER MAN) AND HIS 3, 7, OR 10 CENTERS OF POTENTIAL FORCES

(ĀTMAN, although exoterically reckoned as the seventh principle, is no individual principle at all, and belongs to the Universal Soul; is the AURIC EGG, the Magnetic Sphere round every human and animal being.)

1. BUDDHI, the vehicle of ĀTMAN.
2. MANAS, the vehicle of BUDDHI.
3. LOWER MANAS (the Upper and Lower MANAS are two aspects of one and the same principle) and
4. KĀMA-RŪPA, its vehicle.
5. PRĀNA, Life, and
6. LINGA-ŚARĪRA, its vehicle.

I, II, III, are the Three Hypostases of ĀTMAN, its contact with Nature and Man being the Fourth, making it a Quaternary, or Tetraktys, the Higher Self.

1, 2, 3, 4, 5, 6. These six principles, acting on four different planes, and having their AURIC ENVELOPE on the seventh (*vide infra*), are those used by the Adepts of the Right-Hand, or White Magicians.

1 The Physical Body is no principle; it is entirely ignored, being used only in Black Magic.

3RD.—MICROCOSM (THE PHYSICAL MAN) AND HIS 10 ORIFICES, OR CENTERS OF ACTION

1. (BUDDHI) Right eye.
3. (LOWER MANAS) Right Ear.
5. (LIFE PRINCIPLE) Right Nostril.
7. The Organ of the CREATIVE LOGOS, the Mouth.
8, 9, 10. As this Lower Ternary has a direct connection with the Higher Atmic Triad and its three aspects (creative, preservative and destructive, or rather regenerative), the abuse of the corresponding functions is the most terrible of Karmic Sins—the Sin against the Holy Ghost with the Christians.

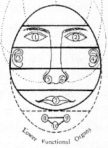

2. (MANAS) Left Eye.
4. (KĀMA-RŪPA) Left Ear.
6. (LIFE VEHICLE) Left Nostril.
7. The Paradigm of the 10th (creative) orifice in the Lower Triad.

These Physical Organs are used only by Dugpas in Black Magic.

FIGURE 2.2. The human microcosm and the Centers of Action. From H. P. Blavatsky, *Collected Writings*, vol. 12, 1889–1890 (Wheaton, IL: Theosophical Publishing House, 1980), 524.

The exact nature and functioning of these Master Chakras, however, is so advanced that it must remain secret for the time being even from the members of the Esoteric Section. Initiates will need to begin with simpler, more accessible teachings until they are prepared for these deeper instructions regarding the subtle body: "When the time comes, members of the E.S.T. will be given the minute details about the Master

Chakras and taught to use them; till then, less difficult subjects have to be learned."[104]

In sum, the structure of the body in the Esoteric Section in many ways mirrors the structure of the Theosophical Society as a whole: just as the initiate is led through progressively more esoteric layers, from the outer Society to the E.S. to the Inner Group, so too, their body is revealed to consist of multiple sheaths, from the gross physical to the most subtle and spiritual, from the lower chakras known to run-of-the-mill yogis to the higher, secret, Master Chakras known only to the E.S., and each becoming increasingly difficult to access or even describe. It is not difficult to see this increasing secretism as a critical part of Theosophy's larger rivalry with other groups in the late nineteenth-century spiritual marketplace. While Freemasons competed for ever more numerous and highly ornamented degrees, other occult groups of this period competed for more esoteric understandings of the cosmos and the human body, mining ever deeper mysteries, each hoping to offer the most secret of the secret.

Conclusions: The Secret Doctrine in the Twentieth and Twenty-First Centuries

Despite her fall into disrepute toward the end of her career, Blavatsky's secret doctrine remains among the clearest examples of the central paradox inherent in most forms of religious secrecy. This is the paradox that we can call the advertised secret, as the active cultivation of a public reputation of concealed knowledge. This paradox involves not only the use of a complex "language of secrecy" and "occult rhetoric" but also the cultivation of an entire occult personality—an occult *habitus* or mode of being that includes dress, comportment, mannerisms, and speech that generates the aura of secret knowledge and hidden power.

As it grew in the last quarter of the nineteenth century, Theosophy developed into a system of multiple complex layers of secrecy—a kind of Russian doll of ever-increasing levels of concealment. Following the formation of the Society in 1875, through the increasingly esoteric volumes of *Isis Unveiled* and *The Secret Doctrine* to the formation of the Esoteric Section and then the still more esoteric Inner Group, Blavatsky elaborated layer after layer of concealment and revelation, leading her disciples ever deeper into the unknown. The result was a successful, influential, but also controversial new offering amidst the occult marketplace of the late nineteenth century. A powerfully double-edged sort of rhetorical device, the advertisement of secrecy in the Theosophical Society was a key part of its popularity but also an important factor in its various scandals and exposés.

Woven from the complex threads of nineteenth-century Orientalism, occult communication with unseen beings, and the claim to reveal the secret wisdom that unites all the world's religions, Theosophy became a kind of archetype for much of the alternative and New Age spirituality of the twentieth and twenty-first centuries. Not only did Theosophy give birth to a variety of offshoots, such as Anthroposophy, but the influence of Blavatsky's occult rhetoric extends to an array of new religious movements of the last century. The claim to reveal the ancient wisdom that illuminates the secret unity of the world's religions runs throughout New Age literature, while the powerful figure of HPB and her communication with secret Masters has inspired much of the New Age phenomenon of "channeling" (communication with entities from other realms).[105]

To cite an example, one of the most successful channelers in contemporary America is the former suburban housewife JZ Knight, who claims to be the medium for a 35,000-year-old being from Atlantis named Ramtha. The message that Ramtha brings, through Knight, is said to be an ancient truth, but one that has been lost and is now much needed in the modern world—namely, the truth of our own divinity, the knowledge that we are all gods.[106] Clearly, Knight is playing on many of the same tropes of secretism and occult rhetoric as had Blavatsky before her: contact with hidden Masters, knowledge from the mystic Orient, and revelation of a lost secret teaching. But she has also cultivated and now skillfully performs an entire occult personality, complete with strange foreign accent, archaic speech, odd mannerisms, and exotic clothing. Perhaps most significant, Knight has become enmeshed in many of the same allegations of fraud and chicanery as had Blavatsky, with her ex-husband accusing her operation of being a farce and a dangerous, money-making scheme. These allegations have in some ways undermined her reputation, yet in other ways have added to the complex aura of "secretism" that surrounds her as a popular channeler.[107]

But this dense mixture of belief, skepticism, concealment, and public exposure is the very essence of the advertised secret. And perhaps no one captured this ambivalent nature of secrecy better than Blavatsky, when she wrote in 1875:

> As a rule, Occultism is a dangerous, double-edged weapon for one to handle, who is unprepared to devote his whole life to it. The theory of it, unaided by serious practice, will ever remain in the eyes of those prejudiced against such an unpopular cause an idle, crazy speculation, fit only to charm the ears of ignorant old women.[108]

✳ CHAPTER 3 ✳
The Seduction of the Secret
EROS AND MAGIC IN TWENTIETH-CENTURY EUROPE

[W]hat is it about secrets that is so compelling and seductive?
ELLIOT R. WOLFSON, "The Occultation of the Feminine and
the Body of Secrecy in Medieval Kabbalah"[1]

*[L]e grand secret de la transmutation de l'énergie animale en énergie
spirituelle . . . n'est autre que l'acte d'amour magique connu par les anciens
Mages d'Egypte et préconisé aujourd'hui par* La Flèche.
MARIA DE NAGLOWSKA, "Une Vision Polaire"[2]

*Fame and secrecy are the high and low ends of the same fascination,
the static crackle of some libidinous thing in the world.*
DON DELILLO, *Underworld*[3]

More than a simple art of concealment or a form of symbolic power,
secrecy is also very often a complex play of *seduction*. In many ways it is a
kind of *ars erotica* that involves a subtle dialectic of lure and withdrawal,
partial concealment and partial revelation, veiling and unveiling, which
has frequently been compared by both mystics and scholars to the playful
dynamic between lover and beloved. As Elliot Wolfson eloquently put it
in his study of secrecy in the Jewish mystical tradition, "The confluence
of concealment and disclosure underscores another essential element in
the nature of secrecy.... I refer to the link between esotericism and eroticism, which is related more specifically to the insight that transmission
of secrets requires the play of openness and closure basic to the push and
pull of eros."[4] In this sense, the seductive nature of the secret comes very
close to what Georges Bataille calls *erotism*. In Bataille's sense, *erotism* is
not a matter of mere nudity but depends precisely on the play (*le jeu*) between clothing and striptease, between taboo and transgression, between

the creation of laws and prohibitions and the delicious overstepping of those boundaries.[5]

In many esoteric traditions, moreover, secrecy is not only tied metaphorically but also quite literally to eroticism, through various forms of sexual rites.[6] In medieval Kabbalah, the union between the Kabbalist and his wife can symbolize the union of the male and female aspects of the Godhead; in Hindu Tantric traditions, sexual union can serve as either the symbolic or literal union of Shiva and Shakti, the divine male and female principles; and in various modern esoteric traditions that have emerged since the mid-nineteenth century, the experience of sexual orgasm has been harnessed as a source of magical power and wielded for a wide variety of material and spiritual ends.[7]

Although it might at first appear marginal and idiosyncratic, the practice of sexual magic ties closely to modern conceptions of sexuality that have developed since the late nineteenth century. As Michel Foucault famously argued in his *History of Sexuality*, the nineteenth century in Europe and England was not a period of silence and repression regarding sexuality; on the contrary, this era witnessed an unprecedented proliferation of new scientific and medical literature on sexuality, which was discussed *ad infinitum* as "the secret."[8] As we see in tomes such as Richard von Krafft-Ebling's *Psychopathia Sexualis* (1886) and the works of Sigmund Freud, sex was seen as the most powerful drive in human nature and the key to understanding all of human society, politics, and even religious life.[9] Taking this modern preoccupation still further, many esoteric movements of the nineteenth and twentieth centuries found in sexuality *the occult secret par excellence*, not just the most powerful force in human nature but the most powerful source of magic and the key to the innermost mysteries of reality. In the words of Aleister Crowley— arguably the most important figure in the modern revival of occultism and magic in the twentieth century—"if this secret [of sexual magic], which is a scientific secret, were perfectly understood ... there would be nothing which the human imagination can conceive that could not be realized in practice."[10]

This chapter examines the intersections between secrecy, eroticism, and magic in early twentieth-century Europe, by focusing on one of the most important but today little-known figures in the development of modern occultism: Maria de Naglowska (1883–1936) (fig. 3.1). Born in Russia, Naglowska came to Paris in the 1920s and became intimately involved in the vibrant artistic, literary, and spiritual circles of the era, such as the Surrealists—who had their own fascinations with sex, magic,

FIGURE 3.1. Maria de Naglowska.

and the occult.[11] Not only was she a friend and probably lover of the far-right traditionalist philosopher, Julius Evola (who also wrote extensively about sexual magic), but her lectures and writings are said to have attracted the likes of André Breton, Man Ray, Michel Leiris, Georges Bataille, and other key intellectuals of prewar France.[12] While there is now a small amount of scholarship on Naglowska,[13] I argue that her work needs to be understood more specifically in the context of French intellectual and artistic life of the 1920s and 1930s, amidst the rich foment of occultism, Satanism, Surrealism, and politics in the years immediately prior to the Nazi invasion of France in 1940.[14] Perhaps most important, her work shares much with Bataille's influential writings on mysticism, death, and sexuality and deserves more recognition as a significant female precursor to his rather male-centric concept of *erotism*.[15]

Drawing on earlier traditions of occultism and Satanism in late nineteenth-century Europe,[16] Naglowska made exquisite use of the seductive power of secrecy. From her first publication of *Magia Sexualis*, the combined tropes of sex and secrecy formed the heart of Naglowska's writings. Naglowska's work played explicitly with themes that were clearly provocative, transgressive, and scandalous for her time. These included her invocation of Satan as a key figure in her metaphysical system, her reference to herself as a "Satanic woman," and her practice of sexual-spiritual techniques such as erotic ritual hanging.[17] Perhaps her most unique innovation was to synthesize these many elements into a powerful, dangerous, and seductive *secret*—and specifically, the secret of transforming the Satanic aspect of human nature into the Divine, precisely through women and through the alchemical work of sexual magic. For Naglowska, the deepest theological secret is that Woman herself is the third term in the Trinity; and the secret of ritual practice lies in the power of sexuality, which reconciles God and Satan, transforming the latter into the former.

Together, all of these elements helped to create the aura of dangerous power, mystery, and exotic transgression that surrounds Naglowska's work, a combined perfume of sex, death, and mystical ecstasy that pervades her writings as well as those of many writers in the Parisian scene of the 1930s. As such, Naglowska endowed the secret with an erotic dimension that went far beyond even the advertised secrecy of Blavatsky or the adorning silence of the Scottish Rite. While she is a relatively obscure figure today, her writings helped inspired a whole wave of sexual magicians, who now flood the shelves of Barnes and Noble and Amazon .com with an array of new mixtures of esotericism, eroticism, and the promise of divine knowledge through the secrets of sex. Indeed, Naglowska's writings have seen a certain renaissance in recent years, being republished in English translations with exotic covers and sold next to *The Secrets of Western Sex Magic*, *The Art of Sexual Ecstasy*, and other popular paperbacks.[18]

"A Satanic Woman": Naglowska and the Occult Milieu of the Early Twentieth Century

Naglowska's biography is much less well known or documented than Blavatsky's, and therefore, like her religious system itself, remains much more of a tantalizing secret. What we know of her life comes primarily

The Seduction of the Secret 83

from the work of her disciple, Marc Pluquet, along with a few other historical fragments.[19] Born in St. Petersburg, she was the daughter of the province governor of Kazan in a prominent Czarist family; yet she was orphaned at the age of twelve after her mother died of an illness and her father was murdered by a nihilist. Raised and educated at Smolna Institute, a girl's school for daughters of nobility, Naglowska's apparent gifts as a medium and mystic were noted from a very early age. Various rumors suggest that at some point in Russia she came into contact with the infamous occultist and political advisor, Rasputin, and was involved with the Khlisty sect, which was known for its sexual rites.[20] Naglowska, we should note, would later claim that the primary inspiration for her unorthodox ideas came not from any occult source but from a mysterious Catholic monk, whom she claims to have met in Rome.[21]

As a young woman, she fell in love with a Jewish violinist named Moise Hopenko; however, her relatives refused to bless a marriage with a Jewish commoner, so the lovers left for Berlin and later settled in Geneva, where they married and had three children. A committed Zionist, Hopenko abandoned the family for Palestine in 1910, and Maria was left to scrape together whatever income she could by working as a translator, a private schoolteacher, and a journalist. She became a target of suspicion because of her radical political ideas — a complex mixture of anarchism, socialism, and nationalism — for which she was imprisoned and then expelled from Switzerland.[22]

After leaving Geneva, Naglowska relocated to Rome in 1920, where she met the controversial Traditionalist author and far-right ideologue, Julius Evola. Many believe that she and Evola probably had a love affair, and many also suggest that she was involved with Evola's secret magical group known as UR.[23] Although Evola was later critical of Naglowska — particularly of her delight in referring to Satan and Satanism — the two shared an intense interest in sexual magic, and Evola later published his own major tome on *Metafisica del sesso* or *The Metaphysics of Sex*, in which he discusses her work at length.[24]

Returning to Paris in 1929, Naglowska was denied a work permit but took up residence in a small Montparnasse hotel, which was something of a hotbed for a variety of artists, activists, and occultists. She quickly gained a reputation in these circles for her quite avant-garde teachings on Satanism and sexual magic. Presiding over daily meetings with a devoted circle of admirers, she founded an initiatic order called the Confrérie de la Flèche d'Or ("Brotherhood of the Golden Arrow") in 1932 and was involved with another esoteric order called the Groupe des Polaires. Her meetings were said to have been attended by many of the most avant-garde and notorious authors, writers, painters, and philosophers of the day, including Man Ray, William Seabrook, Michel Leiris, Georges Bataille, André Breton, and other key figures in the Surrealist movement.[25] Around this time, she began to publish her journal, *La Flèche* ("the Arrow"), which dealt explicitly with sexual magic and whose first issue contained an article by Evola. In 1936, Naglowska left Paris quite suddenly for reasons yet unknown. As Hans Thomas Hakl notes, it is possible that she left the city after one of her followers died by accident during the "rite of hanging" or erotic asphyxiation, which, as we will see below, was part of the higher degrees of her magical system.[26]

While Naglowska had initially been involved in radical movements and was later connected with Evola's Traditionalism, the social and political views expressed in her inner circle appear to be distinct from either of these. In an article on "Notre Thèse Sociale" published in *La Flèche* in 1930, we find an idealistic description of premodern societies, of which Traditionalists such as Evola would probably have approved: those societies were imagined as hierarchical, organized in a pyramid with laborers at the bottom, followed by merchants, warriors, and priests at the very top as the most just and wise.[27] Such a hierarchical, well-ordered model of society has been largely destroyed with the onset of modernity and its leveling chaos (a point with which Evola also would have agreed). However, while Evola hoped to return to a kind of pagan political order modeled on imperial Rome, *La Flèche* concludes that such a hope is foolish and impossible in the contemporary context, and that we must instead strive for a more inward and spiritual response to the "anarchy and barbarism" of the modern world.[28]

Naglowska probably strikes many contemporary readers as an intriguing yet ultimately marginal and idiosyncratic figure; however, in the broader context of spiritual, literary, and artistic movements of the early twentieth century, she is better understood as a clear reflection of the larger fascination with occultism, magic, sex, and Satanism that ran through the French cultural scene of these decades.[29] Like America and England, as we saw in the previous chapters, France witnessed an intense revival of occultism since the mid-nineteenth century, beginning with Éliphas Lévi's classic works and continuing in later writers such as Gérard Encausse (a.k.a. Papus) and Joséphin Péladan. This interest in the occult carried over into new artistic movements of the twentieth century, particularly the Surrealists. André Breton, for example, was fascinated with occult themes, collecting hundreds of volumes of mystical and esoteric literature. In his *Second Manifesto of Surrealism*, he even compares the goals of Surrealism to those of the medieval alchemists: "the philosopher's stone is nothing more or less than that which was to enable man's imagination to take a stunning revenge on all things, which brings us once again, after centuries of the mind's domestication ... to liberate once and for all the imagination by the 'long immense reasoned derangement of the senses'"[30] In their broader quest for the "marvelous," the Surrealists drew inspiration from the works of Lévi, medieval alchemical writings, alchemy, Tarot, Gnosticism, Tantra, and Shamanism, "not only as subject matter but influencing production and technique."[31]

At the same time, there was also a powerful interest in Satanism and the darker side of the occult throughout nineteenth and early twentieth-century France. Satanic themes had already appeared in decadent poetry, such as Charles Baudelaire's classic "Litanies of Satan" (1857), where Lucifer is portrayed as a sympathetic and even compelling figure. "Prince to exile," Baudelaire writes, "you have been wronged; Defeated you rise up ever stronger.... You who even to lepers and accursed outcasts teach through love a longing for Paradise."[32] Yet as Robert Ziegler notes, Satanic themes pervade French literature toward the end of the nineteenth century. Perhaps the most famous Satanic novel ever written was J. K. Huysmans' *Là-bas* ("Down There"), which described a black mass in intimate, sensual detail and became an instant best seller.[33] Satanic themes also appear throughout visual art of this era, for example in the work of the Belgian artist Félicien Rops, whose series, *Les Sataniques* (1880), solidified the association between radical evil and the lustful, deceptive, and destructive powers of women. By the end of the nineteenth century, ideas of the devil had begun to saturate the French popular imagination; as we see in works such as Docteur Bataille's *Le Diable au XIXe Siècle*, there was a vast conspiracy theory that Satanic cults were roaming the countryside, performing bloody rituals and engaging in all manner of sexual perversion. Indeed, "so deep was concern over the spread of devil worship that the Catholic Church published *La Revue du Diable*, whose mission was the exposure of clandestine Satanic practice."[34]

Writing in the early twentieth century, Naglowska clearly inherited this larger cultural imagining of Satanism, sexuality, and femininity. Yet she would also add her own unique contribution: a developed system of sexual magic and a complex cosmology in which Satan played a pivotal role.

The Secrets of Sexual Magic: Eros and the Occult

Naglowska's writings on sexual magic are part of a much larger body of esoteric literature that spread throughout Europe, England, and the US from the mid-nineteenth century onward. For Naglowska, as for many esoteric groups of this period, sexual energy was described as an "enormous occult force," one that is inherently dangerous but also one that can be controlled to achieve illumination.[35] Indeed, the very first issue of *La Flèche* opens with this first-page header: "Nous ouvrons le Livre de la Vie pour dévoiler le raison occulte de l'attrait sexuel" or "we open the Book of Life in order to reveal the occult reason for sexual attraction."[36]

Of course, the use of sexual symbolism and erotic imagery has a long and complex history in Western esoteric literature; since at least the earliest Hermetic and Gnostic texts, sexual union was used as a metaphor for the ineffable mystery of divine spiritual union. In Gnostic works such as the Gospel of Philip, the return of the soul to heaven is described as a kind of spiritual wedding, the "mystery of the Bridal Chamber"; and it appears that followers of Philip may also have practiced some form of mystical sexual union between male and female that mirrored the union of the soul and its heavenly counterpart. Meanwhile, the Jewish mystical tradition of Kabbalah often used erotic symbolism to describe the union of the Torah and her lover, the human Kabbalist, or to symbolize the union of God with his bride, the community of Israel. Later, during the Italian Renaissance, many of these Hermetic and Kabbalist traditions came together, and key authors such as Masilio Ficino would use the language of Eros to describe the workings of magic itself; for both Eros and magic work by the law of attraction, the bringing together of things by their inherent similarity.[37]

However, it is really not until the late nineteenth century that we find a fully developed system of magic in which sexual union is not simply a *metaphor* but an *actual physical technique* used to create magical effects. As we noted above, nineteenth-century medical and psychoanalytic literature consistently identified sex as *"the secret,"* as the most powerful and dangerous force in human nature, and as the key to unlocking the depths of the human psyche.[38] Late nineteenth-century occultists took this idea in a much more literal direction, developing whole new techniques of magic based on the power of sexuality. Probably the first and most important author to describe the magical use of sex was the American Spiritualist, Paschal Beverly Randolph (1825–75), who influenced a wide array of esoteric traditions and erotic occult movements for the next century. Born the son of a white father and a mother of mixed race, Randolph was orphaned at a young age and grew up penniless on the streets of New York City. As a young man, he worked aboard sailing vessels and traveled widely throughout Europe and the Middle East. In the course of his wanderings, he claimed, he was initiated into a variety of esoteric traditions, including the practice of sexual magic, which was revealed to him by a mysterious dark young woman: "One night—it was in far-off Jerusalem or Bethlehem, I really forget which—I made love to, and was loved by, a dusky maiden of Arabic blood. I of her, and that experience, learned ... the fundamental principle of the White Magic of Love."[39] Shortly thereafter, he claimed, he also became affiliated with a group of fakirs, which may have been a branch of the unorthodox mystical order of the Nusa'iri, a group long persecuted by orthodox Islam because of its alleged Gnostic sexual rituals.[40]

Whatever his primary inspiration, Randolph began to teach a form of sexual magic that would have a profound impact on much later esotericism in England, Europe, and the US. For Randolph, the sexual instinct is the most fundamental power in the universe, for it is the natural attraction between positive and negative forces that flow through all things. The experience of orgasm is, consequently, the critical moment in human consciousness and the key to magical power. Indeed, at the moment of sexual climax (ideally a mutual orgasm), the soul is suddenly opened to the powers of the universe, and anything one desires can potentially be achieved:

> The moment when a man discharges his seed—his essential self—into a willing or unwilling womb is the most solemn, energetic, and powerful moment he can ever know on earth....
>
> Whatsoever he shall truly will and internally pray for when Love, pure, divine, natural, passional or volitional, is in the ascendant, that moment the prayer's response comes down.[41]

Randolph lists a wide array of ends toward which sexual magic may be directed, ranging from the most mundane and this-worldly to the most sublime and transcendent. These include increasing the brain and body power of an unborn child, influencing one's wife or husband, regaining youthful beauty and energy, prolonging life, attaining "supreme white magic," furthering "financial interests, schemes, lotteries, etc," and attaining "the loftiest insight possible to the earthly soul."[42] While Randolph died in relative obscurity (possibly by his own hand), his writings on sexual magic helped inspire a huge wave of erotic mysticism and esoteric orders, including the Hermetic Brotherhood of Luxor and the Ordo Templi Orientis, and occultists such as Crowley. Indeed, by the early twentieth century, sex had become in many ways "*the* secret," not just in medical and psychoanalytic discourse but in esoteric and occult practice as well.[43]

While not the first to write about the subject, Naglowska was surely one of the most important figures in the spread of sexual magic as a modern occult technique. One of Naglowska's most enduring contributions to the history of modern esotericism was her publication of *Magia Sexualis*, which was ostensibly a "translation" of Randolph's work. The term "translation" is placed in quotes here because the work is more of a summary of some ideas drawn from Randolph with a large amount of other material drawn from authors such as Péladan and occult orders such as the Cénacle d'Astarté and the Société Egyptienne Secrète.[44] Naglowska's translation was also a crucial source of income for her during her lean years, when she was without the support of a husband or regular employment. Like Blavatsky's Theosophical works, *Magia Sexualis* was a clear example of the "advertisement of the secret" and was prominently featured in ads in *La Flèche*. Significantly, however, the ads for the text ascribe the most explicit discussions of sexual magic not to Naglowska but to the "mysterious mulatto" from America:

> This mysterious mulatto, who lived in the last century in the United States, was part, among others, of the secret society known by the name of the B.H. of L. [Hermetic Brotherhood of Luxor]. . . . He betrays the tradition by hazarding this summary of the occult sciences: *the greatest magical force in nature is Sex* [*la plus grande force magique de la nature est le Sexus*]. The publication "Magia Sexualis" is an extremely rare summary of manuscript notes, completely unedited, on Sexual Magic. The sexual rites of millennial secret societies are scientifically reduced to experimental analyses and practical recipes of stupefying efficiency. The results of his research . . . will fascinate not only amateurs but also the knowledgeable man of science.[45]

Just as Randolph has ascribed the origins of his sexual magic to exotic sages in the Orient, so too, Naglowska has ascribed her secrets of sexual magic to a mysterious mulatto in America. In both cases, the dark and sensual power of magic is seen as coming from a distant, mysterious — and racialized — source.

This seductive advertisement of the secret (which is itself an *erotic* secret) continued throughout the publication of *La Flèche*.[46] Thus a 1932 issue of the journal includes an ad for Naglowska's new book, *Le rite sacré de l'amour magique,* promising both a special price and even a signed copy for generous supporters: "we will offer a volume in grateful tribute, with the author's autograph, to all the friends who supported *La Flèche* in its difficult initial period. We will offer it with the exceptional price of 5 francs to all subscribers who have paid us at least 10 francs."[47]

The text of *Le rite sacré*, however, is anything but a straightforward manual of sex magic. Rather, it is a highly allegorical novel that uses elements of fantasy, fairytale, and elaborate symbolism to convey the deeper mysteries of sexuality and the path to salvation. The story centers on a young woman named Xenophonta who lives in a castle in the mountains and is raped by a Cossack named Misha. Her purity, patience, and self-sacrifice, however, ultimately redeem Misha, revealing that "a genuinely pure woman who has dedicated herself to a higher Force ... and does not want anything for herself can save the most violent man and turn him into a sage. And she can do this by satisfying his carnal desire."[48] Xenophonta repeatedly describes her love for Misha as a kind of self-immolation and sacrificial offering; thus, as she rubs herself against his body, she says she feels "the need to sacrifice myself. Oh! The voluptuousness of sacrifice!"[49] Then, after they consummate their union, a heavenly chorus sings: "Contemplate the flesh offered in holocaust.... Consider the voluntary offering, O powers of heaven, of the stars and of the earth, and recognize that this work is beautiful."[50] Significantly, however, their sacred union appears to take place while Xenophonta has either "slept, or been unconscious," making her a largely passive participant in the rites and one without sexual pleasure of her own (a point discussed in more detail below).[51] Nonetheless, their union is praised as a perfect fulfillment of the most sacred and secret ritual of erotic magic, a kind of divine alchemy leading to transformation and divine rebirth. Again the heavenly chorus sings, "Yes, Glory to Mishaël! And glory to his Bride.... Glory to the man and the woman who lent themselves to the realization of this cycle of magical love, according to the will of the Master of Life, the Wise Alchemist."[52] The novel is thus a key illustration of Naglowska's skillful use of the seductive power of the secret and the secret power of seduction, employing veils of allegory to convey a deeper mystery, while also revealing that mystery to be the divine power of sex itself.

This seductive power of the secret was carried over from Naglowska's fictional tale into the esoteric order she established, the Confrérie. Like most Masonic and other initiatory orders, the Confrérie was modeled on a hierarchy of three grades, though hers ascended through grades of sexual knowledge and achievement as well as esoteric knowledge. The lowest of these was the *Balayeur*, or "Dustman," a title that referred to a kind of symbolic interior cleaning or purification.[53] The second degree was that of *Chasseur Affranchi* ("Free Hunter"), who underwent a paradoxically non-orgasmic sexual rite based on *coitus reservatus*. The male initiate was to be joined with a female partner who served as both his sacred lover and spiritual guide, and the two would make love, though refraining from orgasm.[54] Finally, the third degree was entitled *Guerrier Invincible*, or "Invincible Knight," in which the initiate was led into the most esoteric sexual rites (discussed in more detail below).[55] Throughout her work, Naglowska makes it clear that these rites must be shrouded with utmost secrecy, containing as they do the most powerfully dangerous mystery of love itself: "the priestesses, entrusted to the influence of the Golden Arrow, surround their ministry with impenetrable secrecy, in such a way that, until the last minute, no one knows where the rite ... will take place, nor the name or other details about the woman."[56]

The Secret of the New Religion:
The Trinity and the Divine Feminine

Throughout her writings of the 1930s, Naglowska presented her teachings as nothing less than a new religion—the religion of the "Third Term" (*la troisième terme*), based on a kind of female-centric reworking of the Christian Trinity. Naglowska believed that the world was ready to receive the true secret message that the third term is none other than Woman (*la Femme*), who is both wife and mother, source of both love and life:

> The teachers of the Christian Church have named these three respectively: the Father, the Son, and the Holy Spirit ... but we say: the Father, the Son, the Woman [*la Femme*]. We could also say ... the Descent, the Suffering in the body, the New Ascent....
>
> We also know that humanity is the arena for the projection of the Divine Comedy in three acts: the generation of the Son by the Father, or the fall of the divine into creation; the desecration of the Father by the Son, or the painful affirmation of the Son through created forms; the glorious return of the Son to the Father, thanks to the Wife, or the work of divine rebirth....
>
> The hour approaches when everyone will know the secret, and that is when the selection will be made. Because there will be those who will succeed and those who will not succeed.
>
> This will depend on the inner purity that each will bring to the liberating test. It will be the baptism of the new religion, the Religion of the Third term.[57]

As such, Naglowska sees our own era history as a key turning point, a transition from the first and second terms of the Father and Son to the "third term" of the divine feminine. This is the secret that the church has kept hidden all these years and is now ready to be revealed openly:

Our epoch is that of the third term, because the divine Ascension is now beginning, and that is why it is only today that our new dogmas can be clearly announced in the public square. Nothing is understandable to all if the hour has not yet sounded. Therefore we give homage to the learned men of the church for having been able to keep the secret until the end....

The complete text of our dogma of the Trinity is presented thus: **We know that the Trinity is holy. We know that they are Father, Son, and Woman, that Their glory is one, and that Their life is eternal.**[58]

Several articles and advertisements in *La Flèche* explain this third era of Woman even more clearly, now linking it specifically to the power of *sex* itself, of which Woman is both the source and defender: "as we have already said many times, the new light that today strikes the world is that of the Divine Mother, protectress of Sex."[59] In this way, the role of sex as "the light of the new religion [*la lumière de la nouvelle religion*]" succeeds the previous religions of the Father and the Son: "a religion of the First Term is always a religion of Reason; a religion of the Second Term a religion the Heart; and a Religion of the Third Term a religion of Sex."[60] In Naglowska's reading of the biblical narrative, Woman is both the cause of our fall from paradise and the key to our salvation. Through her womb, Woman is the doorway through which sensuality and sin entered the world[61] and also the secret gateway leading us back to redemption (see fig. 3.2).[62] As Julius Evola explains this dynamic,

> The woman is thought of as the gate through which it is possible to enter into the sphere of death or life. In the fall, sensual pleasure "became the magnet that draws man toward women, not for the conquest of life (which equals God) but for the conquest of death (which equals Satan), and Eve ... became the battle field of the struggle between life and death." At the decisive point of this trial, man sees his "bride" again and is invited to immerse himself in her, the female once more ... [T]he woman is presented as the *Ianua Coeli*, or Gateway to Heaven, and as the essential instrument for freedom.[63]

Here again we see the dynamic of secrecy and revelation, the claim to profound hidden knowledge and the desire to reveal it openly, which was also evident in Blavatsky's writings. The time is now finally ripe to reveal this ancient hidden secret. The key difference, however, is that the secret now is also a sexual secret and closely tied to the rising power of women.

Naglowska's writings on the divine feminine did not occur in a vacuum

FIGURE 3.2. "La Femme et le Serpent," from Maria de Naglowska, *Le Mystère de la pendaison* (Paris: Éditions de la Flèche, 1934).

but were very much part of larger spiritual, cultural, and political contexts that saw a new interest in the power of women. Since the mid-nineteenth century, women had begun to play a central role as mediums in the huge wave of Spiritualism that spread rapidly across the US and France; meanwhile, in England, a new revival of pagan witchcraft emerged in the 1940s with the founding of the first modern Wiccan covens, in which women played central roles as priestesses and the Great Goddess held center stage.[64] Meanwhile, in the more secular political realm, France like England and the US, saw the rise of many new waves of feminism, which began at least at the time of the French Revolution and continued with the suffrage movement of the early twentieth century. The more developed forms of modern feminism would not emerge really until after World War II, particularly with the publication of Simone de Beauvoir's landmark *Le Deuxième Sexe* in 1949. Yet Naglowska's *Troisième Terme* seems only tangentially related to these political movements, with which she does not appear to have been directly engaged. Rather, as Michele Olzi suggests, her unique brand of "Satanic feminism" emerged in the 1930s, shortly before the more sophisticated work of de Beauvoir and others, and so might best be thought of as a kind of "proto-feminism."[65] At the same time, Naglowska also added a more radical spiritual and sexual dimension to her feminism, linking it to both the divine power of Woman as a divine force and the transformative power of sex itself.

Yet if Naglowska's "Satanic feminism" seems progressive and liberatory in ways that were ahead of its time, it is also oddly conservative and traditional in many respects. Whereas Randolph had argued that the mutual orgasm of both male and female was the most powerful form of magic, Naglowska is actually much more chaste in her view of the woman's role. As she explains in an article entitled simply "Dogme" in *La Flèche* in 1933, men and women are exact opposites both physically and mentally, and their sexual organs and minds are polarized like the two ends of a magnet: "The sex of man belongs to God (Affirmation of Life), the sex of the woman to Satan (Negation of Life). The head of man belongs to Satan, the head of woman (Intelligence) to God." She then explains that this is why men should achieve orgasm during sexual union while women should not, since the latter would then be a dangerous inversion of the polarity. Instead, the woman should offer herself up like a selfless, sacrificial immolation in order for the magic to be performed: "This is why a man has the right to sexual pleasure, while the woman does not have this right, and if she usurps it, she commits debauchery. The woman must offer herself to the man without egotism, as an expiatory holocaust. This is the secret of Love Magic."[66] If this is a form of "proto-feminism," it is still quite a long way from de Beauvoir's *Deuxième sexe* published just over a decade later.

At the same time, in addition to its connections to broader social movements of twentieth-century France, Naglowska's *troisième terme* was explicitly linked to specific *political and historical* contexts. In her view, these three ages were not purely metaphysical but were unfolding in human history in the context of Europe in the decades between the two world wars. According to an advertisement published in *La Flèche* in October 1932, the dawn of this new third era of the Mother and sex was imminent: "The third era of the triangle at which we now arrive—

Judaism, Christianity, and now the religion of the third term of Trinity — will begin cosmically at the start of the year 1933." Moreover, this age was closely tied to political events unfolding in Europe at the time. In a long article published in *La Flèche* in April 1933, Naglowska interprets the vicious wave of anti-Semitism then spreading across Germany through the lens of her three ages and three terms of the Trinity. This resurgence of anti-Semitism is the manifestation of a deeper "cosmic truth," reflecting the larger struggle between the First and Second Terms of the Trinity, which has now grown into a horrible conflict: today, "the struggle between the First and Second Terms, the struggle of Gog and Magog, becomes a hideous quarrel.... [T]he anti-Semitic movement that assumes more and more acute forms in Germany has its deepest origins in the great cosmic truth that we have just exposed."[67] And this great cosmic struggle can be resolved only in the Third Term of the Trinity, when the new age of Woman is embraced and the Golden Mass is celebrated:

> Oh Israel, terrible is your loss and terrible your decay. Or will you take the necessary measures to rebuild the New Jerusalem? ... The Third Term is coming, and in its New Light, the new life must be organized. For, in the Third Temple, where the true communion, the triumphant Mass of the Lord, will be celebrated, the twelve tribes of the twelve sons of Jacob must be worthily represented.[68]

Another issue of *La Flèche* from March 1933 begins with an open letter addressed to none other than Pope Pius XI, beseeching him to recognize the idea of this New Age of the Trinity. Noting the rising influence of Mussolini's fascism in Italy, the letter calls on the pope to spread the message of love as the only alternative to nationalism and war:

> The Italian leader, Benito Mussolini, has declared that the new generations need a *mystique*. He offers them that of distant travels and wars for sport.
>
> Are you not in a position to tell him that this is only a derivative, an external consolation, when the disease is inside of man? This disease is called: the absence of love....
>
> Have the courage to reveal the new truth, find the strength to say that man and woman are created for each other, and that in the love of these two lies all Mystery, all Wisdom, and all *Mystique*.[69]

Finally, in its last issue published in 1935, *La Flèche* ran an article entitled "Avant la Guerre de 1936," which makes even more dire predictions about the coming struggle. Published amidst the growing tide of nationalist conflict and the rise of Fascist, Nazi, and other authoritarian regimes in Italy, Germany, Spain, and neighboring countries during the mid-1930s, the article warns that the "two lines of the Triangle are about to intersect with terrible force," and that there will be a major, bloody war—waged both spiritually and physically—within the coming year:

> [T]he year 1935 is the last before great turmoil.
>
> In effect, for twelve more months, men and women can choose their way and orient themselves, according to their will, to the side of the Light or to the side of the Shadows....
>
> The war, in 1936, will be inevitable, because the occult turmoil will require blood on the earth.[70]

Hence the need to reveal this great secret of Woman and to embrace the power of love was at that moment more urgent than ever before in human history.

Satanic Secrets: Occult Rhetoric and the Use of Scandalous Language

Perhaps the primary reason for Naglowska's controversial—and today, increasingly popular—reputation is her explicit use of Satanic language and imagery throughout her work. Not only did she refer to herself as a "Satanic woman," but she also built Satan directly into her complex metaphysical system and her practice of sexual magic. Although she was not herself a "Satanist" according to any modern understanding of the term, "Naglowska often expressed herself in symbolic language. Some of this language was evidently intended to shock and to draw attention to herself and her teachings (two things not easily done in the vibrant and decadent Paris of the 1930s)."[71] Meanwhile, the space where she and her followers gathered was the only known "Satanist Temple" in Paris at that time.[72] Even sympathetic contemporaries such as her (probable) lover, Evola, complained about her use of transgressive imagery, which seemed to reflect her "deliberate intention to scandalize the reader through unnecessarily dwelling on Satanism."[73]

Here I think there are least two factors at play in Naglowska's explicit use of Satanic language. The first is the power of what philosopher Paul Ricoeur calls "semantic shock"—that is, the effect of deliberately jarring, startling, surprising, and even offensive metaphors, which use the deliberate juxtaposition of odd or disconcerting terms to jolt the reader in a sudden new kind of insight. The aim of such semantic shock, Ricoeur suggests, is less a matter of clear communication than of "challenging and even shattering our sense of reality through reflective redescription."[74] As I have argued elsewhere, this sort of semantic shock is a common pattern in the metaphoric language of many esoteric traditions, both in Europe and in Asia.[75]

The second factor at work in Naglowska's invocation of Satan, however, is a larger fascination with and attempted recuperation of the devil that runs throughout modern literature at least since the work of John Milton's *Paradise Lost* and William Blake's *Marriage of Heaven and Hell*. In France, as we saw above, there was a general fascination with Satan, the powers of evil, and the black mass throughout the nineteenth century, from Baudelaire's decadent poetry down to Huysmans's fictional account of the black mass in *Là bas*. However, one key point that emerges in both the works of Baudelaire and Huysmans is that of the eventual turn away from Satan and back to Christ. Once fascinated with flowers of evil, Baudelaire eventually returned to the church; likewise, as Ziegler notes, Huysmans left his occult fascination with the devil and black mass to return to Christ: "In turn-of-the-century France, an encounter with the devil often inspired the seeker to begin a quest for the divine."[76]

While clearly influenced by these earlier occult and literary movements, Naglowska also developed a complicated metaphysical system in which Satan played a pivotal role in both the unfolding of the cosmos and the human path to redemption. In the metaphysical sense, Satan holds an important place in Naglowska's view of both the creation of the world and the unfolding of the divine plan in history. As Hans Thomas Hakl explains, Satan is the necessary dialectical counterpart to God in this system, acting as the power of negation that is essential to creation, and therefore deserves a separate turn of worship by initiates:

> God is Life and Life is God. But Life can generate the world only by means of a dialectical process in which Life is constantly confronted with the negation of Life. This negation is Reason, and Reason is associated ... with Satan, who likewise constantly fights God. But since God actually needs negation—Satan—as his dialectical counterpart in order to create the world, initiates who want to be part of the dialectical process have to serve Satan before they can serve God.... [I]t was also out of the same dialectic between God and Satan that the Son, manifested in Christ, was born.[77]

Satan's role also plays out in the unfolding of history and in the three ages discussed above. Here Satan performs a key role as the dark underside of the age of Christ, the Son. Although Satan's work is embodied in secret orgies and black masses, these are, again, the necessary dialectical counterpart to the Christian Eucharist. Finally, in the third age of the Mother, the work of the Father and Son will be completed and Christ and Satan will be reconciled,[78] ushering in a new "Golden Mass" that will transcend both the white and black masses of God and Devil:

> The symbol of Judaism—a religion of the Father—is the rod hidden in the ark. Its ethic protects reproduction of the species.
>
> The symbol of Christianity—a religion of the Son—is, on the one hand, the cross, and on the other, the sword: renunciation of the sex act and scorn for life. But in the shadow of the Christ, the worshippers of Satan make divine the womb of the woman in secret orgies, which maintain the dynamism of the march forward. The white mass of the transubstantiation is thus attenuated by the black mass of the redynamization of the flesh, which, without that, would become anemic.
>
> The symbol of the third religion—the Religion of the Mother—is the arrow launched toward heaven. The golden mass, which it will establish, will glorify the real love of the flesh, in order to release from the latter the renovating and ascendant spirit, which will make all things new upon the earth.[79]

Rather than simply being destroyed and annihilated, Evil will thus be alchemically transmuted into a higher Good, and Satan will ultimately be redeemed:

> Divinely, the mission of our Triangle consists in redirecting the Spirit of Evil onto the good path, in other words the Redemption of Satan. . . . [W]hile the East applies itself to conquering Evil by its destruction, the true goal of the Christianity of Europe has been from the very beginning exactly the opposite: the victory of Evil itself by means of its transformation into the Good.[80]

This ultimate turn from Satan to God is reminiscent of both Baudelaire's eventual turn from the "Litanies of Satan" back to the church and Huysmans's return to Christ after dabbling in black masses. Once again, "an encounter with the devil often inspired the seeker to begin a quest for the divine."[81] The key difference is that, for Naglowska, Satan is not abandoned and rejected altogether but redeemed, transformed, and reconciled with God. In this sense, her work is more reminiscent of William Blake's ideal of the "Marriage of Heaven and Hell" and also his key idea that the "roads of excess will lead to palaces of wisdom."[82] But what is perhaps most unique about Naglowska's teachings, and what sets them apart from Blake or Baudelaire or most other previous authors, is her injection of a distinctly feminist or "Satanic feminist" interpretation. In what is perhaps her most radical statement, Naglowska also says that her philosophy is nothing less than a "new religion in the world"[83] and that this is itself a kind of "feminine Satanism." Such a Satanic feminism would at once reverse and redeem a "masculine" Satanism. Whereas masculine Satanism is the voice of rationalism that "pushes away the divine," feminine Satanism is the power of love and sexuality that will also embrace the divine and so usher in a new age of wholeness: "in Satan there is also the feminine side.... Feminine Satanism is the principle of the New Birth, and its cry of joy announces the new day. The Word is born in the chaste womb of the Woman; it rises to her head and speaks through her mouth, determining the beginning of a New Era."[84]

The Hanging Mystery: Satan, Sex, Death, and Redemption

Naglowska's use of jarring, transgressive, and yet seductive imagery is not limited simply to words and text, however; rather, it is also a matter of ritual practice. Satan is not a mere rhetorical device in her system but a key stage in the initiate's progress toward ultimate salvation. Just as he plays a key role in the process of creation and in the unfolding of history, Satan is equally critical to the spiritual path of the initiate in Naglowska's esoteric order. Thus in her *La Lumière du sexe*, she allegorically describes the initiatory path to the ascent of a symbolic mountain, which is to be climbed under the guidance of Satan. Undergoing a death and rebirth, their work will be transformed from satanic to divine, just as Satan is to be redeemed and transformed:

> Once they have reached the summit, they will be hanged, with their body falling down the mountain, but they have to blindly trust Satan's promise that they survive the ordeal. Then, ... in the exact moment of their fall their religious service ceases to be satanic and becomes divine; and thus, after having served Satan they start serving God and understand that both services are but one.[85]

The act of hanging described here was not merely metaphorical, however. Rather, it was central to the most infamous practice in the upper levels of Naglowska's Fraternity, known as *Le Mystère de le pendaison* or the Rite of Hanging (see fig. 3.3). Of all her rituals, this was the one most

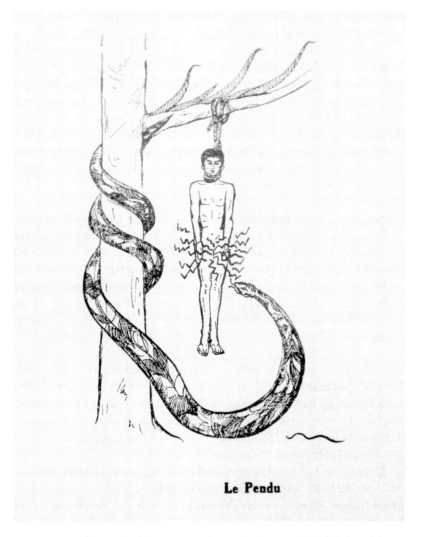

FIGURE 3.3. "Le Pendu," from Maria de Naglowska, *Le Mystère de la pendaison* (Paris: Éditions de la Flèche, 1934).

surrounded by a tantalizing aura of dangerous power and transgression, embodying the seductive nature of the secret more clearly than perhaps any of her other works. Thus, the journal *La Flèche* ran an advertisement for her book *La Mystère de la pendaison*, which warns the reader of the terrible danger of this practice, even as it offers a special price for those brave enough to undertake it: "In order that this important book, which is dangerous, should be read only by people who can understand it, we will reserve it especially for our subscribers, to whom it is offered at the exceptional price of 30 francs."[86]

The Rite of Hanging itself was the difficult and dangerous initiatory ordeal that would lead the initiate from the second degree in the Fraternity—that of *Chasseur Affranchi* (Liberated Hunter)—to the third degree—that of *Guerrier Invincible* (Invincible Warrior). In a classic form of initiatory death and rebirth, the candidate was hung and allowed to dangle in the air, then released at the last moment before death. Afterwards, he was to engage in ritual intercourse with a priestess, experiencing both ultimate desire and ultimate pleasure, which were themselves the result of Satan entering into his body:

> At the moment of this terrible ceremony ... he no longer sees Satan before him and separated from him ... but he is himself Satan, himself the unlimited Force of Negation. And he immolates himself, he accepts in his whole being, top to bottom, the electrifying penetration of the luminous Feminine (religiously purified) at the sublime moment of sacred coitus, for which his Lover is awake. The Man comes away from this test shaken in his Reason, and he is the Sublime Madman of which the secret scriptures speak.[87]

After this encounter with death and ecstasy, he would be a true Invincible Warrior "because he could no longer be tempted by a woman: during his hanging, he had experienced such an extreme lust and such incredible bliss that everything else would have become shallow.... The candidate was to be literally confronted with the total and eternal void, which would inevitably change his perspective forever."[88]

The practices of ritual hanging and erotic asphyxiation were not new. Marquis de Sade described the practice in his classic sadomasochistic novel *Justine*. More than one famous artist had also accidentally died by experimenting with the practice in the eighteenth, nineteenth, and early twentieth centuries, including English author and playwright Peter Anthony Motteux (d. 1718) and Czech composer Frantisek Kotzwara (d. 1791). Closer to our own time, artist Vaughn Bode and actor David Carradine also died by erotic asphyxiation.

Nor was Naglowska the only one to link mystical experience so directly to death and eroticism. One of the most explicit connections between death and sexuality appears in the work of Georges Bataille, the controversial French novelist, philosopher, and head of his own secret society, whom many believe had attended Naglowska's sessions.[89] As Bataille famously argued in his classic work, *L'Erotisme* (1957), there is a deep and fundamental "connection between death and sexual excitement"; for "eroticism itself is nothing other than assenting to life up to the point of death."[90] For Bataille as for Naglowska, sexual union is a form of "immolation," in which the finite individual loses her- or himself in the embrace of the lover, and the narrow confines of the ego are shattered in the ecstatic experience of boundless continuity:

> The embrace restores us ... to the totality in which man has his share *by losing himself*. For an embrace is not just a fall into the animal muck but the anticipation of death. ... The totality reached ... is reached only at the price of a sacrifice: eroticism reaches it precisely inasmuch as love is a kind of immolation.[91]

For both Bataille and Naglowska, the secret is not simply eros but the deep link between eros, death, and mystical ecstasy, in which the self is confronted with its own blissful annihilation. While it is perhaps impossible to say whether Naglowska was a direct influence on Bataille or simply part of a larger intellectual milieu, her insights into death and sensuality did precede Bataille's *Erotisme* by at least two decades.

Perhaps one key difference between Naglowska and Bataille, however, was that her hanging mystery was itself only the prelude to a final ritual, which was imagined but probably never actually performed. The final rite was to be the "Golden Mass" mentioned above, which would transcend both the Black Mass of the Satanists and the White Mass of the Church. Imagined as a rite of sexual magic involving four women and three men, the Golden Mass would be the ritual fulfilment of the new Age of the Third Term of the Trinity. In February 1935, she held a "Preliminary Golden Mass," in which the sexual union was performed symbolically rather than literally; apparently, this was intended to be a dry-run for an actual sexual rite that was never completed before she disappeared and the fraternity dissolved.[92] As such, it remains yet another—perhaps Naglowska's final—tantalizing and elusive secret.

Conclusions: The Erotic Nature of Secrecy and the Secret Nature of Eros

To close, I would like to reflect more broadly on Naglowska's key role in the development of religious secrecy and the complex interplay between eros, concealment, and disclosure. While Naglowska was surely not the first author to link sexuality and esotericism, she did articulate perhaps the most explicit identification between the two, both in her practice of sexual magic and in her esoteric rhetoric itself. From the first publication of *Magia Sexualis*, Naglowska's writings were filled with the seductive dynamic of lure and withdrawal, the promise of tantalizing secret knowledge, and the continuous deferral of the final secret for all but the most dedicated initiates. Using Satanic rhetoric in particular, she surrounded her secrets with an aura of powerful danger and transgressive allure, leading the initiate progressively toward the most dangerous secrets, including ritual hanging and erotic asphyxiation. With her seductive mixture of sensuality, death, and mystical union, she anticipated many of the ideas later articulated by Bataille and others a few decades later.

While Naglowska is a fairly obscure figure today and mostly known only to scholars of early twentieth-century esotericism, her influence has been widespread and profound. Her *Magia Sexualis* is surely one of the most influential texts on sexual magic ever published and helped trigger the massive growth in various forms of erotic mysticism that spread throughout Europe, England, and the US for the next eighty years. Particularly in the wake of the 1960s and the sexual revolution, Western sexual magic was increasingly confused and often identified with Hindu Tantra — usually with a healthy dash of the *Joy of Sex* and the *Kama Sutra* thrown in — giving birth to a vast number of works such as *Sex Magic, Tantra and Tarot: The Way of the Secret Lover, Secrets of Western Tantra: The Sexuality of the Middle Path*, and *Demons of the Flesh: The Complete Guide to Left-Hand Path Sex Magick*, among countless others.[93] Once imagined as a dark, dangerous, and difficult practice accessible only to the most dedicated occultist, the secret of sexual magic is now widely accessible in mass market paperbacks and on myriad websites across the Internet. In the process, the practice of sexual magic appears to have lost much of its Satanic aura and is today more a matter of liberated openness and sexual pleasure than of divine immolation in the *Mystère de la pendaison*.

Yet perhaps Naglowska's most lasting contribution is her seductive use of the language of secrecy itself. More than simply an advertisement, secrecy in Naglowska's work is also a deeply erotic play between taboo and transgression, between chastity and violation, between purity and perversion, with Satan serving as the tantalizing nexus of concealment and revelation. This erotic dimension of the secret is arguably always present in some fashion, as the central dynamic of veiling and unveiling inherent in all forms of concealment.[94] But Naglowska's unique gift is her ability to invest the secret with an aura of dangerous desire, sinful temptation, and delicious pleasure, magnifying both its allure and its mysterious power — intensifying, as it were, that "static crackle of some libidinous thing in the world."

✳ CHAPTER 4 ✳

Secrecy and Social Resistance

THE FIVE PERCENTERS AND
THE ARTS OF SUBVERSIVE BRICOLAGE

*X-UNKNOWN: MEANING TO CONCEAL THE TRUTH.
THE UNCIVILIZED PEOPLE DO NOT KNOW THE TRUTH.
FOR THE POSITIVE BLACKMAN, IT IS U NOW KNOW.*

CLARENCE 13X, "Supreme Alphabet"[1]

*And then you got the five percent
Who are the poor righteous teachers
Who do not believe in the teachings of the ten percent
Who is all wise and know who the true and living god is
And teach that the true and living god is a supreme being black man
   from Asia*

WU TANG CLAN, "Wu Revolution"[2]

*Like prudent opposition newspaper editors under strict censorship,
subordinate groups must find ways of getting their message across,
while staying somehow within the law. This requires . . . a capacity
to exploit all the loopholes, ambiguities, silences, and lapses. . . .
It means carving out a tenuous life for themselves in a political
order that, in principle, forbids such a life.*

JAMES C. SCOTT, *Domination and the Arts of Resistance*[3]

In 1997, the hip-hop group Wu Tang Clan released its double album "Wu Tang Forever," a massive hit record that, despite limited airplay, reached number one in the Billboard 200 chart and sold 612,000 copies in its first week. The album was later certified 4x platinum and sold over two million copies in the US alone. At around the same time, one of the main songwriters of Wu Tang Clan, RZA, also published his own compendium of philosophy and musical analysis entitled the *Wu Tang Manual*, which broke down individual song lyrics line by line to explain their complex references and symbolism. Throughout the songs we find a wide array of subtle and not-so-subtle references drawn from Eastern philosophy, the Bible, martial arts, pop culture, and—most significantly—the Nation of Islam (NOI) and its more esoteric offshoot, the Five Percenters, also known as the Nation of Gods and Earths (NGE).[4]

Founded in Detroit in 1930, the Nation of Islam is an African American new religious movement that spread rapidly among black urban youth throughout the twentieth century; the movement perhaps reached its height of influence in the early 1960s, when the fiery and articulate Malcolm X became its chief spokesman, before leaving the group in 1964.[5] The Five Percenters is an offshoot of the NOI, founded in Brooklyn in 1964 by Clarence 13X, a.k.a. Allah or Father.[6] Taking some of the NOI's esoteric ideas in a more radical direction, Clarence 13X taught that the true God or Allah is none other than every black man. The idea of the "five percent" refers to the belief that 85 percent of the population is enslaved, oppressed, and under control; 10 percent of the population are the rich slave masters who dupe and control the masses; and the few 5 percent are those who are aware of their own true nature as divine beings—indeed, as gods in the flesh—and who have the obligation to awaken the slumbering 85 percent. While the Five Percenters began as a relatively obscure and marginal black urban movement, their ideas rapidly circulated in the 1970s, 1980s, and 1990s, above all through the new genre of rap music and hip-hop culture more broadly, much of which was heavily infused in its early years with the language, symbolism, and ideology of both NOI and NGE.

At first glance, it might seem like a strange transition to move from Freemasonry and the Theosophical Society to the Five Percenters and hip-hop. As we will see in this chapter, however, there are deep historical connections between the Five Percenters' roots in earlier black Muslim movements such as the Moorish Science Temple and esoteric traditions such as Freemasonry, Theosophy, and Islamic mysticism.[7] The Five Percenters also developed a complex system of coded language known as the Supreme Alphabet and Supreme Mathematics that has much in common with other systems of esoteric knowledge transmission, and especially with Freemasonry.[8] Indeed, some scholars have even described the Five Percenters as "a form of African American Gnosticism," sharing with other forms of Gnosis "the mystical perception of transcendent spiritual knowledge that is disseminated and interpreted only by spiritually mature adherents and initiates."[9]

However, what is perhaps most significant about the Five Percenters — at least for the purposes of this book — is their use of secrecy as an instrument of social and political resistance. In one sense, secrecy in the Five Percenters is a powerful source of resistance to a racist and classist society that has consistently targeted young black men as dangerous, disposable criminals. As Simmel famously put it, secrecy often emerges in oppressive conditions as "the correlate of police control" and as a "protection against the violent pressures of central powers."[10] For secrecy often plays a basic protective role, allowing marginal and dissident groups both to bond and to evade the scrutiny of police and legal systems. It can provide what James C. Scott calls a "hidden transcript," or a way "to exploit all the loopholes, ambiguities and lapses" to carve out "a tenuous life in a political order that ... forbids such a life."[11] At the same, secret knowledge for the Fiver Percenters is incredibly empowering for these young men; rather than subhuman, unwanted, social detritus, black men are *Gods*, Allah in the flesh, possessing the knowledge of their true identity and the power to awaken others.[12] It offers both a coded language and an ideology that allows the few who know the truth (5 percent) to mount an incisive critique of the dominant social, economic, and racial order (the 10 percent) while targeting a massive "exoteric" audience of the unawakened (the 85 percent). As such, secrecy here is not simply a kind of symbolic power or capital, but also a subversive and resistant form of power — perhaps a "black market form of capital" — that circulates outside of the dominant symbolic economy.[13]

Yet the role of secrecy here is also more complex than a simple matter of social resistance. While most of the literature on the NGE and Five Percenter rap has been quite celebratory overall — highlighting their spirit of protest, black identity, and social justice[14] — I want to acknowledge the more conflicted and ambivalent role of secrecy in this case. Secrecy in the NGE is also very much about establishing a kind of status and power *within* these cultures of resistance, asserting a source of authority within the black community, within the NOI, and within hip-hop culture more broadly. Much of this status, for example, is clearly *gendered*, with men identified as Gods and women as Earths, and men dominating both the NGE as a movement and Five Percenters rap as a musical genre.[15] The Five Percenters' unique style of esoteric discourse became a key part of what Monica Miller calls a "spiritualized market economy" of competition and status within the hip-hop world — and also, of course, part of a very real material market economy, as hip-hop emerged from an underground musical form into a billion dollar global industry of its own. With the Five Percenters, the "occult marketplace" that began to develop with nineteenth-century print media has now evolved into a full-scale global marketplace, working through transnational media and advertising.

The Five Percenters thus embody a series of profound tensions—tensions between esoteric discourse and public commercial success, between social resistance and new forms of domination. And yet, these tensions are perhaps bound up in the paradoxical nature of secrecy itself, which is always tied to both concealment and disclosure, to both symbolic and material forms of capital.

From Freemasonry to Moorish Science Temple

The Five Percenters are an outgrowth of two other black Muslim movements that emerged in the first half of the twentieth century. Both of these have roots in older esoteric traditions, mostly derived directly or indirectly from Freemasonry, and thus have a surprising amount in common with the otherwise largely "white" tradition of Western esotericism. The first of these, the Moorish Science Temple, was founded in Chicago in the 1920s by a man who called himself Noble Drew Ali. There are various conflicting accounts of Drew's life, most of them mixing—as do the biographies of many founders of new religions—elements of fact with mythology, fantasy, and hagiography. Many sources identify him as Timothy Drew, born in 1886 in North Carolina, either the child of ex-slaves raised by Cherokee Indians or the son of a Moroccan father and a Cherokee mother.[16] At least one scholar, however, has identified him as Thomas Drew, born that same year in Virginia.[17] The narratives of Drew's life appear to have become increasingly embellished over the years, many recounting his remarkable travels overseas and his encounters with various mystical traditions in the Middle East. The most elaborate of these describe a harrowing initiatory ordeal in the Egyptian pyramids, where he was inducted into the most ancient secrets of Egyptian magic:

> There he met the last priest of an ancient cult of High Magic who took him to the Pyramid of Cheops, led him in blindfolded and abandoned him. When Drew found his way out unaided the magus recognized him as a potential adept.... He received the name Sharif [Noble] Abdul Ali.[18]

Many scholars, however, are skeptical of these tales of Drew's journey to Egypt and instead suggest that more likely sources for his religious ideas were much closer to home, coming primarily from Freemasonry and Theosophy. As Fathie Abdat argues, a black Masonic lodge called the Knights of the Jerusalem Temple had been established very close to Drew's home in 1908, while a Theosophy building had also been built nearby. These domestic sources were more likely the inspiration for his esoteric ideas.[19]

Whatever his original inspiration may have been, Drew published a small text known as the *Circle 7 Koran* (not to be confused with the Arabic Koran known to most Muslims).[20] The name "circle seven" comes from the image of the number 7 inside a circle that adorns its cover. Like much of Moorish Science imagery, this draws on esoteric traditions of number symbolism and is said to refer to "the ELOHIM, the angels or 'gods,' called by him 'the Seven Eyes of Allah.'"[21] Much of the *Circle 7 Koran* draws heavily from other sources, including esoteric texts that were popular at the turn of the twentieth century. Roughly half of the text (chapters 2–19) seem to be taken from *The Aquarian Gospel of Jesus the Christ* published in 1908 by Levi H. Dowling, a Theosophical text that purports to recount Christ's travels in India. Dowling's text, in turn, was probably inspired by an earlier work by Nicolas Notovich known as *La Vie Inconnue de Jésus Christ,* which claimed to be based on an ancient manuscript from a Tibetan monastery.[22] Other portions of *The Circle 7 Koran* (chapters 20–44) likely come from the text *Unto Thee I Grant,* edited by Sri Ramatheria, which claims to be the English translation of an ancient Tibetan work obtained from the Dalai Lama.[23] In all of these claims to ancient "Eastern" sources, of course, we are reminded of the elaborate Oriental genealogies of Blavatsky's Theosophical literature.

In addition to its alternative history of Jesus in India, much of the *Circle 7 Koran* also reflects a distinctly esoteric philosophy, with flavors of Theosophical influence.[24] Like Blavatsky's *Secret Doctrine,* this is presented from the very outset as a profoundly esoteric text, one that has long been kept hidden but now may be revealed openly for this day and age:

> The reason these lessons have not been known is because the Moslems of India, Egypt and Palestine had these secrets and kept them back from the outside world, and when the time appointed by Allah they loosened the keys and freed the secrets, and for the first time in ages have these secrets been delivered in the hands of the Moslems of America.[25]

A recurring theme in the text, moreover, is the secret knowledge of the divinity of all human beings and the immediate, direct, unmediated relationship between humanity and God:

When man sees Allah as one with him, as Father Allah, he needs no middle man, no priest to intercede. He goes straight up to Him and says, "My Father God, Allah!" and then he lays his hand in Allah's own hand, and all is well. And this is Allah. You are, each one, a priest.[26]

In addition to these Theosophical and other esoteric sources, however, perhaps Noble Drew Ali's most direct source of inspiration came from none other than Freemasonry and related fraternal orders.[27] Elements of a sort of Westernized Islam and Egypto-philia had been part of Masonry for generations, and these "Muslim" elements became even more pronounced with the founding of the Ancient Arabic Order of the Nobles of the Mystic Shrine—popularly known as the "Shriners." Created by a group of thirty-second degree Scottish Rite Masons in 1876–77, the Shriners incorporated various Americanized Muslim and Egyptian elements that would later be carried over into the Moorish Science Temple.[28]

Although the American Masonic lodges were largely segregationist, black or "Prince Hall" lodges had existed since the time of the American Revolution, assuming names such as the Chapter of the Eastern Star, Order of the Golden Circle, and Knights of the Invisible Colored Kingdom. In 1893, during the famous World Parliament of Religions conference in Chicago, a group of African Americans also claimed to have received initiation from visiting Muslim dignitaries and subsequently established the "Ancient Egyptian Order of Nobles of the Shrine" or "black Shriners." As Wilson notes, photographs of Noble Drew Ali show him dressed elaborately in Egyptian Shriner attire, bearing Masonic headgear and symbols (see fig. 4.1). Clearly the "adorning" function of secrecy was not lost on Ali, who appears to have optimized its symbolic power. Other Moorish Science sources identify Noble Drew Ali as a "Pythian Knight, a Shriner, a Prophet of the Veiled Realm and of course a Thirty-Second degree Mason."[29] Some Moorish Science texts also employ Masonic symbols, including the classic Square and Compass, which is identified with the central "L" in the letters spelling ISLAM.[30] Ali's *Holy Koran*, meanwhile, explicitly refers to the Masonic square and compass, which are part of Jesus's own original carpenter's kit, each implement of which is said to have deeper symbolic meaning. Thus,

[w]e use the square to measure all our lines, to straighten out the crooked places of the way, and make the corners of our conduct square. We use the compass to draw circles around our passions and desires to keep them in the bounds of righteousness.[31]

FIGURE 4.1. Noble Drew Ali. Photographer unknown.

Lastly, we should note that the Moorish Science Temple developed a "catechism" laid out in question-answer format, which bears a close resemblance to the basic format used in introductory literature for new Masons.[32] As Harry Carr shows in his classic study of very early Masonic catechisms from 1696–1730, the standard texts for new initiates followed a question-answer format. For example, the text of the "Grand Mystery of Free-Masons Discover'd" (1725) reads as follows:

Q. What is a Mason?
A. A Man begot of a Man, born of a Woman, brother to a King.
Q. What is a fellow?
A. A companion of a Prince.[33]

Although the structure of the Moorish Science catechism closely resembles Masonic literature, the questions are largely unique to black Muslims. The Moorish Science text adds a distinctly racial element to the questions, identifying dark-skinned Americans specifically with not simply an Arabian but an Angelic genealogy:

57. Who were Adam and Eve? They are the ones who brought about a discord in the Holy city of MECCA and were driven out.
58. Where did they go? They went into Europe.
59. What is the modern name given to their children? Roman.
60. What is the shade of their skin? Pale.
61. Who is guarding the Holy City of MECCA to keep the unbelievers away? Angels.
62. What is the modern name of these angels? Arabian.
63. What is the shade of their skin? Olive.
64. Are the Moorish Americans any relation to those Angels? Yes, we all have the same Father and Mother.

    . . .

71. What is the Higher self? The Higher self is the mother of virtues and the harmonies of life, and breeds Justice, Mercy, Love and Right.
72. Can the Higher Self pass away? No.
73. Why? Because it is ALLAH in man.[34]

As we will see below, this question-answer format was also the primary means of communicating esoteric knowledge in the NOI and even more explicitly in the NGE. Moreover, the claim that the "higher self" is the presence of Allah in man also prefigures the later NGE claim that the black man is himself Allah or God in the flesh.

Supreme Wisdom Lessons and Esoteric
Knowledge in the Nation of Islam

Many aspects of the Moorish Science Temple—including its interest in esoteric symbolism and hidden teachings—were carried over into the Nation of Islam. The founder of the movement, Wallace D. Fard (also known as Wallace Fard Muhammad), was equally if not more mysterious than Noble Drew Ali. Born sometime between 1877 and 1893, Fard's identity, origins, and even ethnicity remain unclear, and there is much debate as to whether he was of Arab, Palestinian, Turkish, African American, or some other descent.[35] According to some historians, Fard was involved with the Moorish Science Temple and even claimed to be Noble Drew's successor;[36] however, his relationship with Moorish Science is also debated, and the NOI today denies that he had any involvement in Ali's movement.

Whatever his background, Fard moved in 1929 to Detroit, a city that, like other industrial cities in the northern US, had become an important refuge for many blacks in the years between the two world wars, as they fled lynchings, racial violence, and poverty in the South. Fard began preaching from door to door, spreading the message that the black man's true religion was Islam, that his original language was Arabic, and that his original identity had been stolen by the white man. The message spread quickly, as Fard attracted a growing following among the city's large and mostly poor African American population, drawing as many as 8,000 members in Detroit alone by 1933.

The chief architect of NOI, however, was not Fard but his chief disciple and successor, Elijah Muhammad (born Elijah Poole, 1897–1975). The son of a minister from Georgia, Elijah Muhammad regarded Wallace Fard as not simply an ordinary man but as the Mahdi—the prophesied end-times redeemer in Muslim theology who will, together with Isa (Jesus), combat evil and rule the world before the Day of Judgment. Indeed, he often referred to Fard as none other than Allah or God appearing in human form and directly incarnate and intervening directly in this world; meanwhile, Elijah Muhammad presented himself as a new Messenger (both claims that are commonly regarded as heretical by more orthodox Muslim, for whom no human can be worshiped as God and for whom the historical prophet Muhammad was the final Messenger).[37]

Even as it grew into a widespread religious movement, the NOI developed a number of more "esoteric" dimensions of belief and practice, many of which have continuities with older esoteric traditions discussed above.[38] One of the most important but little-known documents in the early growth of NOI is a brief text called "The Supreme Wisdom Lessons" (also known as *Secret Ritual of the Nation of Islam*[39]). Originally meant to be an esoteric text for advanced NOI members, the Supreme Wisdom Lessons follow a question-answer format that—as many observers have noted—seems to be based on both the Moorish Science catechism and on the older Masonic catechisms.[40] As Amir Fatir notes, the lessons follow a formula similar to Masonic and other forms of initiation, using esoteric symbolism, paradoxical language, and long processes of memorization to generate an experience of awakening or insight: "Like all initiation systems, the process Master Fard used on Elijah Muhammad is intended to bring about an inner change that lights a spark and suddenly renders understanding. . . . Through memorization and repeated recitation, the true power of the lessons begins to unveil itself."[41]

Like the Masonic catechisms, moreover, the Supreme Wisdom Lessons begin with fundamental questions about the nature of man; and like the Moorish Science catechism, they give this a distinctly racial interpretation, identifying the true or original man with the black man of Asia. Thus, when asked "Who is the Original man?" and "Who is the Colored man?," the correct response is:

1. The original man is the Asiatic Black man; the Maker; the Owner; the Cream of the planet Earth—(Father of Civilization), God the Universe.
2. The Colored man is the Caucasian (white man). Or, Yacob's grafted devil—the Skunk of planet Earth.[42]

Here we should note that the figure of Yacob has its own complex esoteric history. First mentioned briefly in the Supreme Wisdom Lessons, the Yacob story was developed in more detail by Elijah Muhammad in his 1965 book, *Message to the Black Man in America*. As Elijah Muhmmad explains, Yacob was a scientist who lived 6,600 years ago and was responsible for creating whites as a race of "devils." According to this complicated narrative, Yacob engaged in a practice of selective breeding or "grafting" while living on the Island of Patmos (where St. John was said to have been exiled when he received the vision that culminated in the Book of Revelation). Through his experiments in selective breeding, Yacob took the pure black stock of mankind and created a white race by systematically weeding out all the dark-skinned babies and preserving the light skinned ones. Finally, he made a race of men with white skin and blue eyes whose evil spread not only among themselves but to others as well:

The Yakub-made devils were really pale-white, with really blue eyes; which we think are the ugliest colors for a human eye. They were all Caucasian—which means, according to some of the Arab scholars, "One whose evil effect is not confined to one's self alone, but affects others."[43]

While this Yacob story probably strikes most contemporary readers as an anachronistic brand of pseudoscience, it is clearly a powerful form of social critique that attempts to revise, rewrite, and invert many dominant American narratives of race and status. While most nineteenth- and twentieth-century racial narratives consistently portrayed dark-skinned people as either inferior or partially human, the Yacob story redescribes the black man as the original, pure human stock. Conversely, the white man — and particularly the very light-skinned, blue-eyed quintessentially "Aryan" white — is now redescribed as an inferior, polluted, and degenerate imitation of the original man.

In addition to these sorts of quasi-scientific genealogical narratives, the Supreme Wisdom Lessons contain some of the core ideas of the 5, 10, and 85 percent that would later become the basis for the NGE in the 1960s. As the text explains, again in question-answer format:

Who is the 85%?
ANS. The uncivilized people; poison animal eaters; slaves from mental death and power; people who do not know the Living God or their origin in this world, and they worship that they know not what — who are easily led in the wrong direction, but hard to lead in the right direction.

Who is the 10%?
ANS. The rich; the slave-makers of the poor; who teach the poor lies — to believe that the Almighty, True and Living God is a spook and cannot be seen with the physical eye. Otherwise known as the Blood Suckers of the Poor

Who is the 5% in the Poor Part of the Earth?
ANS. They are the poor, righteous Teachers, who do not believe in the teachings of the 10%, and are all-wise; and know who the Living God is; and Teach that the Living God is the Son of man, the supreme being, the (Black man) of Asia.[44]

More than one scholar has noted that these ideas of the black man as the Living God and the "5 percent" as the elite few who possess true knowledge have much in common with older esoteric traditions such Gnosticism and Theosophy. As Swedenburg suggests, the NOI gave these esoteric ideas a racial interpretation or "Afrocentric twist," rearticulated for the position of black men in twentieth-century America.[45] In so doing, they transformed this Gnostic impulse into a powerful source of social critique, which fundamentally inverts the symbolic hierarchy of white over black into one of the black living God over the white devil.

Not surprisingly, because of their radical ideas of black empowerment and resistance to white society, both the Moorish Science Temple and NOI came under intense surveillance by the Federal Bureau of Investigation (FBI) through its COINTELPRO (Counter Intelligence Programs); this included agents infiltrating these organizations in the attempt to destabilize them from within.[46] This pattern continued with other black religious and social movements for the next several decades.

Clarence 13X and the Five Percent Nation of Gods and Earths

By the 1960s, the NOI had become a powerful movement throughout the urban spaces of the US, particularly in cities such as Detroit, Chicago, and New York. Much of the NOI's success in the early 1960s was due to the work of its most charismatic and articulate spokesman, the young Malcolm X (born Malcolm Little, 1925–1965). Through Malcolm X's fiery speeches, NOI emerged as a powerful counterpoint to the more pacifist and Christian branch of the civil rights movement led by Dr. Martin Luther King Jr. (1929–68). Calling for a more militant response to white America, Malcolm X criticized King's moderate goals of integration, invoking instead the language of revolution and black separatism.[47]

Already by 1963, however, the NOI had begun to experience intense internal divisions and splintering. Malcolm X left the movement in 1964 after becoming disillusioned with Elijah Muhammad's leadership, rejecting the NOI's racial views and embracing mainstream Sunni Islam (shortly before being assassinated in 1965). At roughly the same time, in 1963, another former NOI member formed the rival offshoot movement of the NGE.

Born in Virginia in 1928, Clarence Ernest Smith (fig. 4.2) inherited much of the same Masonic background that also informed the development of Moorish Science and NOI. As Wakeel Allah notes, his father was a Prince Hall and Accepted Mason in the local Danville chapter, at a time when "many Black men used the fraternal order as a means to network and uplift themselves."[48] Clarence served in the army during the Korean War and then moved to Harlem on his discharge. In 1961, he embraced the NOI and took the name Clarence 13X, serving as a security officer, a martial arts instructor, and a student minister in the NOI's Mosque No. 7 in Harlem. Like Malcolm X—the outspoken and controversial head of Mosque No. 7 at that time—Clarence 13X began to be monitored by the

FIGURE 4.2. Clarence 13X. Photographer unknown.

FBI, which was increasingly concerned with the NOI's powerful influence among black urban men.[49]

There are several conflicting narratives as to why Clarence 13X parted ways with the NOI. According to some accounts, he had a theological dispute over Wallace Fard Muhammad's alleged divinity. After all, if *all* black man are supposed to be the "living God" (as stated in the Supreme Wisdom Lessons), how could Fard alone be regarded as Allah? Instead,

Clarence 13X changed his own name to "Allah" or "Father Allah" and taught the central message that all black men are God in the flesh.[50] According to other accounts, however, the reasons for his split with NOI were more mundane, having less to do with theological disputes than with his playing craps and drinking, activities the NOI condemned.[51]

Whatever the reasons for his split with NOI, Father Allah began preaching widely to the youths on the streets of Harlem, spreading the central message of the divinity of the black man and the ideal of the 5 percent. In so doing, he was explicitly revealing some of the most esoteric aspects of the NOI, the "Lost-Found Muslim Lessons"—teachings that were originally meant to be completely secret—spreading them promiscuously to a much broader audience of black young men that extended well beyond the existing boundaries of Elijah Muhammad's Nation:

> Father Allah willfully spread Fard Muhammad's secret teachings known as the "Lost-Found Muslim Lessons" to black youth who were outsiders to the NOI. (During the 1960s, NOI members were not allowed to discuss the tradition with outsiders, maintaining a great deal of secrecy about their core beliefs, rituals, and practices).[52]

His reasoning, however, was that it was precisely the young people—the inner-city youths involved in gangs and crime and most lacking in formal education—who most needed this knowledge: "I have not come to the churches because they have their religions. I have not come to the ten percenters because they have their riches. I have come to the Children because they have nothing, the Truth has been concealed from them and theirs is the Kingdom that is to come."[53]

As Tricia Rose persuasively argues, urban centers such as New York during the 1960s and 1970s had been devastated by the changing economic conditions of postindustrialization, as jobs in large factories were increasingly displaced by changes in the global and domestic economies, new international divisions of labor, and new migration patterns. At the same time, postindustrial cities such as New York saw steep declines in federal funding for social services, particularly for poor minorities.[54] In such conditions, the new culture of hip-hop "emerged as a source for youth of alternative identity formation and social status in a community whose older local support institutions had been all but demolished along with large sectors of the built environment. Alternative local identities were forged in fashions and language . . . and in establishing neighborhood crews."[55] Similarly, the Five Percenters offered an alternative form of identity and social status—but they did so at least a decade before the emergence of rap and indeed helped lay the social, linguistic, and ideological groundwork for the latter.

Not surprisingly, the growing influence of the Five Percenters and the idea that all black men are God soon became a source of tremendous controversy. Newspaper accounts of the time were often extremely hostile to the movement, portraying it as a dangerous street gang dedicated to crime, violence, and general mayhem. According to a 1965 article in the *New York Amsterdam News* entitled "Harlem Hit by Five Percenters," this was essentially a deviant hate group, while other papers recounted Five Percenters going on a "window smashing sorté" and beating a man with a pole.[56] Like the leaders of the NOI, Allah was monitored by the FBI, whose agents wrote extensive reports on him, which they forwarded to the Secret Service. Allah was identified as "potentially dangerous," "subversive," and "having evidence of emotional instability."[57] At the same time, the New York City police began to regard Father Allah as a dangerous and perhaps criminally insane individual. His large street gatherings began to attract the attention of the NYCPD Bureau of Special Services, and much of the Five Percenters' early leadership was arrested following an event in June 1965.[58] Clarence was charged with assault, resisting arrest, disorderly conduct, and possession of marijuana, among other offenses. Because he had proclaimed himself to be "Allah," he was confined to the psychiatric unit at Bellevue State Hospital and held on $9,500 bond. There he underwent psychiatric treatment and later was admitted to Matteawan State Hospital for the Criminally Insane (infamous for having some of the worst conditions in America's criminal justice system). He remained at Matteawan for twenty-two months and returned to the streets of New York City in May 1967.[59]

As such, the message conveyed by Father Allah and his NGE appears to have represented profound threat to the dominant order of 1960s America. And this pattern of harassment of Five Percenters for their "dangerous," "deviant," and "insane" ideas has persisted throughout the history of the movement and well into the lives of major hip-hop artists.[60]

Supreme Alphabets and Supreme Mathematics: Subversive Doubling Coding and Black Market Capital

Perhaps the most important aspect of the Five Percenters for our understanding of secrecy is their complex, often ingenious use of coded language.[61] Like most esoteric groups, the Five Percenters use a variety of symbols and terms known only to members, thus drawing clear boundaries between insiders and outsiders, those who know and those who do not; yet more important, they do so in ways that transform, subvert, or "deform" the basic elements of the dominant discourse, such as the alphabet and the Roman numeral system.

Father Allah's teachings were circulated in the form of a text known as the "Book of Life" (also called the "Power Papers"), passed around hand to hand from current members to new recruits. These served as the basis for the Five Percenters' key teachings, esoteric symbolism, and code language, which are still widely transmitted through rap music and hip-hop culture more broadly. This text was also another reason for the ill will between the NOI and NGE, as Father Allah was disseminating the innermost secrets of NOI without the Nation's authorization:

> [T]he Book of Life was central to the bitter feud between the NOI and Five Percent Nation. As a former youth minister for the Nation of Islam's fabled Mosque No. 7 in Harlem, Father Allah was privy to numerous doctrines that were handed down by Fard Muhammad himself and were closely guarded secrets of the NOI's leadership. With Father Allah's departure from NOI, he incorporated these secrets into the Five Percenters' Book of Life.[62]

There are even some allegations that Allah's dissemination of NOI secrets led to his death in 1969.[63] In any case, as we will see below, this tension between secrecy and public disclosure is a theme that runs through the Five Percent movement from its origins to its most recent articulations in hip-hop.

While there were already esoteric elements present in both the Moorish Science Temple and NOI, the NGE went much further in the direction of secrecy, symbolism, and coded language. As Floyd Thomas notes, the movement should perhaps be regarded as a kind of modern Gnosticism, based on an esoteric understanding of the human being and the cosmos: "In keeping with Gnosticism as an esoteric school of thought, the Five Percent Nation philosophy revolves around fundamental principles such as the divine origins of the cosmos; the presence of evil that corrupted humanity; and recovery of humanity by nurturing the inner life of true believers."[64]

The doctrines of the NGE are also communicated in esoteric fashion, through the coded discourse known as the Supreme Mathematics and Supreme Alphabet. Like many esoteric traditions—including Freemasonry, Kabbalah, and Sufism—the NGE uses the letters of the alphabet and the numerals and relations of mathematics in a complex yet playful way to transmit a deeper understanding of the human being and

Secrecy and Social Resistance 119

their relation to the universe. According to Michael Muhammad Knight, the Supreme Mathematics had its roots in another esoteric text of Fard Muhammad called the "Problem Book" or *Teaching for the Lost-Found Nation of Islam in a Mathematical Way.* Another early NOI member and companion of Clarence named John 37X (later Abu Shahid) used this text to develop an early twelve-digit system called Living Mathematics, in which each of the first twelve numbers corresponded to a particular philosophical idea and/or virtue. Thus, 1 = Knowledge, 2 = Wisdom, 3 = Understanding, and so on.[65]

After Shahid was arrested and sent to prison, Knight argues, his early system was developed further by Clarence 13X and his new partner, James "Brother Jimmy" Howard, to create the Supreme Mathematics used by Five Percenters today. The Supreme Mathematics is a ten-digit system that is similar to Shahid's model:

1 = Knowledge	6 = Equality
2 = Wisdom	7 = God
3 = Understanding	8 = Build or Destroy
4 = Culture or Freedom	9 = Born
5 = Power or Refinement	0 = Cipher

Each of these numbers can be broken down into deeper esoteric significance. Thus, Knowledge is number one because it is the "Foundation of all in Existence" and also "the Original [Asiatic Black] Man, who 'knows the ledge' or the boundaries of himself and knows that there is 'no ledge' or no ending to his circumference." Likewise, Wisdom can be broken down into "Wise-Dom" or one who is Wise insofar as he "Speaks Intelligently from the Dome or the Mind."[66]

At the same time, Clarence developed a counterpart system of esoteric code called the Supreme Alphabet, in which each letter corresponds to a key idea and/or virtue. Thus,

A = Allah	J = Justice
B = Be or Born	K = King
C = See	L = Love
D = Divine or Destroy	M = Master
E = Equality	N = Now
F = Father	O = Cipher
G = God	P = Power
H = He or Her	Q = Queen
I = Islam	R = Rule or Ruler

S = Self or Savior	W = Wisdom
T = Truth or Square	X = Unknown
U = Universe	Y = Why
V = Victory	Z = Zig Zag Zig[67]

Like much of Five Percenter esoteric discourse, many terms in the Supreme Alphabet are based on subtle wordplay and double entendre. For example, the letter *B* stands for "Be," as in "to be" or "to be born"; *C* stands for "See", as in "to see" or recognize; *Y* stands for "Why"; and so on. Moreover, each of these can be broken down by a kind of esoteric analysis; *Allah*, for example, is said to consist of "Arm-Leg-Leg-Arm-Head," which is the physical body of the black man as God in the flesh. *Islam* can be broken down into "I-Self-Lord-and-Master." *U* or *Universe* can be broken down into "U N I (you and I) verse," meaning sun and moon, man and woman), etc.[68] At the same time, the Alphabet could also serve as a kind of "stylized slang" and insiders' code language. For example, "To refer to a police officer, Allah might have said 'Cee Cipher Power,' representing the letters C, O and P."[69]

As Miyakawa notes, this esoteric use of numerology and the alphabet may have some precedent in earlier Arabic traditions. Thus she cites the "Arabic science of interpreting mystical meanings from each letter of the Arabic alphabet"[70] called *Hurufa-i-jay-Hurufa-Ab-jay*. However, given Clarence 13X's lack of knowledge of either Arabic or Islamic mysticism, it seems far more likely that the more direct influence was from Freemasonry, which was well known to him and to others in the 1960s. Much like Masonic secrecy, the coded language of the Five Percenters offered a powerful form of authority, legitimation, and "symbolic capital" for many black young men struggling in the postindustrial spaces of New York and other cities.[71] Yet unlike most Masonic systems, this was very much a language of resistance, subversion, and opposition to the dominant hierarchies of white, middle-class America. This kind of capital is circulated not in the dominant economy of mainstream America but in the streets and alleys, gambling dens and bars of postindustrial urban spaces. It is thus perhaps a form of *"black market symbolic capital,"*[72] a powerful, valuable but largely underground and subversive kind of esoteric currency exchanged outside of or beneath the mainstream symbolic economy.

As such, the Five Percenters' creative reworking of the alphabet and number system represents something more profound than just a clever wordplay or secret code; more deeply, I think, it operates much like what Dick Hebdige calls a form of *"subversive bricolage,"* or even what Umberto calls a kind of *"semiotic guerilla warfare."*[73] As Hebdige argues in his study of punks, mods, Rastas, and other groups in postwar England, subcultures often appropriate elements of the dominant culture and signifying system, while reworking them into a new and often resistant or subversive system of meaning: "prominent forms of discourse ... are radically adapted, subverted and extended by the subcultural bricolage."[74] For example, the simple acts of a punk wearing a safety pin through his lip or a Teddy Boy wearing Edwardian suits can be powerful forms of theft and transformation of signifiers, removing an everyday object from its normal place in the scheme of signification and giving it a subversive new meaning: "when the bricoleur re-locates the significant object in a different position within the discourse, using the same overall repertoire of signs, or when that object is placed within a different total ensemble, a new discourse is constituted, a different message is conveyed."[75]

In the case of the Five Percenters, however, this subversive bricolage and semiotic warfare is even more fundamental; here they are transforming and subverting the *basic system of signs itself*—namely, the alphabet and number system—investing the very building blocks of signification with radical new meanings. As Nuruddin aptly observes, the Five Percenters are famous for their creative manipulation of language, subversive wordplay, and mastery of double or triple coding; the aim, he suggests, is precisely to use language in unexpected ways to bring about a shift in perception, a break in ordinary logic, and thus new ways of perceiving reality: "As Conversationalists they are unequaled. The fascinating, even mesmerizing, appeal of the movement to the youth comes from the Five Percenters' eloquent and spell-binding usage of African American inner-city slang. Using the potency and the vitality of the black dialectic they open up new avenues of logic and thinking, or original ways of perceiving the world."[76]

The Five Percenters' subversive play with language and letters is also similar in many ways to the subversive use of letters in the art of graffiti—another classic subcultural youth genre, also closely tied to hip-hop. As Rose suggests, graffiti uses techniques of flow, rapture, and layering to playfully rework ordinary letters into something entirely new: "Letters are double and tripled shadowed in such a way as to illustrate energy forces radiating from the center ... yet, the scripted words move horizontally."[77] As we will see below, rap music uses similar techniques of layering, flow, and rupture, working through sound rather than visual art, but with the same end of transforming conventional language into creative new kinds of signification—often in ways that are subtly coded and illegible to the uninitiated outsider.

Finally, like other forms of esoteric discourse, the Five Percenters' use of coded discourse could serve as powerful form of symbolic "adornment." Thus, alongside the Supreme Alphabet and Mathematics, the Five Percenters developed a key symbol known as the Universal Flag. Consisting of the number 7 (from the cover of the *Circle 7 Koran* and also referring to the significance of 7 as God in the Supreme Mathematics) surrounded by a sun, a crescent moon, and a star, the flag is a dense knot of coded symbolism: the sun here is the black man, also identified with the black number 7 or God; the crescent moon is the black woman, also identified with Earth and Wisdom, the reflected light of knowledge; and the star represents the seed or child, fruit of man and woman.

Like Masonic and other fraternal regalia, the Universal Flag was quickly made into a very literal sort of "adorning possession." As the New York journalist and friend of Clarence 13X, Barry Gottehrer, recalls, he had been asked to make up special pins bearing the Universal Flag for Five Percent members. Because of the growing power and reputation of the movement, however, Gottehrer was very concerned about generating resistance from city hall, which was already alarmed by this new nation of Gods and Earths:

> The Five Percenters designed their own insignia: a black numeral 7 and a star within a larger black and gold star. They asked me to get the design made up into small pins to wear on their shirts or hang on a chain around their necks. There was resistance to this at city hall. With an official medallion, who knows, they might start a recruitment drive, they might start a war. A medallion would give them legitimacy.[78]

Again, in contrast to the regalia of the Scottish Rite Masons, the NGE flag was immediately perceived as a far more subversive and even threatening kind of adornment. Nonetheless, it continues to be worn—often in far more ornate forms—by rappers and Five Percenters today (see fig. 4.3).

The Art of Rhyming between the Lines: Hip-Hop and the Music of the Gods

What began in the 1960s as a small underground urban movement, mostly confined to New York, Chicago, and Detroit, quickly spread nationally and internationally through the medium of music. As Tricia Rose argues, hip-hop emerged in the 1970s from postindustrial spaces and decaying urban centers such as the Bronx, spaces that had been devastated by changing labor patterns and declining federal money for social services. In hip-hop, many black young men found a new kind of identity, commu-

FIGURE 4.3. Five Percenter jewelry. Photo by author.

nity, and status that was largely absent in the postindustrial urban landscape.[79] It is therefore not surprising that early hip-hop aligned closely with the Five Percent movement, which emerged in these same urban spaces just a decade before. As RZA reflects on the birth of hip-hop in his *Wu-Tang Manual*, "About 80 percent of hip-hop comes from the Five Percent. These same brothers are the fathers of a lot of our MC styles.... [I]n a lot of ways, hip-hop is the Five Percent."[80]

Record producer and cofounder of Def Jam, Russell Simmons, also recalls the critical influence of Five Percent ideas in the early development of hip-hop, as it emerged from the streets and prisons of New York into a major artistic form. As he writes in his memoir, *Life and Def*, the language, wordplay, and esoteric references of the Five Percenters were key elements in the birth of rap:

> The Five Percenters are members of a religion that developed in jail among black inmates in the New York area.... [I]f the Nation of Islam is a religion that finds converts in prison, Five Percenters find their converts *under* the prison. That's how street it is.... [I]t never had the discipline or strong organizational structure of the NOI.... It's been very influential over the years in the young black community, because it is very much a religion about talking. Slick, smooth-talking crafty niggas gravitated to

it because the Five Percent religion's membership was built on the ability of its members to articulate their devotion to a strict set of beliefs with as much flair as possible. A true Five Percenter could sit on a stoop or stand on a street corner and explain the tenets of the sect for hours on end—and be totally entertaining![81]

In this sense, Simmons concludes, the Five Percenters were less well known but far more influential than the NOI, at least on the streets and corners of the city:

Listen to rappers from the Brooklyn or the Queensbridge projects ... and you hear Five Percent-speak all in their rhymes. . . . The Nation of Islam is more visible and respectable in terms of its presentation. . . . However, during the period when the gangs I hung out with in the '70s gave way to '80s hip-hop culture, it was the street language, style and consciousness of the Five Percent Nation that served as a bridge.[82]

Emerging in many of the same New York neighborhoods where Five Percent ideas circulated, hip-hop inevitably cross-pollinated with NGE philosophy. Both movements appealed to the same demographics—young black man of the postindustrial city—and both used language, wordplay, and subversive discourse to create new forms of identity and community. The artist Nas describes this period of mutual influence between Five Percenter ideas and hip-hop in his 2001 song, "No Idea's Original":

No Half Steppin' with flat tops when Rakim reigned
Radios on card tables, Benetton, The Gods buildin'
Ask for today's Mathematics, we Allah's children
And this was going on in every New York ghetto
Kids listen, Five Percenters said it's pork in Jell-O
We coincide, we in the same life, maybe a time difference
on a different coast, but we share the same sunlight.[83]

Particularly during the early days of hip-hop in the 1980s, many of the ground-breaking rappers were involved directly in the NGE. Just a few of the more prominent artists include Jay-Z, Nas, Rakim, Busta Rhymes, Wu Tang Clan, Brand Nubian, Poor Righteous Teachers, Gangstarr, Big Daddy Kane, LL Cool J, Big Pun, and Digable Planets. Many others, such as Public Enemy, were involved more closely with the Five Percenter's predecessor, NOI. Five Percenter ideas informed the basic building blocks of hip-hop, giving birth to ubiquitous rap phrases such as "knowledge me," "true mathematics," "peace," "word is bond," and "droppin' science."[84] The greeting "what up, G," originally referred to God, not gangsta, and even much of hip-hop body language has Five Percenter origins. As Fab Five Freddy recalls, "The B-Boy stance originated as a Five Percenter thing. I can remember the way the Gods would stand. The Gods would stand and have one foot there and you'd fold your arms and it was like, Whoa!"[85]

Many rappers from this era recall being initiated into the NGE, a process that involves memorizing and internalizing the teachings of Fard and Allah, learning the lessons, the alphabet and the mathematics by heart. As RZA recounts, "The first thing you have to do is to memorize the 120 questions and answers.... GZA was my teacher and he tested me.... By the end of '82, when I was twelve, I knew the whole 120. You can get tested on these questions and answers at any given moment by any person.... A cipher was held by the brothers standing in a circle testing you—you had to show and prove."[86]

Five Percenter refences run throughout the rap lyrics of the 1980s and 1990s. As *HipHopWired* put it, "Pulsating with Five Percenter vibrations, these lyrical alchemists metamorphosed the base elements of the teachings of the Nation of Gods and Earths into the golden wisdom of their songwriting."[87] One of the first artists to begin using NGE ideas extensively was Rakim (born William Michael Griffin Jr.), who is often praised as the most skilled MC and best rap lyricist of all time. Through his ingenious rhymes and wordplay, the esoteric discourse of the NGE was translated into the instantly recognizable and globally powerful language of 1980s rap. Rakim's tracks such as "Move the Crowd" are replete with Five Percenter references and have as their stated goal the awakening of true self-knowledge in the listener:

> I'm the intelligent wise on the mic I will rise
> Right in front of your eyes 'cause I am a surprise
> So I'ma let my knowledge be born to a perfection
> All praise due to Allah and that's a blessing
> With knowledge of self, there's nothing I can't solve
> At 360 degrees, I revolve.[88]

A scene from the video for the song also shows Rakim in Muslim dress, rapping in front of a large image of the NGE Universal Flag, prominently displaying the "adorning power" of the symbol.

In many tracks from the 1980s and early 1990s, the elements of Five Percenter philosophy are laid out quite clearly for the listener—at least, for the listener who has "ears to hear." Thus, the song "Lost Tribe of Shabazz" by Lakim Shabazz explains the basic ideas of the 85, 10, and 5 percent, articulating both an incisive critique of American society and a call for black young men to wake up and take action:

> Our people will survive America
> My people were took from the motherland
> By the other man
> Brought to the wilderness
> Like a ventriloquist
> Played my people like puppets by plantin' fear in their heart
> Nowadays most of us don't know where to start
> 10% of us can help but don't feel the need
> They love the greed
> And this really bothers me
> 85% of us are totally ignorant
> Walkin' around with the nigga mentality
> 5% of us are ready to die for the cause
> Of course the source is Elijah
> Knowledge of self is what you need to stop the bull
> If you don't get it, I'm held responsible
> Rhymes I make are designed to reach the youth
> I gotta teach, that's why I speak the truth.[89]

In addition to their lyrical presence, NOI and NGE themes are also often woven subtly into the physical landscape of hip-hop of this era, through album covers, packaging, and artwork, often in ways that are quite obscure. As we saw in the case of Freemasonry, there is a sort of "esoteric material culture" of hip-hop, encoded deeply and sometimes rather ingeniously into the more tangible aspects of the genre. For example, the physical disk of Gravediggaz's 1997 album, *The Pick, the Sickle and the Shovel*, is modeled on a tenth-century Persian bowl, around the periphery of which runs Arabic calligraphy that reads: "He who believes in God's mercy is generous."[90] The fact that many of these references are not immediately recognizable to non–Five Percenters is probably intentional. Among other things, the subtle use of Five Percenter terminology is part of a complex code language that helps distinguish between insiders and outsiders, between "those who know" and those who do not, between the true 5 percent who have grasped the truth and the 85 percent who need to be awakened by real knowledge. Finally, as an esoteric language of social and political resistance, it is also a means of communicating NGE ideas to a global audience, yet in ways that fly under the radar and elude the repressive gaze of the 10 percent.

By 1997, Five Percenter ideas had achieved mainstream commercial success, particularly through hugely popular bands such as Wu Tang Clan. Like Lakim Shabazz, Wu Tang's massive hit album, *Wu Tang Forever*, makes extensive and explicit reference to NGE teachings; at the same time, however, it inserts a powerful critique of mainstream religion and its imaginary God—the "spook in the sky"—which only distracts form the knowledge that the true God is the black man himself:

> It was a hundred percent of us
> That came on the slave ships
> Eighty five percent of our people was uncivilized
> Poison animal eaters
> They're slaves of the mental powers
> They don't know who the true and living God is
> Nor their origins in the world
> So they worship what they know not ...
> And now you got the ten percent who are rich slave makers of the poor
> Who teach the poor lies that make the people believe
> That the all mighty true and living God is a spook in the sky
> And you can't see him with the physical eyes
> They're also known as blood suckers of the poor
> And then you got the five percent
> Who are the poor righteous teachers
> Who do not believe in the teachings of the ten percent
> Who is all wise and know who the true and living god is
> And teach that the true and living god is a supreme being black man
>   from Asia
> Otherwise known as civilized people
> Also Muslims, and Muslim's sons.[91]

While the height of Five Percent rap may have been the 1980s and 1990s, the use of NGE ideas has continued well into the twenty-first century. Thus in 2006, Lord Jamar (from Brand Nubian) even released an entire *Five Percent Album*. Featuring the Universal Flag prominently on its cover, the album contains explicitly NGE-influenced songs such as "Original Man," I.S.L.A.M.," "Yakub da Jeweler," and "Supreme Mathematics." The latter track walks the listener through the numerals 1–0, explaining the Five Percenter interpretation and its larger mission of awakening the masses: "Supreme Mathematics, this ain't black magic/I do my work amongst dope fiends and crack addicts/Civilized the savage, eight five's run rampant."[92] Here and in much of later Five Percent rap, we can clearly see that the NGE message has been increasingly "exotericized," that is, progressively transformed from a secret underground street teaching to one now meant for massive global audiences.

If Five Percenter themes feature prominently in hip-hop of this era, they are also typically mixed in with a wide array of other philosophical, religious, and cultural references. Again, they are often "layered" in complex ways amidst a larger "bricolage" of signifiers from a range of sources. The coded references in Wu Tang's lyrics, for example, are particularly eclectic and wide ranging, drawing freely not just from NGE symbolism but also from the Bible, martial arts, Chinese philosophy, and pop culture. We even find occasional references to Masonic symbolism, including the classic square and compass that appeared in the *Circle 7 Koran*. Thus the track "Triumph" includes the line: "Perpendicular to the square, we stand and glow like flare." As RZA explains its deeper meaning, "This is a Masonic reference. They teach that man should stand firm and upright upon his square of earth. So to be upright is to be at a right angle to the square — perpendicular to it."[93] Here the esoteric bricolage comes full circle, taking us all the way back to the Masonic lodge, though, again, in a far more subversive and black-market sort of way.

Resistance, Empowerment, and Authority in
NGE Discourse and Five Percent Rap

It is not difficult to see the esoteric discourse of the NGE and its articulation through hip-hop as a powerful language of resistance, social critique, and empowerment for young black men. As Floyd-Thomas puts it, "Central to the mission of the Five Percent Nation has been an attempt to move beyond a critique of nihilism into a mode of empowerment for poor and working-class African Americans who are otherwise disenfranchised, disaffected and desperate."[94] In this sense, the coded language of the NGE reveals a rather different side of secrecy than we have seen in the Freemasons or Theosophy, a strategy that is deployed not so much to reinforce elite power as to subvert the dominant order and mount a scathing social, political, and racial critique. As Simmel famously observed, one of the primary uses of secrecy for poor and marginal groups is that of concealment or protection from the powers of the dominant regime; and this protective function, in turn, can open the space for the cultivation of a new form of political awareness and the possibility of active struggle against the status quo:

Youthful knowledge, religion, morality, party, is often weak and in need of defense. Hence each may find a recourse in concealment. Hence also there is a predestination of secret societies for periods in which new life-contents come into existence in spite of the opposition of the powers that be.... Accordingly, the secret association was the form in which the germs [of a new political structure] could be protected and cultivated.[95]

This message of resistance and empowerment runs throughout the political rap of the 1980s, and particularly among artists influenced by NOI and NGE. Perhaps the most outspoken and influential of the political rap groups from this era was Public Enemy, who combined NOI's philosophy with a pointed critique of American racism and inequality. From its earliest albums, Public Identity offered an incisive analysis of the ways in which black bodies are dominated and controlled by white society, presenting NOI as a religious force of awakening that is far more powerful than Christianity. As Christopher Pinn explains,

Chuck D. sees the meaning of American society as centering around the control and destruction of black minds and bodies.... Public Enemy outlines this control and the methods for breaking its grip.... The meaning of black religion is found in its support of black identity and consciousness, and its rejection of status quo politics, economics and social relations. Chuck D.'s support of Nation of Islam suggests that black churches ... are not in line with religion's ultimate purpose, and the "Nation's" praxis better fulfills the meaning of religion.[96]

This mix of racial critique, calls for social justice, and celebration of black Islam is perhaps most explicit in Public Enemy's "Party for Your Right to Fight" on the 1988 album, *It Takes a Nation of Millions to Hold Us Back* (1988), which also explicitly invokes Elijah Muhmmad and the teachings of W. Fard Muhammad,

It was your so-called government
That made this occur
Like the grafted devils they were ...
Word from the honorable Elijah Muhammed
Know who you are to be Black ...
To those that disagree it causes static
For the original Black Asiatic man
Cream of the earth
And was here first

And some devils prevent this from being known
But you check out the books they own
Even masons they know it
But refuse to show it, yo.[97]

Here we should also note the subtle reference to the Freemasons, who are described as knowing the truth but concealing it from the masses.

Five Percent rap takes this spirit of critique and empowerment even a step further. By identifying each black man as God in the flesh, Five Percent rap offers perhaps the most radical alternative to a society in which black bodies have been discursively constructed as inferior and subhuman. As Monica Miller observes, black men in America had historically been viewed as only partially human — three-fifths of a white man in the founding of the US — and subject to dehumanizing violence for the next 200 years. By celebrating the black body as Allah, God made flesh, Five Percent rap enacts a remarkable inversion of the symbolic logic of racism: "Thought of in the context of US history, the full humanity of black bodies was deemed by white others as 3/5s human.... Metaphorically speaking, for many blacks, cultural ingenuity and strategic manipulation helps to transform niggas (3/5s) into Godz (5/5s).... For the Five Percent Nation ... the Black Man is god, ALLAH, incarnate, in the flesh."[98] RZA of Wu Tang Clan makes much the same point, though in less academic language. In his *Wu Tang Manual*, he recalls the sense of empowerment that came with encountering the idea that he was not just another poor black kid but a God: "Being in poverty and one of the oppressed people in America, you know you're limited, but you feel like you shouldn't be. These teachers taught us, You are the original man of all civilization. Hearing that when you're a kid, you're like, 'Whoa, Who, me?' It was power."[99]

Gods and Earths: Gender Dynamics and Male Dominance

While secrecy plays a powerful role as a form of cultural critique, self-empowerment, and social resistance in the NGE, it would be naïve to romanticize this as a pure or uncomplicated sort of social justice movement. Rather, like most religious movements, the NGE contains its own internal tensions and contradictions, many of them centering on this very issue of justice and power. As I have noted in my studies of other forms of secrecy and social resistance, even groups that mount the most powerful assaults on social hierarchies and economic injustice often recreate their own internal forms of hierarchy and imbalances of power.[100] As we saw in chapter 1 on Freemasonry, moreover, the rhetoric of equality and freedom is often in tension with new forms of gender, class, and racial hierarchy. In the case of a movement such as the NGE, which so strongly emphasizes the divinity of the black male, it is not surprising that this hierarchization comes out most clearly in gender relations.[101]

The superiority of male over female is built into the esoteric discourse and symbolism of the Five Percenters from the very beginning. Thus, in the Supreme Mathematics, the male is identified with the number seven, the number of God and perfection, while the highest the female can reach is six. In the Five Percenter flag, the male is identified with the Sun and the female with the Moon that revolves around him. The female is also known as a "Muslim," because she submits to Allah, the black male, whereas the male submits to no one since he is God.[102] As Floyd-Thomas notes, the symbolism of the Five Percenters reaffirms and naturalizes these sorts of gender hierarchies because they are now described as not simply arbitrary but as deep mysteries encoded in the very fabric of the universe:

> [M]uch of what is taught within the Five Percent Nation has served to reify modes of patriarchy that are insidious and regressive. For instance, it is important to note that there are only a handful of female Five Percenters in the entertainment industry. Also, unlike her male counterpart, a female Five Percenter is known as a "Muslim" because she bears witness to the fact that her man is Allah and willingly submits herself to the black man.[103]

This male dominance is evident throughout Five Percent rap, both within the music and in the larger industry. As Swedenburg notes, "5% rap remains an overwhelmingly male activity: the only female rappers in this orbit are Lady Mecca of the Digable Planets, Lauryn Hill of the Fugees, and a very minor character in the Wu Tang roster, vocalist Blue Raspberry. . . . Although Five Percenters tend to treat women with respect, their orientation creates little space for . . . the articulation of women's issues."[104]

Lyrically, this gender attitude is pervasive throughout Five Percenter music. As we see in Brand Nubian's "Love Me or Leave Me Alone" from their *In God we Trust* album, the primacy over the Sun over the Moon and of Knowledge over Wisdom is translated directly into male-female relations:

Sayin, "I'ma do my own thing, bein I'm my own King
And it's up to you to follow"
So on your Wisdom I'll shine my light
Bring forth the seed, created in the night
You gotta love me, or leave me alone
. . .
I ain't down for a honey who don't want to submit
Always throwin' a fit, want to talk a lot of shit
But love to get hit from behind
. . .
No hoe, there's no gold, the G-O-D know
The time on the Sun and the Moon and the Stars
Dance to the tune of Lord Jamar
And if you're actin tone def it's your own mental death
Huh, you gotta love me, or leave me alone.[105]

Even in songs that are less misogynistic and more respectful of the female, the primacy of Sun over Moon and the role of the woman as child bearer is still clear. As Lord Jamar sings in "Same Ole Girl,"

I'm the sun, and you're the moon
I plant my seed into your womb
Nine months later, a star will come soon
I'm try'nna build a army like the fifth of tomb
And we can have us a wedding, in May or June
Out in the Bahamas, you're not just my baby mamma
Wifey material, lifey material.[106]

This sentiment is repeated throughout Five Percenter rap. For example, as Poor Righteous Teachers put it in their track "Can I Start This?" from the 1990 recording *Holy Intellect*, the black man is clearly the Sun and the divine Seven around which his queens revolve and to which they submit:

Here's an inorganic, bomb but don't panic.
I'm the sole controller, revolving nine planets.
Yes, I'm manifesting, a blessing from the heavens
Peace, to all the queens, submitting to the seven.
I'm the Asiatic, based on mathematic
You're the jive junkie, sack crack fanatic
Write a knowledge knowledge, wisdom be purified
My wisdom will receive, reflect and amplify.[107]

The esoteric language of the Five Percenters is thus a complex and often double-edged sort of discursive weapon. At the same time that it asserts the divine power of the black male, it also inherently subordinates the black female, who, even when given respect, can only be the Muslim submitting to his divinity, the Earth beneath his Godhood.

Conclusions: Music, Capital, and the Disclosure of the Secret

In the end, the Five Percenters are not only a powerful example of the role of secrecy as a form of social resistance; they are also a striking example of the paradoxes inherent within secrecy. As Derrida reminds us, the secret is always already a negation of itself, precisely because a secret is meant to be revealed, shared, and transmitted to others. Ultimately, "There is no secret *as such*; I deny it. And this is what I confide in secret to whomever allies himself to me."[108] We have seen this paradoxical play of secrecy and disclosure throughout the history of the Five Percenters, beginning with Clarence 13X's dissemination of NOI esoteric teachings and continuing with the proliferation of Five Percent code language through the mass medium of hip-hop. The same "gnostic" teachings that once circulated by word of mouth to street kids in New York now circulate globally through hit records and publications such as the *Wu Tang Manual*.

At the same time, these esoteric ideas have become part of a new kind of "economy of secrets" — one that far surpasses the comparatively limited occult marketplace of Scottish Rite Masonry or Theosophy's competition with the Golden Dawn. Through hip-hop, Five Percent ideas such the Supreme Alphabet and Mathematics have become key aspects of a multibillion-dollar global industry. After all, as Keith Negus observes, rap is not simply a powerful music form and vehicle for social and cultural critique; "Rap is also a very particular U.S. business.... In its struggle against racism and cultural marginalization, and in an attempt to 'live the American dream,' rap has also been created as a self-conscious business activity as well as a cultural form and aesthetic practice."[109] Within this new economy of secrets, where rappers become billionaires and record companies become even richer, one wonders to what degree secrecy still retains its power as a form of social resistance and to what degree it has become reabsorbed — like virtually everything else in the neoliberal world order — into the all-consuming logic of capitalism?[110]

Both critics and fans have lamented this transformation of hip-hop from a street discourse of dissent into a massive commercial industry. In the words of an article from *Hip-Hop Wired* in 2010, "Hip-Hop has lost its way.... While flaunting money and drug game exploits run abundant, the lessons in the music have been submerged since capitalism took over and the jewels have been buried."[111] In particular, this article laments the loss of the original Five Percenter message and its displacement by a message of consumption and display of wealth. A similar narrative of hip-hop's decline is recited by journalist Christopher John Farley, who complains that the music's commercial success has come at the price of its disenfranchisement as an effect medium of resistance:

> Corporate America's infatuation with rap has increased as the genre's political content has withered. Ice Cube's early songs attacked white racism; Ice-T sang a song about a Cop Killer; Public Enemy challenged listeners to "fight the power." But many newer acts ... are focused almost entirely on pathologies within the black community. They rap about shooting other blacks, but almost never about challenging governmental authority or encouraging social activism.[112]

Others see this trend as a continuation of the same move toward commercialization that happened among black radio stations a decade earlier in the 1970s. Just as local black DJ's gave way to large media conglomerates, so too the local power of rap was progressively absorbed by huge corporate entities:

> African-American DJs lost their power as the modern-day *griots* of their communities and as the presenters of hip-hop music and culture. Similarly, with the "discovery" of hip-hop artists by corporate record labels, rap music was stolen from its community, repackaged by money-minded businesspeople looking to create a wider appeal by erasing hip-hop's historic function, and sold back to the streets through marketing ploys such as music videos and Top-40 charts. By the 1980s, hip-hop had become a business and rap music was a valuable commodity.[113]

The critical impulses within the Five Percenters thus exist in deep tension with the forces of capital, power, and patriarchy. But this is perhaps only further evidence that secrecy is never a simple or homogenous phenomenon but always a complex and conflicted one, representing a kind of *knot or linchpin* at the intersection of many different social, political, and economic interests. In fact, this tension between social resistance and commercial success is one that hip-hop artists have engaged directly in their music. It was already captured poignantly in a lyric by AZ in Nas's track "Life's a Bitch" from 1994, which highlighted this shift away from Five Percenter ideals to the pursuit of capital:

Visualizin the realism of life in actuality
Fuck who's the baddest, a person's status depends on salary
And my mentality is money-orientated
I'm destined to live the dream for all my peeps who never made it
'Cause yeah, we were beginners in the hood as Five Percenters
But somethin must've got in us cause all of us turned to sinners
Now some restin' in peace and some are sittin' in San Quentin
Others such as myself are tryin' to carry on tradition.[114]

But this tension is by no means unique to the Five Percenters. It is arguably inherent in the very nature of the secret itself, which is always a complex nexus of both concealment and revelation, both symbolic and material capital, both power to resist and power to dominate.

✳ CHAPTER 5 ✳
The Terror of Secrecy

RACISM, MASCULINITY, AND VIOLENCE
IN THE *BRÜDER SCHWEIGEN*

*I, as an Aryan warrior, swear myself to complete secrecy
to the Order and total loyalty to my comrades.*

Oath sworn by the *Brüder Schweigen*[1]

*Remember, mobility and concealment are the best
weapons in the hands of a Guerilla force.*

MACABA, *Road Home*[2]

A secret society usually possesses significant powers, even terrifying ones.

MARCEL MAUSS, *Manual of Ethnography*[3]

If secrecy can be a powerful tactic of social and political resistance, it can
also easily serve as a weapon of political violence, revolution, and terrorism. Again, as Elias Canetti famously put it, secrecy is an art of concealment that lies at the "very core of power"; and the same tactics of disguise
and dissimulation that allow the predator to stalk its prey can also allow
the insurgent to camouflage identity and cloak an attack.[4]

Examples of religious secrecy and political violence are visible everywhere from the White Lotus Society in China to the Carbonari in Italy,
from the Jugantar movement in colonial India to the contemporary al-
Qaeda and ISIS networks.[5] However, as Jonathan Masters notes, most
of the American media's—and politicians'—focus since 9/11 has been
on underground Islamic terrorist groups, often to the neglect of more
pervasive and potentially more dangerous homegrown American terrorist groups.[6] These include a vast array of white supremacist, militia,
and antigovernment groups, such as Aryan Nations, the KKK and its offshoots, various neo-Nazi groups, neo-Confederates, the diverse groups
associated with Christian Identity, and a rapidly growing number of anti-
Muslim and anti-immigrant movements.[7] According to several recent

studies, the number of deaths caused by these far-right, homegrown extremist groups have significantly outnumbered those by radical Islamist groups. While these groups have their roots in far-right movements since the 1970s, they saw a strong resurgence after the 2001 terrorist attacks; they saw another spike in numbers following the election of the first black president in 2008; and they have now come increasingly out into the open with the election of Donald J. Trump, whose stance on immigration, Islam, and race is widely seen as aligned with if not directly in support of these far-right and white power movements.[8]

Arguably the most spectacular and audacious example of a homegrown, secret, and violent organization in the modern US was the white supremacist criminal group known variously as the Order, the Organization, the *Brüder Schweigen*, or the Silent Brotherhood.[9] Formed in 1983 by Robert Jay Mathews, the Order launched a bold plan to create a separate white nation on US soil, supporting its mission through a spree of robberies, counterfeiting, assassination, and terrorism.[10] Drawing inspiration from earlier right-wing groups such as the Aryan Nations, the National Alliance, the militia manual *The Road Back*, and fictional works such as the *Turner Diaries*, the Silent Brotherhood became the epitome of the secret, racist, antigovernment organization and still provides inspiration for the radical right to this day. Indeed, it "wrote the book on living in the white underground and has served as a blueprint for far-right movements ever since."[11]

As the group's name indicates, secrecy was a key to both the real and symbolic power of the *Brüder Schweigen*. On the most basic level, secrecy served the obvious function that Canetti noted, the tactical use of concealment as the "core of power." Yet beyond this simple tactical role, I suggest, secrecy has at least three further qualities that are particularly important for the understanding of religious violence and terrorism. First, secrecy and esoteric ritual are a key part of the creation of a *sacralized community of violence*—a group bound by initiation, oaths, and commitment to a cause of ultimate significance (in this case, the Order's defense of the Aryan race against the dark-skinned mobs and tyrannical government). Second, secrecy and secret ritual help to create a *sacralized lineage of mythical ancestors*, a chain of initiates extending into the sacred past. In the case of the Order, this lineage includes a fictional predecessor, the group called the Order in the infamous racist novel, *The Turner Diaries*; but it also extends back through an imagined lineage in the Nazi SS and ultimately to the mythic Aryan race itself.

Finally, and perhaps most important, secrecy is key to the creation of a *terrifying aura of power*. As we have seen in the preceding chapters, secrecy can help project a kind of a "magnification of reality, by means of the sensation that behind the appearance of things there is a deeper, mysterious reality."[12] In the case of the Order, the creation of this secret white supremacist community was also part of an attempt to recover some of the power—both symbolic and material—lost by white males in the rapidly shifting context of 1980s America. In the face of what Abby Ferber calls "white man falling," or the seeming loss of white male dominance in late twentieth-century America,[13] secret brotherhoods such as the *Brüder Schweigen* provided at least the fantasy of *"significant powers, even terrifying ones."* As Simmel aptly puts it, "The secret society protects the decaying as well as the growing development. The flight into secrecy is a ready device for social endeavors and forces that are about to be replaced by new ones.... [The secret society] exploits the psychological fact that the unknown itself appears to be fearsome, mighty, threatening."[14]

To conclude, I suggest that the example of the Silent Brotherhood offers key insights into our own historical moment in the first decades of the twenty-first century, when this sense of "white man falling" first reached its height of anxiety (with the election of President Obama) and then seemed to find its greatest champion (in Donald Trump). The racist and nationalist sentiments that once fueled secretive, underground groups such as the *Brüder Schweigen* have been increasingly legitimated and emboldened through the rise of Trump, the "alt-right," and white nationalist media outlets such as Breitbart, now openly promoted on a broad public stage. Today we perhaps need to fear not so much the silent but the increasingly *vocal and visible* brotherhoods that espouse the same far-right, racist, and violent ideals.

Racist Roots: William Pierce, the National Alliance, and Cosmotheism

The *Brüder Schweigen* emerged out of a complex network of white power groups and militias that had been steadily increasing in influence throughout the 1970s. As Kathleen Belew suggests in her history of the movement, white power "united a wide array of groups and activists previously at odds, thrown together by tectonic shifts in the cultural and political landscape," bringing them together around the idea of an all-white nation and an increasing hostility toward the federal government.[15] The roots of these underground racist groups go back much earlier, of course. As we saw in chapter 1, the grandfather of most of these racist brotherhoods was the Ku Klux Klan, which drew inspiration from Freemasonry but which developed in an explicitly white supremacist political direction in the decades after the Civil War. Following World War II, another wave of white nationalist movements spread across the US, first with the American Nazi Party, founded by George Lincoln Rockwell in 1959, and then with groups such as the Aryan Nations, founded by Richard Butler in 1974.[16] Despite their differences of religious affiliation and political goals, virtually all of these groups combine white supremacy, hypermasculinity, and militant religiosity—in most cases surrounded by secrecy and the aura of fearsome power that comes with it.

One of the most influential figures in the racist right during the late twentieth century—and perhaps the most important for understand the birth of the Order—was William Luther Pierce III (1933–2002) (fig. 5.1). A highly educated and articulate man, Pierce also led some of the most virulent white supremacist movements in America and, perhaps more important, wrote some of the most widely read white supremacist fiction. According to the Southern Poverty Law Center, Pierce was "America's most important neo-Nazi for some three decades" and "the movement's fiercest anti-Semitic ideologue," who continues to inspire far-right racist and nationalist groups to this day.[17] Others have called him the "'ghost in the machine' whenever serious acts of violence are contemplated or undertaken by American National Socialists" and a key inspiration for most violent far-right groups since the 1970s.[18]

Born in Atlanta, Pierce described his family as a formerly aristocratic southern lineage that had fallen from the upper tier of white society as a result of mixing with lesser races. As his biographer, Robert S. Griffin recounts,

> Pierce describes his mother's ancestors as members of the aristocracy of the old South. Her great-grandfather was governor of Alabama and Attorney General of the Confederacy during the Civil War. After the war, the family lost their genteel status and lived a working-class existence.[19]

This sense of the decline of white aristocratic society would seem to be reflected in much of Pierce's later racial theory and throughout his fiction.

After receiving his doctorate, Pierce taught briefly at Oregon State University from 1962 to 1965. However, Pierce was sickened by the civil rights and antiwar movements of the 1960s and turned to far-right politics, joining the American Nazi Party and serving as an aide and close confidant to its leader, George Lincoln Rockwell—even writing a biography of the neo-Nazi icon.[20] Pierce was also deeply influenced by the writ-

FIGURE 5.1. William Luther Pierce III. Photo by Robert Hartnell from Wikimedia Commons.

ings of Savitri Devi (born Maximiani Portas), a Greek-French writer who was one of the key exponents of occult Nazism and a brand of far-right esotericism that blended National Socialism with Hinduism and Nordic racial ideology.[21] After Rockwell's assassination in 1967, Pierce became associated with the National Youth Alliance; and then when the latter movement split in 1971, he formed the National Alliance. At its height of influence in the 1980s, the National Alliance was estimated by the Anti-

Defamation League to be "the largest and most active neo-Nazi organization in the nation.... In the past three years there has been evidence of NA activity in no fewer than 26 states across the country."[22]

In Pierce's mind, the National Alliance was intended to serve as a kind of political vanguard in a war against the cultural decline of contemporary America—a war, in short, for white racial redemption. "The fact of the matter," Pierce said in an interview, "is that we are engaged in a war for the survival of our people."[23] Modern white men, in his view, had become emasculated, feminized, and softened, leading to a general decline in society and to a loss of white values, particularly a warrior spirit:

> Not only has society lost its artistic sense and reverence, it has also lost much of its warrior spirit, argues Pierce. Pierce decries the large numbers of soft, dependent men he observes today.... Pierce says that a true man has a firm sense of personal dignity and self-worth and is strongly self-reliant. In contrast to men of this sort, true men, real men, Pierce finds many of today's men given to self-abasement and to be "weepy and submissive"—which turns Pierce's stomach to see in any man.[24]

Alongside the more explicitly political National Alliance, however, Pierce also created his own religious movement called Cosmotheism in 1978. Pierce bought a 400-acre piece of property in West Virginia as the site of the Cosmotheist Community Church, which also served as the headquarters of the National Alliance. With its key symbol of the "life" rune, Cosmotheism is a kind of panentheistic worldview, which sees God as the life force flowing through the universe and working its way to greater and greater self-consciousness through the process of evolution. At the summit of this evolution of the life force are those individuals who have realized the divine consciousness within themselves, becoming tools for the cosmos coming to know itself: "The members of the community of Divine Consciousness, the Awakened Ones, the People of the Rune, serve in a new way, which is the way of higher man, the way of true reason. They are conscious agents of the Creator's Purpose.... Through their service they resume the ascent toward their destiny, which is Godhood."[25] Yet Pierce's Cosmotheist vision is also an explicitly racist view of the evolution of the life force through nature, an evolution toward white racial superiority, even divinity and godhood. Man's striving toward divine consciousness is part of the larger collective urging of the "race-soul"; thus Pierce warns against mixing with "the stock of an alien soul," which will "spread its spiritual poison" and corrupt that stock spiritually: "He shall keep his stock pure; he shall not permit his blood to mix with that of other stocks, for each stock follows a different course along the Path of Life. When stocks are mixed, the inner sense of direction is lost and with it the potential for attaining Divine Consciousness."[26] Pierce also frankly admitted, however, that part of the reason for creating the explicitly "religious" Cosmotheist Church was simply bureaucratic and a matter of good business. Among other things, he notes that tax exemption was a consideration: "We are going to have to do this in a business-like way. What we really are is a church—we're like one anyway. So why don't we call ourselves a church, because there are some advantages to that. For one thing, we won't have to pay taxes."[27]

Finally, Pierce's racist ideology reached a wide popular audience through the genre of white power music. In 1999, he purchased Resistance Records, which "came to dominate the white power music scene and also became the biggest moneymaker in the [National Alliance] empire," promoting itself as the "Soundtrack for the White Revolution."[28]

Imagining "the Order" in The Turner Diaries

Pierce's influence among radical groups in the US is deep and wide ranging. Both directly and indirectly, his racist, violent, and quasi-religious ideas have found their way into much of the discourse of the extreme right over the last forty years. But perhaps its greatest impact has come not through the works penned under his own name but through two fictional books written under the pseudonym of Andrew Mac-Donald, The Turner Diaries and Hunter. The former work, in particular, has been one of the most widely read and circulated works in the white supremacist world. A dark, violent fantasy about the creation of a terrorist secret society aimed at antigovernment resistance and the creation of a white nation, the Turner Diaries has often been called the "Bible of the racist right" and has become a seminal work for virtually every radical racist group since the mid-1970s (see fig. 5.2). The National Alliance itself promoted the book as nothing less than a "Blueprint" and a "Handbook for White Victory."[29] As Belew notes, "This narrative, outlining a strategy that is dependent on secrecy, loyalty and violence, would become the sustaining myth of a real-life Order dedicated to a violent war on the state, and a guidebook for decades of white power terrorist violence."[30]

First published in serial form in the National Alliance publication *Attack!* between 1975 and 1978, the Turner Diaries are presented as the journals kept by Earl Turner from the autumn of 1991 until his death two years later. The historical context in which the Turner Diaries were written is

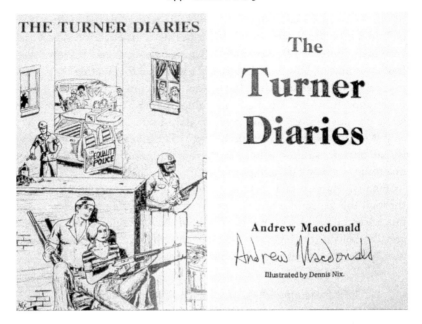

FIGURE 5.2. Original title page of the *Turner Diaries*. Photo by Dennis Nix.

not insignificant. In the aftermath of Watergate and the Vietnam War, the book reflects an intense cynicism and suspicion of the federal government; and in the wake of the civil rights movement, the book also reflects an intense paranoia toward all nonwhite groups and the threat of an increasingly integrated society. The story begins with a series of oppressive acts by the federal government, including strict gun control legislation and drastic forms of racial integration. The government has become increasingly totalitarian, corrupt, and run by blacks and Jews; meanwhile, the American public has become too brainwashed by the media to put up much resistance, "marching in mental lockstep with the high priests of the TV religion."[31]

The opening scene of the book is a striking depiction of the sense of white victimization and antigovernment paranoia—and, one might add, a fantastic inversion of the historical reality of 1970s America. Four black men burst into Turner's apartment and ransack his belongings; while they look to Turner like common thieves, they have been designated by the government as "special deputies." Meanwhile, black neighborhoods have been exempted from these raids.[32]

Sickened by this totalitarian government and this duped and brainwashed populace, Turner joins a resistance group called the Organization, which is dedicated to unseating this oppressive regime. An "underground group," the Organization develops increasingly strict measures to protect its identity and to ensure the loyalty and secrecy of its members. "Our security rests primarily in our changed appearances and identities," Turner recounts. "We've changed our hair styles and either dyed or bleached our hair." Meanwhile, any members who violate the Organization's tight discipline are expelled, as are any who compromise its secrecy or violate its "rule against loose talk about Organizational matters."[33] In many ways, the government and the Organization seem to be caught in a strange dynamic of mutual paranoia, surveillance, and secrecy. While the Organization becomes more powerful, Turner notes that the System's "paranoia is really showing" as the police and FBI begin stopping thousands of citizens on the streets to prove their identity. Meanwhile, the Organization also begins to tightly screen its recruits for possible infiltrators, moles, and traitors: "the Organization has developed a testing process for new underground recruits. Its function is to determine the recruit's true motivations and attitudes and to screen out those sent to us as infiltrators by the secret police."[34]

Eventually, Turner is admitted into the inner circle of the Organization, an elite, esoteric group simply called the Order. With his entry into the Order, Turner is introduced to the secret and explicitly religious dimension of the Organization, realizing that he is now not just a soldier but a "bearer of the Faith" and an instrument of "God in the fulfilment of His Grand Design":

> As members of the Order we are to be bearers of the Faith. Only from our ranks will the future leaders of the Organization come....
>
> The Order ... will remain secret, even within the Organization, until the successful completion of first phase of our task: the destruction of the System. And he showed us the Sign by which we might recognize one another.[35]

Entry into the Order follows the model of an initiatory ordeal, complete with robes, candles, sacred oaths, and a ceremonial death and "rebirth." Donning a "monk's robe," Turner is brought before a high priest and is made to swear "a mighty Oath." With the other initiates, Turner is given a necklace with a pendant that contains a cyanide capsule, signifying his willingness to make the ultimate sacrifice for the Order:

> And then we swore the Oath — a mighty Oath, a moving Oath that shook me to my bones and raised the hair on the back of my neck....

Major Williams placed a gold chain with a small pendant around each of our necks.... Inside each pendant is a tiny, glass capsule. We are to wear them at all times, day and night.

Whenever danger is especially imminent and we might be captured, we are to remove the capsules from the pendants and carry them in our mouths. And if we are captured and can see no hope of immediate escape, we are to break the capsules with our teeth. Death will be painless and almost instantaneous.

At the end of the ceremony, Turner feels that he has been given a wholly new life: "Now our lives truly belong only to the Order. Today I was, in a sense, born again."[36] Specifically, he is reborn as a real *man*, a white man joined spiritually and physically with a true brotherhood: "*real men, White* men, men who are now *one* with me in spirit and consciousness as well as in blood."[37]

Turner's initiation into the Order clearly draws on many older ritual themes, both historical and imaginary. In this ceremony, we can detect elements drawn from KKK initiation ceremonies, the Aryan Nations initiation (see below),[38] and probably also some reference to the Nazi SS initiation ceremonies. The SS, of course, had its own rituals of initiation and a "kith and kin oath," in which one swore "obedience unto death so help me God [*Gehorsam bis in den Tod, So wahr mir Gott helfe*]."[39] Throughout the text, moreover, Turner frequently draws comparisons between the Order and the SS.[40] In another remarkable inversion of history, Turner describes the loyal SS members as tragic victims who were tortured at the hands of cruel US soldiers and Jewish interrogators. When Turner is captured by the FBI and tortured by a Jewish intelligence agent, he recalls the same cruel fate suffered by the noble SS and other Nazis after World War II, comparing himself to Adolf Eichmann: "I remembered the horrible photographs ... of German prisoners who had had their eyes gouged out, their teeth pulled, their fingers cut off, and their testicles smashed by sadistic interrogators, many wearing US Army uniforms, prior to their conviction and execution by military courts as 'war criminals.'"[41]

The role of secrecy and initiation in the *Turner Diaries* is more than simply a rhetorical flourish or a kind of adolescent fantasy, however. For the character Turner (and perhaps for Pierce), it represents a deep communion with a white brotherhood, a community of racially and sexually pure men who are united in both blood and spirit, at once linked back to their ancient and pure racial past and looking forward as the vanguard of a new generation:

Knowing fully what was demanded in character and commitment of each man who stood before me, my chest swelled with pride. There were no soft-bellied conservative businessmen assembled for some Masonic mumbo-jumbo; no loudmouthed, beery rednecks letting off a little ritualized steam about "the goddamn niggers"; no pious, frightened church-goers whining for the guidance or protection of an anthropomorphic deity. These were *real men, White* men, men who were now *one* with me in spirit and consciousness as well as in blood.

As the torchlight flickered over the coarse gray robes of the motionless throng, I thought to myself: These are the best men my race has produced this generation.... In them are combined fiery passion and icy discipline, deep intelligence and instant readiness for action.... They are the vanguard of the coming New Era, the pioneers who lead our race out of its present depths and toward the unexplored heights above.[42]

Secrecy in the *Turner Diaries* thus forges the bonds of a community that now seems greater and more powerful than the mere sum of its parts—one filled with "significant powers, even terrifying ones." Ultimately, for Turner, the secret community of the Order even offers an immortality that goes beyond that offered by having children: the immortality of the race itself:

The Order has a life which is more than the sum of the lives of its members. When it speaks collectively ... something deeper and older and wiser than any of us speaks—something which cannot die.[43]

He gained immortality for himself ... when he faithfully fulfilled his obligation to his race, to the Organization and to the holy Order which had accepted him into its ranks. And in so doing he helped greatly to assure that his race would survive and prosper, that the Organization would achieve its worldwide political and military goals, and that the Order would spread its wise and benevolent rule over the earth for all time to come.[44]

The actual activities of the Order as it wages its war against the System are merciless, violent, and devastating. Not only do all nonwhites need to be expunged from the US, but even most whites deserve to die, having become traitors to their own race. Whether the poor rednecks who are left to die in bomb blasts or the university professors who are "strung up" for their intellectual treason, even most whites won't be spared the coming wars: "We must understand that our race is like a cancer patient undergoing drastic surgery in order to save his life. There is no sense in asking whether the tissue being cut now is 'innocent' or not."[45] In the apocalyptic conclusion to the book, the Organization seizes Vandenburg Air Force Base, along with its nuclear missiles. In a final suicide mission, Turner flies a small plane armed with a warhead into the Pentagon, and the epilogue closes with a brief description of how the System quickly disintegrated afterwards. In 1999, the "New Era" is ushered in by horrific bloodshed spreading not just across North America but across the globe, beginning with revolution throughout Europe:

> [A] cleansing hurricane of change swept over the continent, clearing away in a few months the refuse of a millennium or more of alien ideology and a century or more of profound moral and material decadence. The blood flowed ankle-deep in the streets of many of Europe's great cities momentarily, as the race traitors, the offspring of generations of dysgenic breeding and hordes of *Gastarbeiter* met a common fate. Then the great dawn of the New Era broke over the Western world.[46]

The European revolution is followed by massive nuclear strikes on China, which sterilize sixteen million square miles of the earth's surface from the Ural Mountains to the Pacific and from the Arctic Ocean to the Indian Ocean.[47] Ultimately, the Order's once small and secret community of white brothers triumphs in the reconquest of the Western world and the complete annihilation of the entire nonwhite, non-European half of the globe.

Since its publication, the *Turner Diaries* has inspired a great many white supremacist, extremist, and homegrown terrorist movements. In addition to the *Brüder Schweigen*, it provided a blueprint for the largest terrorist attack on US soil prior to 9/11—the Oklahoma City bombing in 1995.[48] When Timothy McVeigh was apprehended and arrested, the police found pages from the novel in his car, and the bombing appears to have been modeled on a bombing described in Pierce's fictional account. Meanwhile, after the Oklahoma City attack, "Pierce predicted, or maybe hoped, that resentment of Jews, minorities and others would lead to terrorism 'on a scale the world has never seen before.'"[49]

The Road Back: A Guerrilla Handbook for the Order

The *Turner Diaries* has clearly had a lasting impact on all segments of the racist right since the book's publication. Like Timothy McVeigh after him, Robert Jay Mathews had also read and enjoyed the book, even circulating it to fellow members of the *Brüder Schweigen*. Indeed, many media reporters and several scholars have suggested that Mathews's "Order" was thus directly modeled on the fictional Order of Pierce's novel.[50]

However, while the *Turner Diaries* and its author were clearly one influence on the birth of the *Brüder Schweigen*,[51] their importance has perhaps been exaggerated. As Schlatter notes, Order members such as Richard Scutari later argued that "the media's attention on The Order's use of the *Turner Diaries* is unfounded. He claims that, though members thought it was a great read, it was a novel and not a blueprint for Order activities"; instead, Scutari stated that the battle plans for the movement came from a lesser-known booklet from 1973 called *The Road Back: A Plan for the Restoration of Freedom When Our Country Has Been Taken Over by Its Enemies*.[52] Published under the name Macaba—a pseudonym of Ethan K. McCabe—the *Road Back* has been widely circulated among right wing and militia groups since the mid-1970s and provides a simple but very clear model for organizing a guerrilla movement. According to the author's grandson, McCabe had been involved in military intelligence (in some unspecified capacity) and then went on to be involved in the Minutemen militia group.[53] As Mathews would a decade later, Macaba presents a relentless indictment of contemporary American society and government, which is now so corrupt and tyrannical that it must be countered with bloody resistance: "The government against which our forces of resistance are working is in the last stages of transition into an alien dictatorship. Those persons responsible for this state of affairs have spun a web of conspiracy throughout the world."[54]

Secrecy, Macaba explains, is the primary tactic in guerrilla warfare, which can only be fought through dissimulation, concealment, and covert action. Guerrilla war, he writes, "is a war of surprise, deceit and coordination"; and thus "mobility and concealment are the best weapons in the hands of a Guerilla force."[55] Indeed, secrecy and security are critical at all levels of the guerrilla organization, particularly when attracting new initiates to the group:

> It is secure against detection, and infiltration. . . . Infiltrators must not be allowed to penetrate. . . . Only personal acquaintances should be considered for membership. Broadcast methods of recruitment should be shunned like poison . . .
>
> Identities of all persons in the organization must be kept secret until the prospect has actually been recruited. After recruitment, the lowest echelon of leadership will provide the contact for the recruit—this is the level of Team leader.[56]

Finally, the text also offers elaborate instructions on ways to disguise oneself and ultimately to create an entirely new secret identity: "If you simulating, and you are a good actor, you will have created a new identity."[57] Macaba advises the guerrilla fighter to alter his appearance with sun tan, weight gain or loss, tattoos, change of posture, and change of mannerism; then of course he will have to obtain false identification papers, a false driver's license, a false credit record, and so on.[58] Ultimately, one must create a kind of dual identity, constructing an entire false alter ego to mask one's true identity as a resistance fighter. He should establish a "duality" in his identification:

> You now possess two social histories instead of one ... Move to anyplace but California. On the way to your new habitat, in some convenient place, make the full physical transformation into our new identity.... Now you are ready for a complete existence in a new role as Mr. X–or whatever your name is....
>
> Avoid unnecessary public exposure. Do not cultivate any close friends. Avoid situations where you may be fingerprinted or have your photo taken. Change living quarters frequently.[59]

Although it reveals no specific religious affiliation, Macaba's text does make frequent religious references. The cover image of the booklet is a crusader-like shield with a red cross, with crossed spears behind it. In the dedication, the author writes that he hopes that "this book, with the help of God, will strengthen the arms of those who fight for liberty." Meanwhile, he also names the current leaders of the US as "Evil men" whose conspiracy and "political prostitution" leave us no other choice but bloody revolution.[60]

In general, however, Macaba seems less interested in religious ideology than in creating the most effective organization for the guerrilla army. Macaba's guerrilla force is structured in an elaborate esoteric hierarchy, divided by power and access to information. The two basic units are the Band and the Teams underneath the Band. Beneath each of these are series of sublevels, such as the second in command, the Band Executive Officer, the Underground Support Section, the Communications Man, and so on. Each of these levels, in turn, is guarded by strict security and a closely controlled flow of information to protect the secrecy of the entire unit.[61]

While the *Turner Diaries* provided an inspiring fictional manifesto for the coming white revolution, the *Road Back* provided the nuts-and-bolts details on how to actually create a secret, underground army. In both

FIGURE 5.3. Robert J. Mathews. Courtesy of Getty Images, Bettman Collection.

texts, however, secrecy is a central theme in the imagining of a unified white brotherhood bound by common a spirit and filled with an aura of terrifying power.

The Silent Brotherhood: The Order, from Fiction to Reality

It was from this rich mix of white supremacist rhetoric, underground militias, racist fiction, and guerrilla manuals that the *Brüder Schweigen* was born. Mathews, the movement's founder and driving force, is frequently described as "a clean-cut young man," originally from Arizona with a history of right-wing associations that began in high school[62] (see fig. 5.3). As a teenager, Mathews joined a youth chapter of the John Birch Society and soon began reading works such as Spenglar's *Decline of the West* and

Wilmot Robertson's *Dispossessed Majority*. In 1974, Mathews moved his family from Arizona to Washington State, buying a fifty-three-acre plot of land near Metaline Falls, where he formed his first group called the Sons of Liberty, an anticommunist, paramilitary, survivalist order. Over time, Mathews also became increasingly critical of Christianity—which he saw as an obstacle rather than an aid in the affirmation of white identity—and, like other white supremacists, turned to Norse paganism as an alternative religious and racial worldview.[63]

Mathews clearly felt a strong attraction to the ideas of William Pierce. After writing to Pierce, Mathews became a member of the National Alliance and then continued to correspond with Pierce until the two men met in 1981.[64] He is also said to have frequently discussed the plot of the *Turner Diaries* and handed out copies of the text to anyone who had not yet read it.[65] Pierce would later describe Mathews in words of rare high praise, calling him the ideal racial activist—a "strong, sturdily built man with a warm, open face," who was interested in practical solutions to deal with "the malevolent enemy that was trying to wipe out our race, as its tribal god had commanded in the Old Testament."[66] In the end, as Pierce eulogized him,

> Mathews declared war on the enemies of our race, went underground with a handful of companions he called the Silent Brotherhood and began fighting. His fight lasted until he was burned to death by a secret police task force a little over a year later.[67]

The Order itself was born in the early 1980s, as a result of two key events. The first was the signing of a document called the Nehemiah Township Charter and Common Law Contract in 1982. The aim of the Charter was essentially to create a civil body with sovereignty over a specific territory, thus establishing self-rule as opposed to ZOG (the Zionist Occupied Government). Signatories to the document included not only Mathews but some of the most important figures in the radical right of the 1980s— almost a "who's who of the Christian Identity Movement and racist right"—including Richard Butler of the Aryan Nations, militia leader Robert Miles, and future member of the Order, Randolph Duey.[68]

The second key moment in the rise of the Order was a seminal speech given by Mathews at a meeting of the National Alliance in 1983. In it, Mathews powerfully articulated his vision of an organized Aryan resistance, a small, disciplined group with the determination and resources to overthrow the entire ZOG system.[69] Calling on white "yeoman farmers" as the true embodiment of the "Aryan work ethic and a living monument to masculinity," he declared war on the "filthy lying Jews and their parasitical usury system." At the same time, he also warned that Christianity was perhaps the greatest obstacle in the war against the ZOG system, decrying the "stranglehold that churches have on rural America" with their useless theological baggage.[70] Mathews concluded his speech with a direct appeal to white masculinity, challenging his Aryan brothers to reclaim the lands their forefathers fought and died for:

> Stand up like *men* and drive the enemy into the sea! Stand up like *men* and swear a sacred oath upon the green grass of our sires that you will reclaim what our forefathers discovered, explored, conquered, settled, built and died for! Stand up like *men* and reclaim our soil![71]

Mathews's vision in this speech became formally established later that year as the group variously called itself the Order, the Organization, the Silent Brotherhood, or the *Brüder Schweigen*. This last name was taken from a well-known book on the history of Hitler's SS, *Wenn Alle Brüder Schweigen*. The book's title in turn comes from a famous German patriotic song penned 170 years earlier, which contains the line "Wenn alle Brüder schweigen und falschen Götzen traun, wir woll'n das Wort nicht brechen . . ." (When all brothers fall silent and trust in false idols, we will never break our word).[72] The first meeting of the Order was held in Mathews's home in the summer of 1983, with a small group consisting of various men on the far edge of the racist right. These included several "disaffected members of the Aryan Nations Church who had . . . tired of straight arm salutes and worship of Hitler, Klansmen looking for action instead of words, and one survivalist."[73] Eventually the Order would grow to almost forty men, attracting Christian Identity churchgoers from Colorado, several National Alliance members, a couple of members of the John Birch Society, and a few Christian Constitutionalists.

The dramatic inauguration of the Order, however, took place at a now infamous ceremony on Mathews's property in October 1983, as Mathews and eight other men gathered for a secret rite of initiation. Among those present were Richard Kemp, William Soderquist, Ken Loff, and David Lane. According to the account of Tom Martinez, a member of the Order who later became an FBI informant, "nine men met in a wooden building that had been constructed at the rear of Bob Mathews's property outside Metaline Falls. There the men formed a circle and greeted one another, right arms outstretched in the Nazi salute."[74] Some suggest that the number nine for the members of the initiation was also significant in relation to Odinism and Norse mythology: "He was mindful that Odin learned nine magic songs and hung for nine nights on Yggdrasill, the world tree, to acquire the wisdom of the dead."[75] A woman then placed a baby boy in the middle of the circle, while the men followed Mathews in swearing a sacred oath.[76] Adapted from the Aryan Nations oath,[77] this was essentially a vow in the name of God Almighty to protect the complete secrecy of the Order, to pledge complete loyalty to one's brothers, and to fight tirelessly to defend the Aryan race and to destroy its enemy the Jew:

> I, as a free Aryan man, hereby swear an unrelenting oath upon the green graves of our sires, upon the children in the wombs of our wives, upon the throne of God Almighty, sacred be His Name ... to join together in holy union with those brothers in this circle and to declare forthright that, from this moment on, have no fear of death, no fear of foe, that I have a sacred duty to do whatever is necessary to deliver our people from the Jew and bring total victory to the Aryan race. I, as an Aryan warrior, swear myself to complete secrecy to the Order and total loyalty to my comrades. ... And furthermore, let me witness to you, my brothers, that if I break this oath, let me forever be cursed upon the lips of our people as a coward and an oath breaker. My brothers, let us be His battle axe and weapons of war. Let us go forth by ones and twos, by scores and by legions, and as true Aryan men with pure hearts and strong minds face the enemies of our faith and our race with courage and determination. We hereby invoke the blood covenant, and declare that we are in a full state of war and will not lay down our weapons until we have driven the enemy into the sea and reclaimed the land which was promised to our fathers of old, and through His will and our blood, becomes the land of our children to be.[78]

A number of things in this dramatic initiation ritual deserve discussion here. The most obvious is the appeal to religious authority—God Almighty and His sacred Name—which is then turned toward an explicitly racist ideology—the righteous Aryan warrior in his struggle against the evil Jew and his minions. The second most notable feature of the oath is the gender dynamic at play: a group of male Aryan warriors gathers to invoke weapons of war, with a male infant—brought by a woman—placed at their center of the *brüderbund*, promising to fulfill the vows of their holy forefathers and to save the future nation for their own children. It would be difficult to find a more perfect distillation of the complex ideologies of white supremacy, anti-Semitism, and patriarchy—not to mention the intense anxiety of the "white man falling" syndrome—in a single ritual performance.

Historians of religions have long observed that initiation ceremonies of this sort tend to be modeled on a past mythic ideal that is invoked and then replicated in the present. As Mircea Eliade notes in his classic work on initiation, such rites typically reenact some original mythic and "transhuman model," such as a sacred narrative about the history of a people or the creation of the world in its present form: "in order to become a man, it is necessary to resemble a mythical model."[79] And such initiations also usually involve some form of symbolic death and rebirth—that is, a new "birth into a higher mode of being" in which one is introduced to "sacred history." For example, as we saw in chapter 1, the third-degree initiation for Freemasons reenacts the death of Hiram Abiff, the chief architect of the temple of Solomon, which is the model for the Masonic Lodge. In the case of the *Brüder Schweigen*, the initiation is invoking and reenacting several layers of mythic precedent: first, the initiation in the novel, the *Turner Diaries*, which is modeled on SS initiations, which were modeled on the many other occult initiatory practices drawn mainly from Freemasonry and related fraternal orders. The "new birth" here is not simply into some transcendent concept of sacred history, but also a very specific ideological view of history driven by an explicitly white supremacist, anti-Semitic, antiliberal, and patriarchal worldview. "They thought of themselves as an elite military force, but also as the men responsible for protecting and propagating the white race."[80]

The Secret War: The Spectacular Success and Downfall of the Silent Brotherhood

In a remarkably short span of time between 1983 and 1984, the *Brüder Schweigen* undertook a bold series of criminal and terrorist activities. The group pursued a six-step strategy, which involved paramilitary training, fundraising (through robbery and counterfeiting), purchase of weapons, distribution of money to white power groups, assassination of targeted individuals, and expansion into cells to avoid persecution.[81] Developing a complex esoteric structure—modeled in large part on Macaba's *Road Back*—the Order established paramilitary camps in Idaho and Missouri, heavily supplied with guns, ammunition, all-terrain vehicles, dogs, army K-rations, and computers.[82] At the same time, it launched a series of small bank robberies and quickly progressed to the robbery of $500,000 from a shopping mall and $3.8 million from a Brinks armored car in Ukiah, California. Like the Order in the *Turner Diaries*, the *Brüder Schweigen* ran a sophisticated counterfeiting operation and engaged in more explicitly terroristic acts, such as bombing the largest synagogue in Idaho and assassinating a Jewish radio talk-show host, Alan Berg. The group also had an assassination list that identified a wide range of targets, including Henry Kissinger and members of the Rockefeller and Rothschild families, among others.[83]

Shortly before his death, Mathews wrote a letter in which he outlined his vision of the Order's real mission. In his mind, this was nothing less than a *secret war* against the federal government, which had been using its own secret tactics to squelch dissenters like him. While the FBI and other agencies had been developing increasingly powerful and invasive techniques of surveillance, loyal American patriots had been expanding their own, equally and ultimately far more effective networks of secret organization, preparing a vast underground network that would one day undo the power of this corrupt state regime. Significantly, we should note, Mathews linked his decision to fight this secret war directly to the birth of his first male child. His son's birth awakened in him the awareness that white men must take up arms to fight for their legacy in America — above all, to fight against the secret conspiracy hidden within the government that was working covertly to destroy the white race:

> By the time my son had arrived, I realized that White America, indeed my entire race, was headed for oblivion unless White men rose and turned the tide. The more I came to love my son, the more I realized that unless things changed radically, by the time he was my age, he would be a stranger in his own land.... I came to learn that this was not an accident, that there is a small, cohesive alien group within this nation working day and night to make this happen....
>
> A secret war has been developing for the last year between the regime in Washington and an ever growing number of White people who are determined to regain what our forefathers conquered, settled, built and died for. The FBI has been able to keep this war secret only because up until now we have been doing nothing more than growing and preparing. The government, however, seems determined to force the issue, so we have no choice left but to stand and fight back.[84]

The Order's activities, in turn, inspired one of the largest and most expensive criminal investigations in FBI history, involving a full quarter of the Bureau's manpower and costing over $1 million. Mathews was finally hunted down and killed in a firefight on Whidbey Island, Washington, in December 1984, while the remaining members of the Order were rounded up by 1987. All told, there were some seventy-five arrests and sixty-seven separate criminal charges ranging from robbery and arson to bombings, counterfeiting, and murder. Apparently, the group had even more ambitious terrorist plans in the works before these arrests, including a "sabotage against dams, water supplies, utility and communications lines.... They stopped Mathews only four months short of attempting the shutdown of a major U.S. city through terrorism."[85]

Despite its brief career and catastrophic ending, however, the *Brüder Schweigen* lived on in the popular imagination of the radical white supremacist subculture, helping to inspire a new wave of antigovernment, anti-Semitic, and racist fervor that is still with us today. In the words of George Hawthorne, the singer of the white power rock band RaHoWa (or "Racial Holy War," one of the best-known bands on the Resistance Records label), "it was of unfathomable significance.... It marked the radicalization of the right wing."[86] Mathews, meanwhile, has grown into something of a "larger than life" figure since his death, achieving the status of a kind of "legendary Aryan warrior martyr. In poems, artwork and the lyrics of White Power music, Mathews is hailed throughout much of the Aryan revolutionary world."[87]

The Secrets of Racist Paganism: David Lane and Wotansvolk

Among the many movements inspired by the *Brüder Schweigen*, one of the most widespread and influential today has been Wotansvolk, a racist form of neopagan Odinism or Wotanism created by David Lane. After his arrest for involvement in the *Brüder Schweigen*, Lane was sentenced to 190 years in prison. Not long into his sentence, he cofounded Wotansvolk, together with his wife, Katja, and artist, Ron McVan, in 1995, with its headquarter in Idaho. Before coming to the *Brüder Schweigen*, Lane had also passed though the John Birch Society, the KKK, and Christian Identity, finally developing his own form of mystical, esoteric Odonism. Called by many admirers a "prisoner of war" and even the "Nelson Mandela of the White revolution," Lane remains one of the most influential figures of the white supremacist underground to this day.[88] His colleague, McVan, meanwhile, is a talented and prolific artist, who has crafted an impressive array of Odinist artifacts, amulets, Thor's hammers, drinking horns, wood sculptures, Viking art, shields, and paintings that have added an important cultural and aesthetic dimension to the movement.[89]

While Odinism had existed for some time as a Norse-inspired neopagan movement, Lane's Wotansvolk articulated its most explicitly racist and anti-Christian version. In his view, Christianity is a religion of weakness, subservience, and superstition, while Wotanism is the original religion of the white race, an ideology of strength and racial power: "Wotansvolk's mission is not only to recover the European's indigenous religion, long suppressed by the vile forces of Christianity, but to prepare for a violent revolution to preserve the white race."[90]

Combining Norse mythology with white supremacist ideology and a conspiratorial view of the US government, Wotansvolk is part of a broader lineage of racist pagan movements that derive from the German Ariosophists, which, as we saw in chapter 3, provided much of the occult symbolism for the Nazis. Lane's new articulation of these ideas is embodied in his key texts, the *14 Words* and the *88 Precepts*. The fourteen words read as follows: "We must secure the existence of our people and a future for white children." Lane also wrote a second fourteen-word slogan that runs: "Because the beauty of the White Aryan woman must not perish from the earth." Both of these short statements embody the key themes that run throughout the white supremacist underground in the US: these include not simply the ideology of Aryan racial superiority but also a clearly masculine, patriarchal ideal of protecting the white woman and, through her, the white male's descendants.

Significantly, Lane also links his Wotansvolk movement directly to the same lineage of secret societies and initiatic wisdom invoked by the Scottish Rite, Theosophical Society, Evola's UR group, and other esoteric traditions. Using much the same language as Albert Pike, Lane suggests that initiates in every age have had to conceal their teachings from the oppressive powers of both religions and political authorities; yet, following Blavatsky, he also believes that these initiates have been secretly guided by a Great White Brotherhood of Masters, revealing this wisdom tradition throughout each historical era:

> [I]nitiates into ancient wisdom preserved true knowledge throughout the many centuries of persecution by tyrants of both church and state. . . . Among them are Druids, Priests of Egypt, Initiates such as Pythagoras and Plato, the first Christians who were either Gnostics or related adepts, Cathars, Knights Templar, Teutonic Knights, Rosicrucians, early Masonic Orders and unknown initiates into Hermetic philosophy. In the first millennium before the Christian era, the secret teachings were kept alive in the Mystery Schools and corresponding Mystery Religions which were found from Tibet in the East to Uppsala, Sweden in the West. Among the many Mystery religions, all concealing the secret teachings, were Odinism, Mithraism, Zoroastrianism, and Gnosticism . . .
>
> Fortunately, mankind has always had secret friends who opposed tyrants, past, present and future. They have been called the Watchers, Adepts, Initiates, Hermetic Philosophers, the Great White Brotherhood.

... They have given us alphabets, languages, measurements, religions, music, art, ritual, books, medicine, science and more. Unrecognized ... they secretly guided and moderated.[91]

Indeed, Lane links his own racist order to both the KKK and Pike's Scottish Rite, which he sees as the *original template* for the tactics of secrecy that have allowed the white race to survive for so long in the US, despite its fierce oppression:

> The much-revered Nathan Bedford Forrest, a founder of the Ku Klux Klan ... was a high ranking, initiated Mason. His closest friend and mentor was Albert Pike, master of the entire Scottish Rite and author of the Masonic bible called "Morals and Dogma." The motives of rank and file Klansmen were White survival, but the big picture is different. The White race had to be kept alive in America until it could be used to conquer the world.... The methods of secrecy used by the Klan are straight from Masonry, as is the name.... So, the Ku Klux Klan was formed ... to keep the White race alive another 150 years in America.[92]

These secret brotherhoods, however, have always been the targets of political and religious persecution, from ancient attacks on dissident philosophers down to the most recent assaults on religious communities such as the Branch Davidians at the hands of the Bureau of Alcohol, Tobacco, Firearms and Explosives and the FBI: "Be it the poison of hemlock, the headsman's axe, burning at the stake, Federal infernos in Waco, Texas ... the inquisitors' rack or any number of other devices throughout history, the tyrant tolerates no competition."[93] But it is precisely their ancient and secret wisdom, "known to a few for thousands of years, mercilessly persecuted for 1700 years," that can still perhaps "return the world to sanity" by restoring the natural order and hierarchy among the races today.[94]

While various forms of Odinism or Wotanism have spread widely throughout white supremacist circles, they have perhaps been most successful in the prison system. As Mattias Gardell notes, Lane and his cohorts helped inspired "a pagan revival among the white prison population, including the conversion of whole prison gangs to the ancestral religion.... Partly due to the reputation of Lane and its association with the legendary *Brüder Schweigen*, Wotansvolk's name-recognition is high among the Aryan prison population."[95] Largely through Lane's pagan reworking, the legacy of the *Brüder Schweigen* continues, arming new generations of white men with an ideology that at once explains their sense of racial decline while also promising a return to lost power through racial brotherhood.

Conclusions: The "Vocal Brotherhood," from the Order to the Alt-Right

To conclude, I would like to make some broader comments on the recent resurgence of far-right white supremacist movements in our own generation. As we saw in this chapter, secrecy played a powerful sort of double-edged role for the *Brüder Schweigen* and related movements among the white supremacist underground. Secrecy, in effect, served as both the explanation and the radical solution for the "white man falling" syndrome. On one hand, secrecy allowed the *Brüder Schweigen* to imagine themselves to be a *persecuted minority*, marginalized and driven underground by a government run by blacks, Jews, immigrants, and women. But on the other hand, secrecy also allowed them to imagine themselves to be an elite vanguard, the noble few *remasculinized* warriors who are now working secretly to save the white race. Again, in Simmel's terms, secrecy is often a tactic deployed by groups who are waning in status and significance, allowing them to imagine themselves to be "fearsome, mighty, threatening," even as their actual power and stature declines.

Yet if secrecy was a key tactic for white supremacist movements of the 1980s and 1990s, it seems much less critical for those of our own historical moment. While much of the American media continues to focus on the threat of secret Islamic extremists, reports from the FBI and other agencies indicate that the threat of homegrown, far-right, and white supremacist groups may be far greater.[96] And, increasingly, these movements appear to be operating not so much deep underground but often very much out in the open, broadcasting their message loudly, and at times with direct or indirect political support.

Thus, on August 11–12, 2017, a wide array of far-right organizations in the US — including white supremacists, white nationalists, KKK, neo-Confederates, neo-Nazis, and various militias — gathered in Charlottesville, Virginia, to protest the removal of a statue of Robert E. Lee from Emancipation Park. The protests had been orchestrated by Richard Spencer, perhaps the most vocal white supremacist in America today, who also claims to have coined the term (with some dispute) "alt-right." Spencer runs the far-right National Policy Institute as well as the website alternative-right.blogspot.com.[97] Marchers in this "Unite the Right" rally chanted racist and anti-Semitic slogans, openly carried semiautomatic weapons, and displayed Swastikas, confederate flags, and anti-Muslim banners. Violence erupted when the marchers clashed with counter-protestors, which resulted in more than thirty injuries and one death, after a man tied to white supremacist groups drove his car into the crowd.

Spencer has since spoken on various large college campuses, such as Florida State, which helped give his extremist agenda a massive public stage. While he espouses many of the same racist and nationalist ideas as the *Brüder Schweigen*, Spencer's views are now far more explicit and un-apologetic. There is no particular secrecy here — indeed, he presents his racist ideology proudly on the Internet for a global audience to peruse. Perhaps the most striking transformation from the white supremacist movements of the 1970s and 1980s (such as National Alliance, *Brüder Schweigen*, or Wotansvolk) to the present is that the former still felt a need for secrecy, silence, concealed communication; the latter, conversely, are able to broadcast their message of hate openly and widely. Indeed, "the radical right was more successful in entering the political mainstream last year than in half a century."[98]

The white nationalist message of the alt-right has also achieved a highly vocal and visible public platform through the work of new media sources such as Breitbart News. Founded in 2007, Breitbart achieved per-haps its peak of influence under the management of Stephen K. Bannon, who also served as Donald J. Trump's key campaign strategist during the 2016 election. Proudly calling itself "platform of the alt-right," Breitbart has been infamous for its viciously anti-Muslim and anti-immigration rhetoric, publishing articles such as "How Migrants Devastate a Commu-nity," "Muslim Immigrants Secretly Hate Christians, Seek to Outbreed Them," and "Political Correctness Protects Muslim Rape Culture."[99] Per-haps most significant, Breitbart is not shy about tracing its own intellec-tual roots in some of the infamous and controversial far-right thinkers of the past — including many of those involved in European fascist and occult movements. According to Breitbart's "Conservative Guide to the Alt-Right," this is a movement that proudly identifies its connections to figures such as ultra-traditional, "super-fascist" Julius Evola (along with the journalist H. L. Menken — also known for his anti-Semitic and pro-Nazi views — and white nationalist Sam Francis):

> There are many things that separate the alternative right from old-school racist skinheads (to whom they are often idiotically compared), but one thing stands out above all else: intelligence. Skinheads, by and large, are low-information, low-IQ thugs driven by the thrill of violence and tribal hatred. The alternative right are a much smarter group of people — which

perhaps suggests why the Left hates them so much. They're dangerously bright.

The origins of the alternative right can be found in thinkers as diverse as Oswald Spengler, H. L. Mencken, Julius Evola, Sam Francis, and the paleoconservative movement that rallied around the presidential campaigns of Pat Buchanan. The French New Right also serve as a source of inspiration for many leaders of the alt-right.[100]

White supremacists such as Spencer were openly enthusiastic when Bannon was first named Donald Trump's chief campaign strategist and then, following the election, was made White House chief strategist and (briefly) a member of the US National Security Council. "Strategist is the best possible position for Steve Bannon in the Trump White House," Spencer wrote. "Bannon will answer directly to Trump and focus on the big picture, not get lost in the weeds."[101] If Spencer represents the "coming out" of far-right white supremacist views into the public sphere, Bannon and Breitbart represent their full entry both into mainstream public discourse and into the halls of power. As Potok notes, Bannon's Breitbart News is, "fundamentally, a recent rebranding of white supremacy for public relations purposes, albeit one that de-emphasizes Klan robes and Nazi symbols in favor of a more 'intellectual' approach. With Bannon's appointment, *white nationalists felt they had a man inside the White House*."[102] While Bannon's career in the White House was short-lived, he has remained an influential figure on the national stage, continuing to espouse his nationalist message and supporting political candidates who reflect his ideals.

However, surely the most stunning evidence of the "mainstreaming" of white nationalist ideology has been election of President Trump. As the Southern Poverty Law Center put it in its annual report on hate groups in the US, "Trump's run for office electrified the radical right, which saw in him a champion of the idea that America is fundamentally a white man's country."[103] The Center's report cites a wide array of Trump's statements and actions that have been enthusiastic cheered by the racist right: not only did Trump begin his campaign with a speech that characterized Mexican immigrants as rapists and drug dealers; he retweeted white supremacist messages filled with false statistics about black people;[104] he repeatedly called for a "complete ban on Muslims entering the country"; and in the aftermath of the Charlottesville tragedy, he repeatedly refused to condemn the neo-Nazis, instead insisting that there was "blame on both sides," while also comparing the removal of Lee's statue to the removal of a statue of George Washington.[105] Trump's electoral victory, meanwhile was celebrated by white supremacists such as Spencer as "a victory of identity politics," while neo-Nazis such as Andrew Anglin put it even more boldly: "Our Glorious Leader has ascended to God Emperor."[106]

Trump's use of incendiary rhetoric on the political stage and his rise to the White House appear to correlate closely with an increase in both hate groups and racial violence over the last two years. According to the Southern Poverty Law Center's detailed reports, the number of "hate groups" in the US has risen dramatically in the last two decades, from 602 in the year 2000 to over 900 in 2016. These include a wide array of anti-immigrant, anti-LGBTQ, Christian Identity, KKK, neo-Nazi, neo-Confederate, racist skinhead, and white nationalist groups; the largest increase, however, had been among anti-Muslim groups, which had increased from 34 in 2015 to 101 in 2016, while hate crimes against Muslims had spiked 67 percent during that same time period.[107] In just the first ten days after the November 2016 election alone, some 900 hate crimes were reported, followed by another 1,863 between November 9 and March 10, 2017, including murders of black, Muslim, Indian, and other minorities; vandalism of mosques and synagogues; and posting of white supremacist literature throughout college campuses across the country.[108]

Of course, the spread of white supremacist violence is by no means limited to the US but has spread globally, from Anders Breivik's attacks in Norway in 2011 to Brenton Harrison Tarrant's assault on two mosques in New Zealand in 2019. Both of these last two attacks, we should note, were accompanied by highly visible "manifestos" that were circulated globally online.[109] Moreover, many white supremacists overseas look to the US for either inspiration or at least common cause; thus, when Tarrant released his rabidly xenophobic manifesto before slaying forty-nine people at mosques in Christchurch, he described himself as a "supporter of Donald Trump ... as a symbol of renewed white identity and common purpose"; both his document and his video of the shooting spread virally through social media.[110]

The racist and violent ideology of the *Brüder Schweigen* is still very much alive and well in the twenty-first century. Increasingly, however, it circulates not so much through silence and secrecy but through loud, public pronouncements, including those from the highest offices in the land. Perhaps today we are no longer dealing with a "white man falling," working silently through underground brotherhoods, but instead with a new form of "white man resurgent," screaming loudly in mainstream media outlets and political platforms.

❋ CHAPTER 6 ❋

The Third Wall of Fire

SCIENTOLOGY AND THE STUDY OF
SECRECY AS AN HISTORICAL PROCESS

*This utterly astounding level reveals the truth you need to know—about yourself
and your power as an Operating Thetan, and the actual fulfillment of the Aims of
Scientology. . . . Before long you'll be crossing through the doors that open
to the highest states of OT on New OT VIII Truth Revealed.*

"OT VIII: Truth Revealed"[1]

*[S]ecrecy (that lies at the very core of power) [is] a powerful stimulus to
creativity, to what Simmel called the magnification of reality, by means of
the sensation that behind the appearance of things there is a deeper,
mysterious reality that we may here call the sacred, if not religion.*

MICHAEL TAUSSIG, "Transgression"[2]

The preceding chapters have explored an array of different modes of
secrecy, ranging from adornment and advertisement to social resistance
and terrorism. Yet in many cases, secrecy is by no means a static phenomenon but instead one that changes and morphs over time, shifting in
relation to changing social and cultural contexts. Religious secrecy is also
very much a *historical process* that is bound up in a complex dialectical
relationship with the larger political, economic, legal, and governmental
structures in which it is enmeshed.[3] The same secrets that might in some
cases serve as a form of "adornment" or symbolic capital may in other
cases become a source of *embarrassment, exposé, scandal,* and *litigation.*[4]

This chapter explores this aspect of secrecy as a historical and dialectical process in the complex case of the Church of Scientology. From the
church's first appearance in the 1950s, popular media accounts and journalistic exposés have made a great deal of the role of secrecy in this complex movement. Recently dubbed "America's most secretive religion," the
church has also been the target of numerous critical documentaries such
as the BBC's "Secrets of Scientology" and many others.[5] However, de-

spite this intense media attention to the secretive aspects of Scientology, relatively little serious scholarly analysis has been done on the deeper role of secrecy in this movement or to the complex ethical and epistemological challenges involved in the attempt to examine aspects of new religious movements that are confidential or off limits to outsiders.[6]

A great many aspects of Scientology are shrouded in layers of secrecy, concealment, obfuscation, and/or dissimulation. The founder of the Church of Scientology, L. Ron Hubbard (1911–1986), was quite secretive about his own biography, and many of the details of his life's narrative were later proved false; he also spent the last years of his life in hiding, when he was wanted by the FBI and other agencies.[7] Scientology was highly concerned with internal surveillance, and in the early 1960s it developed a practice called Security Checks designed to identify potentially subversive members within the organization.[8] The church had its own sophisticated intelligence bureau called the Guardian's Office that was engaged in fairly remarkable acts of espionage, including the infiltration of the IRS and other agencies during the 1970s.[9] Finally, Scientology developed highly esoteric levels of advanced training called the Operating Thetan levels or OT, which claim to reveal the ultimate secrets of the human spirit and the past history of the universe.[10] During its first few decades, Scientology might even have been described as a kind of *Cold War religion*. That is, it reflected and often *epitomized* the larger concerns with secrecy, information control, and surveillance that pervaded the US during the 1950s and 1960s.[11]

This chapter, however, focuses on just one aspect of Scientology's complex teachings: OT VIII, the last and highest of the Operating Thetan levels released by the current church. OT VIII is claimed to release the "total freedom and power" of the human spirit,[12] yet ironically, it has received little serious attention by scholars of religion. Thus far, most of the scholarly and journalistic attention has focused on the infamous Xenu narrative contained in OT level III, which was infamously satirized in the American TV show *South Park*.[13] Despite its rather provocative and highly sensationalized science fiction narrative, however, the Xenu story is not the most interesting or controversial of the OT materials that have leaked to the media; it is arguably only the tip of the "esoteric iceberg," as it were.

Here I want to make two arguments. The first is that Scientology is not only an especially good example of religious secrecy, it is also a particularly acute example of the *methodological problems* involved in the study secrets. It is perhaps the epitome of the *"ethical and epistemological double bind of secrecy"* that we discussed in the introduction.[14] As we saw above, this double bind involves the following dilemma: How can an outsider ever really know the content of a tradition that is secret or closed to non-members? And should one even try? Even if one *were* an insider, could one in good conscience reveal those secrets to a broader public audience? Moreover, is the very *attempt* to penetrate the secrets of another tradition an act of violence—that is, a form of intellectual imperialism or a kind of cultural theft?

Again, I do not think there is any easy way out of this ethical-epistemological double bind, but I do think that there are at least some alternative strategies for dealing with it. In the case of Scientology's advanced OT materials, I suggest that we shift our gaze away from the elusive *content* of the secret—which, we will see, is both epistemologically and ethically problematic—and instead focus on the more visible *forms and strategies* through which secret knowledge is revealed and concealed.[15] While we cannot say much with certainty about the content in this case, we *can* say quite a lot about the forms and strategies through which secret information is partially displayed and largely obfuscated, advertised and withdrawn, the ways in which the "aura of secrecy" is constructed, transmitted, and protected.

Thus, my second task in this chapter is to retrace the *history of a secret*, by pursuing five historical moments and five strategies through which Scientology's esoteric knowledge was constructed and transmitted from the late 1960s to the present. Over the last five decades, this esoteric knowledge has been progressively transformed from an "advertised secret" and a kind of "adorning possession"—similar to what is discussed in chapters 1 and 2—to an increasing source of litigation, liability, embarrassment, and ultimate irrelevance. Finally, to conclude, I will suggest that the case of Scientology offers some much broader theoretical insights into the study of religious secrecy in a comparative context.

The Background of the Secret: From Early Dianetics to the Church of Scientology

The Operating Thetan materials are a fairly late innovation within the Church of Scientology, which was first incorporated in the US in December 1953. The church's founder, L. Ron Hubbard, first made his career as an enormously prolific author of science fiction and fantasy tales during the 1930s and 1940s, emerging as one of the most widely published writers of the "Golden Age" of sci fi.[16] Indeed, he wrote so much and so quickly that he was forced to publish under a wide array of pseudonyms, such as Winchester Remington Colt, René Lafayette, Legionnaire

148, and many others. As more than one observer has pointed out, there are many continuities between Hubbard's early science fiction tales and his later Scientology writings, which also include large amounts of what Hubbard called space opera material—that is, discussions of life on other planets, alien races, and the past history of the universe going back billions and even trillions of years.[17]

Hubbard also had a keen interest in occultism, magic, and paranormal phenomena, which appear as frequent themes in many of his early stories.[18] Following his career in the Navy during World War II, in fact, Hubbard became actively involved in a series of magical rituals with a young engineer and rocket scientist named Jack Parsons (1914–1952) in southern California.[19] And this episode, we should note, remains one of the most controversial and much-debated periods in Hubbard's already controversial biography. Jack Parsons was a student of the work of Aleister Crowley (1875–1947), arguably the most important figure in the revival of occultism and magic in the twentieth century, and he was a member of Crowley's magical group, the Ordo Templi Orientis.[20] Parsons in fact was performing a series of rituals called the Babalon Working that aimed to create a "magickal child" or "moon child"—a supernatural offspring that would become the embodiment of ultimate power. The rite was intended first to identify a woman who would serve as Parsons's partner in esoteric rites and ultimately as the incarnation of Lady Babalon, who would in turn become impregnated with this magical child of ultimate power. According to Parsons's records from March 1946, Hubbard was as an intimate participant in the Babalon Working and even acted as the "Scribe" or voice for Lady Babalon, who spoke through him during the rites.[21]

The magical collaboration between Parsons and Hubbard was short-lived, however. Parsons and Hubbard, together with Parsons's girlfriend Betty (Sara Elizabeth Northrup, 1924–1997), had entered into a partnership called Allied Enterprises, with the plan of buying yachts on the East Coast, sailing them to California, and then selling them for a profit. Yet Hubbard ended up running off with Betty, along with over $20,000 of Parsons's money that had been put up for the yacht-selling plan.[22]

Perhaps the most remarkable part of this whole story about Hubbard, Parsons, and secret magical rites is that the Church of Scientology acknowledged that all of this *really did happen*. In an article published in the *London Sunday Times* in 1969, the church claimed that these rites actually did take place, but that Hubbard had been sent in on a special "military mission" to break up this secret black magic group. This he successfully did, the church reported, by rescuing the girl (Betty) and shutting down this occult operation.[23] It is worth noting, however, that neither the Church of Scientology nor any independent researcher has provided any evidence for this claim.

But in any case, whether Hubbard really was engaged seriously in these occult rituals or whether he was sent in as a secret military agent, this incident is worth keeping in mind for the latter part this chapter. As we will see, today there is tremendous debate as to whether these occult themes reappeared in Hubbard's later writings on Scientology, including the advanced OT materials that are discussed below.[24]

In 1950, Hubbard turned his attention from science fiction to what he dubbed a new science of the human mind called Dianetics.[25] Derived from the Greek words *dia* and *nous* meaning "through the mind," Dianetics claimed that all of our problems come from the mind, and therefore all of the solutions to our problems can be resolved through a proper understanding of the mind. Dianetics was hugely but briefly successful in the years 1950 and 1951—indeed, it was really the first great American self-help book and pop-psychology manual, which leapt to the top of the *New York Times* best-seller list and remained there for many weeks, spawning a kind of "Dianetics craze" across the US. But the initial fervor of the Dianetics fad quickly fizzled as a popular movement, and its parent organization, the Hubbard Dianetic Research Foundation, went bankrupt by 1952. However, it was quickly replaced by a new and explicitly "religious" movement, which Hubbard called the Church of Scientology and formally incorporated in 1953.[26]

Both the early Dianetics movement and the later Church of Scientology use a basic technique called auditing, in which an individual works with a trained counselor called an auditor to identify areas of unconscious pain and trauma (called engrams). Auditing involves the use of a device called the e-meter or electropsychometer, which works much like a lie detector and is designed to help the auditor identify problem areas and painful memories in the mind by asking questions and observing the reactions on the meter (see fig. 6.1).[27] Once these problem areas and negative memory traces have been identified and talked through with the auditor, they are "cleared" from the mind. And, when all of one's negative memory traces have been identified and examined, one achieves a state called Clear—an optimum state of mental, physical, and personal well-being.[28]

In the late 1960s, Hubbard then introduced even higher levels of increasingly esoteric training called the Operating Thetan levels.[29] The term "Thetan" refers to our spiritual self or true identity as an immortal spirit, and Operating Thetan or OT means a spirit that is increasingly free

FIGURE 6.1. L. Ron Hubbard. Photo by Chris Ware. Courtesy of Getty Images, Hulton Archive.

from the limitations of the material universe. Eventually, an OT is said to acquire supernatural abilities or super powers, such as the ability to "exteriorize" or travel outside the body, clairvoyance, telekinesis, and various others.[30] Scientology has a map of the spiritual path called the Bridge to Total Freedom, which begins with the lower-level Dianetics auditing and then leads to the higher and confidential OT levels. The church's official "Bridge" lists fifteen of these secret OT levels, though only eight of them have thus far been released, and it is unclear today whether the other seven were ever completed before Hubbard's death.

One of the most common criticisms of Scientology is that these higher levels of confidential training become quite expensive. Early lists of these materials in the late 1960s ranged from $75 for OT I to $875 for the higher OT levels; yet throughout the 1970s, 1980s, and 1990s their costs increased rapidly.[31] According to a 2009 list of fees and registration rates from the church's Flag Services Organization in Florida, the costs below level OT run from $6,800 per 12.5 hours of auditing to $56,100 per 150 hours of auditing. Then, above OT III, costs run from $7,800 per 12.5 hours to $64,350 per 150 hours. The individual OT levels themselves, according to this list, range from $2,800 to $13,600.[32] The total costs to complete OT training varies depending on the amount of auditing an individual Scientologist requires to move through each level. However, conservative estimates suggest that rising to OT VIII would require a minimum of $350,000 to $400,000.[33] And that is without including the various other courses, books, and materials offered, such as the latest model E-meter (the Mark Super VII Quantum at $4,650) or various texts, recordings, and DVDs, ranging in price from several hundred to several thousand dollars.[34]

Most of the media attention has focused on just one of these Operating Thetan levels, OT III. This was leaked to the press in the 1980s and allegedly tells the story of the past history of the universe going back 75 million years. This level is also called the First Wall of Fire, which was extremely difficult for Hubbard to attain and purports to reveal the cause of human suffering on earth. As we read in one advertisement for this level, "A research accomplishment of immense magnitude, OT III has been called 'the Wall of Fire.' Here are contained secrets of a disaster which resulted in the decay of life as we know it in this sector of the galaxy. The end result of OT III is truly the stuff of which dreams are spun: The full return of self-determinism and complete freedom."[35] The main character in this tale is an evil emperor named Xenu (or Xemu in some versions of the story), and it involves a complex narrative of a Galactic Confederacy, atomic bombs, volcanoes, and other elaborate "space opera" details.[36] While this is indeed a fascinating story, it is not really the most interesting or potentially volatile aspect of the OT materials.

Indeed, the truly interesting and complicated mysteries go well beyond the widely known and often-ridiculed Xenu story. OT VIII is the most controversial of the OT levels and is the last one that the church has released (and some argue is the last one Hubbard completed before his death). This is also called the third and final Wall of Fire, which promises to reveal the ultimate truth of our existence and restore the full power of the Thetan or spiritual self. Rather surprisingly, however, this key portion of Scientology's esoteric materials — which is supposed to be the ultimate secret of Hubbard's teachings — has never been examined critically by contemporary scholars.

This OT VIII level was completely secret until 1990, when a Scientologist named Steven Fishman was involved in a complex legal case involving the claim that he had committed fraud to pay for his Scientology auditing. In the course of the court proceedings, all of the OT materials became part of the public court record, and, not surprisingly, they were then quickly leaked to the press and eventually onto the Internet.[37] Initially, the Church of Scientology claimed rights to *all* of the Fishman materials, including OT VIII; but it later amended its claim to exclude the version of the OT VIII text in the Fishman affidavit, claiming that it was a forgery.[38] Meanwhile, there is also the larger question of the OT materials beyond OT VIII, from OT IX to XV, which have to date never been released but which the current Scientology head, David Miscavige, claims to have in his possession.[39]

The Third Wall of Fire:
The OT VIII Text from the Fishman Affidavit

So let us examine the text from the OT VIII materials in the Fishman affidavit. Again, this is the material from the court proceedings and has been ruled (after much litigation) to be in the public domain, so one can now find it easily on the Internet. It is a fairly long document, but I want to focus on just a couple of key paragraphs from this text, which is dated May 5, 1980, and is explicitly labeled "CONFIDENTIAL" in capital letters. In this document, the author seems to make the remarkable claim to be the future Buddha Metteya or Maitreya, who is predicted to come at the end of this cosmic era. This is a claim, we should note, that Hubbard had made in a previous document from the mid-1950s entitled *Hymn of Asia*[40] (moreover, similar claims to identify the future Buddha had previously been made by other new religious movements, most notably by the Theosophical Society[41]):

> With the exception of the original Buddhism, virtually all religions of any consequence on this planet, mono- and pantheistic alike, have been instruments to speed the progress of this "evolution of consciousness" and bring about the eventual enslavement of mankind. As you know, Siddhartha Gautama never claimed to be anything more than a man. Having caught on to this operation, he postulated his own return as Metteyya, part of which prophecy will have been fulfilled upon the passing of L. Ron Hubbard.[42]

If this claim were not remarkable enough, however, the same text *also* appears to identify Hubbard with the figures of Lucifer and the Antichrist (a reference that may also reflect the influence of Theosophy[43]). Hubbard's mission in this world, the text claims, is actually to *derail* or *prevent* the biblical narrative of Jesus's Second Coming described in the book of Revelation. The text also weaves the narrative of the Second Coming with aspects of Hubbard's space opera cosmology, such as an ancient civilization called the Galactic Confederacy and another, more sinister, alien civilization called the Marcabians:

> No doubt you are familiar with the Revelations section of the Bible where various events are predicted. Also mentioned is a brief period of time in which an arch-enemy of Christ, referred to as the anti-Christ, will reign and his opinions will have sway.... This anti-Christ represents the forces of Lucifer (literally, the "light bearers" or "light bringer"), Lucifer being a mythical representation of the forces of enlightenment, the Galactic Confederacy. My mission could be said to fulfill the Biblical promise represented by this brief anti-Christ period. During this period there is a fleeting opportunity for the whole scenario to be effectively derailed, which would make it impossible for the mass Marcabian landing (Second Coming) to take place.[44]

The text then goes on to present a fairly severe criticism of Jesus, who is described essentially as a "lover of young boys" who had an anger-management problem:

> For those of you whose Christian toes I have stepped on, let me take the opportunity to disabuse you of some lovely myths. For instance, the historic Jesus was not nearly the sainted figure [he] has been made out to be. In addition to being a lover of young boys and men, he was given to uncontrollable bursts of temper and hatred.[45]

Finally, in what is perhaps the oddest portion of the document, the text concludes with a promise about L. Ron Hubbard's future incarnation on planet Earth. Here the author claims that Hubbard will return to this world not simply with a spiritual mission but also a *political* one, which is really his final secret:

> I will return not as a religious leader but a political one. That happens to be the requisite beingness for the task at hand. I will not be known to most of you, my activities misunderstood by many....
>
> So there you have it. The secret that I have kept close to my chest all these years. Now you too are part of this secret....[46]

We should emphasize that the Church of Scientology initially claimed ownership of all of this OT VIII material, but then stated that it was a forgery.[47] Moreover, the version of the OT VIII text that was later leaked to sources such as Wikileaks is completely different from this version contained in the Fishman affidavit.[48] So the status of this text—with its extremely controversial claims about Jesus, the Antichrist, and Hubbard's political role—remains quite unclear. Even ex-Scientologists who had achieved OT VIII and then left the church disagree as to the authenticity of this text, some claiming that it is the original work of Hubbard and others that it is a forgery. In one recent book, ex-Scientologist George Witek (a.k.a. George White) states that about half of the OT VIII level Scientologists he interviewed said this was the real version of the text, and about half said it was fake. Witek, we should note, claims this is the real one that he received in 1988.[49]

The authenticity of this text therefore remains quite uncertain. However, for critics who want to find continuities between Hubbard's early involvement in occultism and the later Church of Scientology, the text in the Fishman affidavit would lend great support to the idea that Hubbard was still immersed in magic, occultism, and in the works of the Aleister Crowley discussed above. Crowley, for example, was also quite critical of Christianity, and he had also called himself by the "Antichrist-like" title of the "Great Beast 666."[50]

Now, to make things still *more* complicated: all of this still leaves open the question of whether there is any additional OT material *beyond* OT VIII. This would seem to be indicated on the church's official Bridge to Total Freedom, which lists the levels OT IX through OT XV. These levels would presumably be even *more* esoteric and more inaccessible to non-Scientologists. Today, however, it is not really known whether these upper levels from IX to XV even exist—not even by most Scientologists, including former high-ranking members who have recently left the church. The current Scientology head, David Miscavige, claims to have these remaining OT levels written in Hubbard's hand safely in his possession, simply waiting for the right moment to release them.[51] But many ex-Scientologists, such as Mark Rathbun (who was the chief lieutenant under Miscavige before he left the church) claim that this is simply a lie and that there are no additional levels beyond OT VIII.[52]

So what we have in the OT VIII materials is really an extreme example of what I have called the ethical and epistemological double bind of secrecy. Not only is the attempt to pry into Scientology's advanced materials ethically problematic, it is also a *massive epistemological quagmire.* I think we can justifiably examine materials that have been made part of the public court record, such as the documents in the Fishman affidavit; yet determining their authenticity at this point seems difficult if not impossible. Indeed, it seems unlikely that even Scientology's current leadership could say with certainty whether the OT VIII materials in the Fishman affidavit are fraudulent or genuine since their alleged author has been dead for thirty years.

The History of a Secret, from the 1960s to the Present

Again, I don't think there is any simple way out of this double bind of secrecy. However, my approach here is basically twofold. First, I suggest that we shift our gaze from the *content* of the secret to the more visible *forms and strategies* through which secret information is constructed, maintained, and transmitted.[53] This does not mean that the content is nonexistent or unimportant but, in many cases, *unknowable and/or ethically problematic*. Here I follow Simmel's seminal insight that secrecy is a *sociological form* that is independent of its contents. In other words, even if we can't always say much about the *content* of a secret, we can still say quite a lot about the *forms* through which secrecy operates, the *mechanisms and strategies* through which secret information is concealed, revealed, and transmitted. And second, I will retrace the *history* of this particular secret and its strategies of concealment through *five historical moments*. Some of these moments in the history of Scientology reiterate several of the other modes and strategies of concealment that we have seen in previous chapters; yet they also reveal the ways in which the power of secrecy can change dramatically over time, even becoming a source of shame and embarrassment rather than adornment, status, or capital.

1. THE ADVERTISED SECRET: PROMOTING THE OT ESOTERIC MATERIALS IN THE 1960S AND 1970S

The first key moment and strategy in this history is what I call in chapter 2 the "advertisement of the secret," or the public announcement of esoteric knowledge. As we saw in the case of the Theosophical Society, most forms of religious secrecy involve the paradoxical fact that a secret is always partially known and partially revealed.[54] As Mary H. Nooter observes in her work on secrecy in African art, cultural forms such as masks, emblems, and figures draw attention to secret knowledge at the same time that they conceal its content. In effect, they *broadcast* secrecy and "publicly proclaim the ownership of privileged information while protecting its contents"; for "to own secret knowledge, and to show that one does, is a form of power."[55]

This sort of broadcasting of the secret is something that we see throughout Scientology publications during the late 1960s and early 1970s. As glossy magazines such as *Advance!* proudly declare, the OT levels reveal the most secret and powerful insights into the past history of the universe, offering the keys to our spiritual liberation and the means to ever greater spiritual powers. As one promotion puts it, "L. Ron Hubbard found the key and taped out the exact path—that path is Operating Thetan. Here the secrets of this sector of the universe are revealed."[56] These advertisements use a variety of dramatic imagery to illustrate the state of OT, such as doors in the starry heavens opening onto brilliant white light, angels flying into the heavens, individuals on the bridge of a space ship hurtling through the stars toward a glowing white OT symbol and a large space craft with the OT symbol floating above a distant planet, with the slogan: "The Sky is the Limit: Regain Yourself and Your Full Ability. GO OT."[57]

Hubbard, these advertisements explain, had to struggle and suffer to pass through this "Wall of Fire," but now we can all follow him through it to total liberation. As we read in one promotional ad from *Advance!* magazine in 1977, describing the awesome revelations promised by the First Wall, OT III:

> A catastrophe occurred 75 million years ago that still has a tremendous impact on our lives and civilization today.... L. Ron Hubbard was the first being to penetrate the mystery of its existence and find a way through this "Wall of Fire" for others to follow. On the other side you will find freedom ... and the full return of self-determinism. You will understand the terrible fate that has gripped this planet and why Man has previously failed (before Scientology) to answer the riddle of his own existence.[58]

These advertisements are consistently accompanied by testimonials from various Scientologists who describe their remarkable experiences and achievements upon reaching the OT levels. These range from fairly mundane experiences, such as a greater sense of well-being and enjoyment of life, to more supernatural experiences, such as seeing disembodied spirits, journeying into the future, and even controlling the weather.[59] Others describe healing their sick pet cats and goldfish or fighting fires from a distance through the power of the Thetan.[60] "I love it," as one enthusiastic member testified, "like Superman!"[61] One of the most common experiences described in advertisements for the OT materials is the ability to "exteriorize" or separate the Thetan from the physical body and then travel at will around the earth or even into outer space. According to a testimonial from a Scientologist named John Bruce that was advertised in *Advance!* magazine in 1975,

> A couple of weeks ago I received a letter from home (in Rhodesia) saying that my sister was seriously ill with double pneumonia and was in hospital. Well, I decided, since I had just completed OT III, to do something about it. So I exteriorized and located my sister's body. I sent a great whopping intention over for the body to heal and immediately felt better about the situation.[62]

OT VIII was first advertised in publications from the early 1970s for a fee of $500, but the ads noted that it was "not yet released" (already by 1978, however, the fee had increased to $1,326.65 "when released"[63]). Later advertisements promote the profound importance of OT VIII in even more explicit and grandiose terms, as an "utterly astounding level" that reveals all the secrets of "yourself and your power as an Operating Thetan, and the actual fulfillment of the Aims of Scientology."[64] Opening the secrets of OT VIII is promised to carry the Scientologist through the final Wall of Fire into the deepest mysteries of the human self and the universe: "When you reach New OT VIII Truth Revealed, you have stepped across the threshold taking you into ... vistas never even dreamed of and glories no past glory ever surpassed."[65]

In short, the advertisements for OT that we see throughout Scientology publications consistently work to accomplish two strategic goals: first, they make it very clear *that* a tremendously powerful secret exists and must be obtained; and second, they always do so by very carefully not saying anything specific about *what* that secret might be.

2. THE SECRET AS MATERIAL AND SYMBOLIC "ADORNING POSSESSION" IN THE 1970S AND 1980S

The second moment in this history of the secret is what I call in chapter 1 a kind of "adorning possession." As we saw in the case of Scottish Rite Freemasonry, the secret often serves as a form of adornment, which paradoxically enhances and exaggerates the status of the one who holds it precisely by virtue of what it conceals. Just as fine clothing or jewelry enhances one's status by *covering* parts of the body, the possession of secret knowledge can enhance one's status through its power of concealment.[66]

Again, this adorning function is more than metaphorical; it is often quite *literal*. In the case of Scientology, the individual rising through the

OT grades not only acquires ever greater status and abilities, but also may purchase a wide array of specially branded OT jewelry to signal and display their advanced status. As shown in a 2009 *Dianetics and Scientology Catalog*, these include the OT pendant ($150), OT pendant with diamond ($285), OT ring with diamonds ($475), OT earrings ($350), Gold OT bracelet ($2,100), and large OT bracelet with diamonds ($3,200).[67] Again, the acquisition of concealed knowledge is often both a social and a very physical kind of adornment, or a kind of "material esotericism."

In this sense, Scientology's OT materials are a particularly obvious illustration of Bourdieu's concept of "symbolic capital," as well as the ways in which material capital tends to be converted into nonmaterial capital, and vice versa. As we saw in the introduction, Bourdieu uses the term "capital" to refer to "all the goods, material and symbolic . . . that present themselves as rare and worthy of being sought after in a particular social formation."[68] Symbolic capital, however, is a form of wealth that tends to conceal and mystify the material power behind it, just as, for example, the claim to having "good taste" in wine or clothing at once conceals and yet also legitimates the real economic capital required to buy such goods. As a kind of "denied capital," it "disguises the underlying 'interested' relations to which it is related by giving them legitimation."[69] Moreover, the acquisition of symbolic capital is typically linked to a very real exchange of *material capital*: for example, the investment in an expensive university bestows the linguistic, cultural, and social capital that come with a good degree; the investment in an expensive piece of artwork or a fine bottle of wine brings the capital of taste and distinction, and so on. Scientology's intense focus on secrecy in the OT materials seems to be a particularly clear example of this sort of capital and its exchange. Not only does the secrecy surrounding the OT levels transform this material into a kind of *scarce resource*, that is, a good that is "rare and worthy of being sought after";[70] at the same time, this material clearly links to a complex system of economic exchange, which runs into the thousands and tens of thousands of dollars.

It seems likely that this aspect of symbolic capital was at least *in part* the attraction of Scientology for the many celebrities and actors who joined the movement beginning in the 1970s, such as John Travolta, Tom Cruise, Kirstie Alley, Isaac Hayes, and many others. As we see in the extremely opulent Scientology Celebrity Centres such as the one in Hollywood,[71] becoming a Scientologist was for many rising stars a kind of symbolic capital and "adornment," in both a figurative and literal sense — that is, at once a form of status and also a means of social networking in the film and music industries. At least at its peak in the 1970s and 1980s, Scientology really did provide a certain status and symbolic capital for many actors, musicians, and entertainers, allowing them to enter into a network of successful, wealthy, and well-connected individuals. As journalist Lawrence Wright observes in his popular work on Scientology and Hollywood, the church offered members a very powerful sort of insider network: "especially in Hollywood, awarding them an advantage in a ruthless competitive industry."[72] Of course, as we will see below, this is probably less true today, as Scientology has now lost much of its symbolic power and caché and is arguably as much a *liability* as a sign of status.

3. THE LITIGATION OF THE SECRET IN THE 1990S

The third period in this history is what I call the "litigation of the secret," or the transformation of the secret into an object of intense legal dispute. Beginning in the late 1980s and 1990s, the Operating Thetan materials became the focus of several major lawsuits when they were leaked by ex-Scientologists and then found their way to the media and eventually onto the Internet.[73] Indeed, the church established its own Religious Technology Center (RTC), whose stated aim is "protecting the Scientology religion's trademarks and advanced religious scripture."[74] The RTC became involved in several intense legal disputes over the circulation of the OT materials, which it claims are not only copyrighted and trade secrets but also confidential religious texts.

In November 1985, the confidential OT texts were first introduced as evidence in court in a case brought against the church by ex-Scientologist Larry Wollersheim. Although Scientology attorneys argued forcefully that the disclosure of the materials violated the group's religious freedom, the Los Angeles Superior Court judge issued an order making the documents public at the clerk's office. In response, some 1,500 Scientologists crammed the court buildings, swamping workers with hundreds of requests to photocopy the documents in an attempt to ensure that the materials were not made public. Yet in spite of these efforts, the *Los Angeles Times* obtained copies of the OT materials and revealed them in an article in November 1985.[75]

In 1993, Wollersheim cofounded the website "Fight Against Coercive Tactics Network" (FACTNet) designed to expose Scientology's activities. Having amassed some twenty-seven gigabytes of material on Scientology, FACTNet was hit with intense legal threats from the church. The church's argument was that the confidential OT documents were both copyrighted materials and trade secrets (that is, information that has economic value from not being generally known); the disclosure of these secrets, it claimed, could cause "irreparable spiritual injury if a rival church . . . were allowed to disseminate them."[76] On August 22, 1995, a federal court ordered a raid on the homes of Wollersheim and another ex-Scientologist, Robert Penny, led by two US marshals. This resulted in the confiscation of all of Wollersheim's and Penny's computers, software, and dozens of boxes of paper files. The legal battle over FACTNet, however, dragged on for another four years until a settlement was reached in 1999.[77]

The confidential OT materials became part of the court record in a second case involving former Scientologist Steven Fishman, the source of the infamous Fishman Affidavit discussed above. In 1990, Fishman was convicted of mail fraud — a crime that, he alleged, he had been brainwashed into committing to pay for his Scientology auditing. Fishman was then quoted in a *Time* magazine article as stating that he not only had been involved in an enormous scam to pay for his Scientology training but even had been ordered by the church to kill his own psychiatrist.[78] The church in turn sued Fishman for libel, and, in the course of the trial, Fishman submitted sixty-nine pages of the confidential OT materials, including secret documents all the way up to OT VIII.

Once again, copies of the materials were placed in a Los Angeles court file that was to be publicly available for two years. As in the Wollersheim case, church members undertook a remarkable effort to maintain the documents' secrecy throughout that period "by alternately checking out the files each day and retaining them until the clerk's office closed."[79] Yet once again, even with these intensive measures by the church, copies of the documents were made and soon found their way onto the Internet. The Fishman documents became the object of intense legal debate not only in the US but also in the Dutch courts, when Dutch journalist Karen Spaink put them on the Internet and then promptly faced charges that her actions violated copyright and trade secrets. The Dutch courts, however, ruled three times in the journalist's favor, and so the Fishman materials and their version of OT VIII remain easily available to this day.[80]

Various other lawsuits both large and small were filed against a wide array of critics, ranging from mega-media empires such as *Time* magazine down to ordinary college students. One of my undergraduate students, in fact, had posted some of the OT materials on his personal website and then promptly received a threatening letter from Scientology's lawyers, who had his entire website and email service terminated.[81] However, these aggressive tactics of litigation appear to have had little real effect on the circulation of the OT materials and have arguably even backfired.

4. THE LIABILITY OF THE SECRET: SECRECY AS A SOURCE OF SCANDAL AND EMBARRASSMENT

The fourth moment in this history is what I call the *"liability* of the secret," or the gradual transformation of secret information from a source of status and power into a source of embarrassment.[82] In Scientology's case, this began in the 1990s and 2000s, as more and more of the OT materials inevitably found their way into cyberspace and began proliferating wildly. Today, a Google search on the keywords "Operating Thetan" produces about 64,900 hits, while a search on "Xenu" produces another 898,000. Perhaps the height of this embarrassment was the 2005 episode of the cartoon satire *South Park*, which dramatized and mercilessly ridiculed the OT III story about emperor Xenu.[83]

This widespread dissemination of Scientology's secrets may well prove to be the greatest challenge to the church's survival in the twenty-first century. As one ex-member, Robert Vaughn Young puts it, the Internet may well prove to be Scientology's "Waterloo" — that is, a deeply entrenched, extremely messy, bloody, and costly battle that the church cannot possibly hope to win.[84] As Gerry Armstrong commented in an interview with me in August 2009, this may well be "the last generation of Scientologists" since young people today grow up on the Internet, live increasingly in cyberspace, and obtain all of their information online.[85] It is difficult, he thinks, to foresee great numbers of converts coming from a generation that has access not just to the secret OT levels on hundreds of websites but also to Netflix series and *South Park* clips that expose or even ridicule Scientology's beliefs and practices.

Scientology and its secret materials also became a major target of attack and ridicule by the loose collective called Anonymous, which champions free speech on the Internet. In addition to protesting the church in physical space, the Anonymous group has been active in cyberspace. According to a video message uploaded to YouTube in 2008, the Anonymous group is dedicated to nothing less than the "destruction of Scientology in its present form,"[86] and its members have been active in circulating confidential Scientology documents as broadly as possible. In fact, one Anonymous member sent me over forty DVDs of data and a massive hard drive filled with virtually all known documents — texts, magazines, audio recordings, movies, ephemera, old mimeographs, FBI files, and various other materials — ever gathered on the church. While Anonymous has not necessarily succeeded in destroying Scientology, it has helped to fundamentally undermine the role of secrecy in the church by aggressively disseminating basically all available digital information — including the most confidential materials — to a vast global audience.

5. THE EMBARRASSMENT AND THE
OCCULTATION OF THE SECRET

Finally, the fifth period in this history is what I will call the "embarrassment and the occultation of the secret," which is largely what we see in the Church of Scientology today. Over the last two decades, few Scientology spokespersons have been willing to even acknowledge much less discuss things like the Xenu story or other confidential OT materials. In one of my classes at Ohio State, for example, my graduate teaching assistant arranged for a prominent Scientologist to speak to our group. When the students asked him about Xenu and OT III, he claimed to have never even heard of it (which seems impossible for anyone after 2005). Meanwhile, in a famous interview with ABC News in 2009, Scientology spokesman Tommy Davis was asked repeatedly about the OT materials and the Xenu story; after refusing to answer any questions about these documents, he grew increasingly agitated and finally removed his microphone and walked off the set (Davis later left the Church of Scientology and is now among the ex-members).[87]

In its promotional materials and websites today, Scientology typically emphasizes the more public and "exoteric" aspects of the church, such as its ability to help personal lives, build families, and further careers, as well as its outreach and charitable work. "Scientologists come from all walks of life," the church's current website proudly announces, "They are concerned about social problems and support numerous social betterment programs, which provide effective drug-abuse rehabilitation, improve educational standards and help reduce crime and moral decay."[88] Its online materials, for example, prominently feature the work of outreach groups such as the Volunteer Ministers, who help with disaster relief and aid in various problems of daily life. As we read on the Volunteer Ministers website, this is not some esoteric or obscure elitist religious practice; rather, "Scientology offers practical solutions to help you improve conditions in your life and the lives of those around you," ranging from "resolving marital strife" to "managing a company for optimum success."[89]

While the tantalizing power of the OT levels was advertised and promoted quite prominently in publications of the 1960s, 1970s, and 1980s, they are now more often *downplayed* in favor of the more public and noncontroversial aspects of Scientology. Amidst the glowing testimonials from current Scientologists of all ages and ethnicities featured on its websites and introductory promotional materials, one has to actively search to find any mention of the OT levels, and even then, they are described in vague and nonspecific language.[90] In sum, the secret itself has largely receded from public view. While the OT levels are still very much a part of the upper levels of the elite, esoteric tier of advanced Scientology, they are largely obscured and/or removed from public display in the vast majority of the church's more visible media, such as websites, local organizations, and publications for circulation outside of the OT community. In short, they have been progressively occulted—that is, subjected to a new kind of esotericism, a new concealment of powerful but dangerous secret knowledge.[91]

Conclusions and Comparative Comments

To conclude, I would like to briefly discuss the broader implications and also the limitations of the approach that I have suggested here. This focus on the forms and strategies of secrecy and this emphasis on the history of the secret should, I hope, have many comparative implications for the study of secrecy in other traditions. We have already seen in the preceding chapters that the role of secrecy as an "advertisement" and an "adornment" has numerous parallels in other traditions, ranging from Jewish mysticism to African and Afro-Caribbean religions to Freemasonry, Theosophy, the Golden Dawn, and other modern esoteric traditions.[92]

Perhaps more important, however, the "litigation of the secret" is also a phenomenon that we see increasingly in the twenty-first century, as many religious movements have begun to adopt the same structures, logics, and legal tactics as large multinational corporations. Similar legal battles have been fought, for example, over many forms of Yoga, such as Bikram Yoga, which also claims to hold trademarks over its sequences of postures.[93] Another example is the Osho International Foundation, which has claimed trademarks and copyrights over the works and meditation techniques of the Indian guru Osho; indeed, it has claimed rights over the name "Osho" itself and fought a major legal battle with a rival group that used "Osho" in the domain name of its website.[94] It is not a stretch to imagine that these sorts of legal disputes over intellectual property, trademarks, and trade secrets may well become some of the defining issues of twenty-first-century religious life.[95]

Finally, what I have called the "liability of the secret" and the "embarrassment of the secret" are also common patterns that we see, particularly in movements that are undergoing a period of decline or transformation. The case of American Freemasonry is, again, an obvious example of this pattern. In its early development in the US, Freemasonry contained a huge amount of occult symbolism and ritual, along with elements drawn from Kabbalah, alchemy, and Hermeticism. Yet today, Freemasonry is largely an innocuous and quite "domesticated" fraternal organization in which secrecy and esoteric ritual is largely a curious anachronism.[96]

A similar historical trajectory is seen in the development of Mormonism in the US from the nineteenth century to the present. As historian Michael Homer has recently argued, early Mormonism was deeply entwined with Freemasonry, which was a foundational element in the secret ceremonies and other key elements of the Mormon church in the mid-nineteenth century. Yet as Mormonism grew into an established and increasingly "mainstream" tradition, Mormons progressively distanced themselves from Freemasonry, downplaying or "airbrushing" out the esoteric dimensions of Mormon ritual in favor of a more respectable, transparent, and "all-American" public identity.[97]

We could surely cite many other comparative examples here, such as recent work on Australian aboriginal traditions, Hindu and Buddhist Tantra, Jewish Kabbalah, and many others. But the key point I want to make is that the *content* of the secrecy in each of these cases would obviously be very different and historically variable; yet, the *forms and strategies* through which secret knowledge is concealed, transmitted, revealed, and transformed *over time* may well turn out to be remarkably similar across cultures and historical periods. They may not be universal "archetypes" in Mircea Eliade's sense,[98] but they may at least provide a useful starting point for interesting cross-cultural comparative work.

Lastly, I also want to acknowledge the *limitations* of the approach that I've outlined here and this focus on form and strategy rather than content in the study of secrecy. After all, one might legitimately ask: Aren't there cases where the content of the secret really *is* important and really *is* knowable? For example, it is well documented that Scientology's intelligence bureau, the Guardian's Office, was involved in very real acts of espionage against US government agencies such as the IRS during the 1970s.[99] Many ex-Scientologists, such as Marc Headley, Nancy Many, Gerry Armstrong, Leah Remini, and others, have also accused the church of shocking physical abuse and human rights violations in its disciplinary program called the Rehabilitation Project Force (RPF).[100] Many readers will probably legitimately ask whether these are not also secrets that need to be investigated thoroughly by critical historians of religions.

To this I would answer: yes, of course. There are indeed forms of religious secrecy that require a different methodological approach, and there are many cases where a focus on hidden *content* would be more directly relevant. Moreover, there are also cases—for example, allegations of abuse and human rights violations, as we see in Scientology's controversial RPF program—where pursuing the hidden content is neither impossible nor necessarily unethical. At least in cases of potential abuse and violence, the pursuit of the hidden content may indeed be the *ethically imperative* option, despite the many epistemological obstacles. Although I have not undertaken that sort of analysis in this short chapter, I encourage other critical scholars to do so.[101]

✴ CONCLUSIONS ✴
The Science of the Hidden

SECRECY AND THE CRITICAL STUDY OF
RELIGION IN AN AGE OF SURVEILLANCE

As Bachelard so neatly put it, "there is no science but of the hidden."
The sociologist is better or worse equipped to dis-cover what is
hidden depending on . . . the degree of interest he has in uncovering
what is censored or repressed in the social world.

PIERRE BOURDIEU, *Sociology in Question*[1]

To every great politics belongs the arcanum.

CARL SCHMITT, *Roman Catholicism and Political Form*[2]

But this secrecy . . . has become a god in this country, and those people who have
secrets travel in a kind of fraternity . . . and will not speak to anyone else.

J. WILLIAM FULBRIGHT[3]

This book has never pretended to be a comprehensive study of religious
secrecy in all its myriad forms. The preceding chapters have covered only
a small fragment of the possible types of religious concealment that might
be explored, surely in greater detail and with richer nuance than I have
attempted here. Nonetheless, even from this brief overview, we can see
that secrecy has hardly receded in the last 200 years, waning amidst an
increasingly disenchanted, demystified, and transparent modern world;
on the contrary, it has arguably expanded and proliferated wildly, giving
birth to a vast array of secret societies, occult movements, underground
currents of resistance, terrorist networks, and many others. At the same
time, we see that secrecy is neither a simple nor singular thing, but instead a highly varied, complex, and shifting phenomenon, even within
a single religious movement. Lying as it does at the critical intersection
between knowledge and power, secrecy often serves as a kind of "linchpin" that can be deployed for a wide array of different social, political, and

religious ends. This book has explored just a few of these uses of secrecy, ranging from "adornment," "advertisement," and "seduction" to "social resistance" and "terror"; but even from these limited examples, we can see that secrecy represents a kind of dense *knot or node* lying at the intersection of many tangled relations of knowledge and power, which could perhaps be represented schematically as shown in figure 7.1.

Surely, we could also add other modes of secrecy that were not discussed in this book. For example, we could mention the role of secrecy in the attempt to preserve indigenous traditions from political persecution (for example, concealment of the Sun Dance, the Peyote ceremony, and other Native American rituals in the face of persecution from the US government[4]); the role of secret societies in the construction of gender (for example, men's secret societies in Papua New Guinea and other indigenous societies[5]); or the role of secrecy in the concealment of sexual abuse (such as in the Catholic, Baptist, and other churches); among others.

While my analysis in this short book limits itself to examples from the last 150 years in the US and Europe, my hope is that the various strategies and modalities of secrecy explored in these chapters will have much broader comparative implications. They might help, for example, to shed light on the "seductive" power of secrecy in non-Western esoteric traditions such as Hindu and Buddhist Tantra;[6] or to study the dialectics of revelation and concealment in Jewish mysticism;[7] or to illuminate the "adornment of silence" in other examples of material esotericism, such as religious masks in African and other indigenous traditions;[8] or to explore the role of secrecy as social resistance in other marginalized communities, such as Afro-Caribbean traditions; or to interrogate the "terror of secrecy" in any number of contemporary extremist movements around the world. Finally, perhaps one of the most pressing questions for the comparative study of religion today is the "litigation of the secret," as more and more groups claim copyright and trademark over valued religious

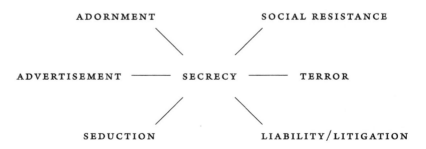

FIGURE 7.1. Secrecy as a linchpin in relations of knowledge and power.

practices and knowledge. As we see in cases ranging from multimillion-dollar industries such as Bikram Yoga to more esoteric groups such as the Urantia Foundation, debates over intellectual property have emerged as some of the most complex, contested, and yet increasingly pervasive features of religious life in the twenty-first century.[9]

As I suggest in the introduction, my aim here is not to assert some sort of grand universal archetypes in an Eliade-an sense but to offer a more modest and ground-up sort of comparative model that might allow us to see common strategies as they play out in very specific historical, social, and political contexts. Yet without making any sweeping universal claims, I do think we can say that secrecy is not simply accidentally or tangentially related to religion; rather, it is intimately related to various forms of religious symbolism, ritual, institutional hierarchies, and arguably to very nature of religious authority itself.[10] While this book has focused on a series of nonmainstream movements that were probably not previously known to some readers, the power of secrecy and the strategies of concealment that we have examined here are every bit as relevant to the understanding of so-called mainstream traditions. Secrecy, as the philosopher Charles Barbour has persuasively argued, is an essential feature of all social interaction and human discourse. As the central dynamic of withholding and disclosing information, secrecy structures all of our relations in one way or another:

> [S]ecrecy ... is a condition of our relations with others, or a condition of interaction, and we can only reveal ourselves to one another, and indeed to anything other ... in so far as, at the exact same moment, we conceal as well. ... [S]ecrecy is not simply one kind of social interaction among many, or one way that we might decide to engage with the world. ... [I]t also a general "form of association [*Vergesellschaftung*]." It is something that structures all of our engagements and all of our relations with everything. ... There is always some secret.[11]

In a similar way, I submit, secrecy is inherent in the very nature of religion itself, insofar as there is "always some secret" in religious experience and practice;[12] concealment and unknowing are as critical to the workings of religion as are knowing or revelation. For what is religion if it is not precisely the power that is attributed to some unseen presence and the authority that comes from the claim to profound, mysterious, largely hidden forms of knowledge? By this I mean not simply the idea of the sacred as a great numinous mystery but the claim to an unseen source of supra-human authority, which is invisible, largely unknowable, but still deeply compelling, serving as an ultimate source of motivation for billions of people across the globe.

To conclude, I would like to make some broader comparative comments on the role of the academic study of religion in our current historical moment. Writing more than fifty years ago in the context of the Cold War, the sociologist Elias Canetti recognized the growing power and threat of secrecy, noting the development of military secrets such as the atomic bomb and the dictatorial threats to democracy spreading worldwide:

> It is only today that we fully realize how dangerous secrecy can become. In different, but only apparently independent spheres, it has become loaded with more and more power. Scarcely was the human dictator dead whom the whole world had united to fight, than the secret turned up again in the shape of the atomic bomb, more dangerous than ever.... [Mo]dern technical secrets are the most concentrated and dangerous that have ever existed. They concern *everyone*, but only a tiny number of people have real knowledge of them and their actual use depends on a handful of men.[13]

Today, Canetti's warnings seem not only prescient but eerily, disconcertingly relevant. The dangers that we face in the early twenty-first, however, are ones that Canetti could probably not have imagined in the early years of the Cold War. Not only do we now face a far more diffuse nuclear threat, but we also witness the spread of terrorists and ethnic nationalists worldwide, as well as increasingly antidemocratic movements in even the most established democracies. Perhaps more alarmingly, we also face the rapid expansion of a vast and immensely powerful national security apparatus that operates increasingly outside of public scrutiny and wields ever more sophisticated instruments of surveillance.[14]

The task of the historian of religions is therefore perhaps today more urgent than ever. Here I again follow the lead of Bruce Lincoln and his idea of a "critical history of religions," which always pays close attention to the human, situated, interested, temporal, and material dimensions of discourses that claim to be supra-human or transcendent. For "there is a significant political dimension to all religious discourse, and ... it is not only possible but important to render this visible so that it may be subjected to critical analysis."[15] This critical approach to the history of religions is closely allied with Bourdieu's model of reflexive sociology, which he describes as a "science of the hidden" — that is, an attempt to illuminate and analyze relations of power that have been masked or mystified in the social order:

There is, therefore, a political dimension to ... what sociology should do in the modern world.... Acts of research, no matter how seemingly mundane, are acts of struggle, conquest, and victory over taken-for-granted assumptions of social life: scientific research is a struggle against all forms of symbolic domination.[16]

In the twenty-first century, however, this science of the hidden increasingly needs to be directed not only at religious groups who use the stratagems of secrecy to conceal problematic behavior—such as abuse within the Church of Scientology or pederasty in the Catholic Church or the terrorist networks of white supremacists. Equally, it needs to be directed at those state—and now also corporate—entities that wield ever more powerful technologies of surveillance while also clothing themselves in ever deeper layers of secrecy.[17]

Secrecy, Spectacle, and Cyberspace: Religious Terrorism in the Digital Age

The study of religious secrecy faces an array of new challenges in the twenty-first century. Among others, the rapid expansion of new information technologies has allowed for exponentially more powerful and diverse means for the concealment, control, and dissemination of knowledge. In short, the early modern "economy of secrets" described by Jütte has been largely absorbed within a much larger economy of information, which has radically transformed all aspects of twenty-first-century life—including religion and its complex relations with the political sphere.

Some of the most sophisticated and (tragically) effective uses of information technologies have been made by religious extremist and terrorist networks around the globe. As we saw in chapter 5, secrecy is central to most forms of religious terrorism, both as a practical strategy and as a means of creating the aura of fear that makes otherwise small and marginal groups appear to possess "significant powers, even terrifying ones." What is particularly striking about forms of terrorism since the 1990s, however, is their use of technology to orchestrate violence on a mass scale and often with an explicit aspect of dramatic performance, theater, and spectacle.[18] The al-Qaeda network, for example, not only made effective use of secrecy to mount a devastating attack on the most powerful nation on earth using little more than ordinary box cutters as weapons,[19] it also made effective use of new information technologies to plan, finance, and carry out the attack. Indeed, even as it called for a return to a maximalist version of Sunni Islam, al-Qaeda was also strikingly modern in its use of email, satellite television, and electronic transfers of funds to operate covertly and mobilize resources across the globe. We might even say that terrorist networks like al-Qaeda are ironically "postmodern" in their highly decentralized structure, which is largely disconnected in physical space and yet have global reach.[20] Through the power of information technologies, al-Qaeda was able to create a kind of "virtual *umma*," circulating through the invisible networks of cyberspace:

> Once entrenched in Afghanistan in the late 1990s, al-Qaeda managed its international operations with ever increasing sophistication and audacity. Directives were encrypted in a quaint corporate language — terror was "commercial activity," bin Laden was dubbed "the contractor" — . . . but at the same time, made use of the Allied Forces' cryptographic systems used in World War Two. Al-Qaeda . . . was from the start a modern virtual organization, or more properly a modern network with a decentralized cell structure.[21]

However, the power of information technologies has not been limited to its ability to conceal the activities of terrorist networks. On the contrary, in keeping with the larger power of secrecy as "advertisement" and "seduction," social media has also been one of the most useful tools in promoting, marketing, and recruiting for extremist groups. Perhaps the most effective use of this sort of advertisement has been made by al-Qaeda's more radical successor, known variously as Islamic State, ISIS, ISIL, or Daesh. In addition to using new technologies in the obvious ways, such as circulating invisible networks of information and funds, ISIS has made extremely effective use of social media to recruit foreign fighters from around the world to join its work in the Middle East.[22] Finally and most infamously, ISIS also used social media as a terrifying yet seductive advertisement by publicly releasing videos of the beheadings of foreign journalists, which quickly spread virally across the globe. While the practice of public beheading surely has precedents in earlier Muslim and other traditions, its recent use by ISIS is clearly part of a new tactic of spectacular terrorist performance — not simply as a means of provoking fear but as a kind of grisly advertising, made possible by the omnipresence of YouTube and other platforms.[23]

Again, it would be a mistake to focus solely — or even primarily — on Islamic extremism online. As we saw in chapter 5, white supremacists have emerged as an equal if not greater threat than Islamic terrorist groups worldwide, and they have made perhaps even more effective use of social media to coordinate and spread their ideologies. As media and technology expert Joan Donovan suggests, the recent proliferation of white supremacist groups and violent attacks has been directly tied to the rise of social media platforms, particularly Facebook: "The outbreak of public organizing and violence by white supremacists relies on the infrastructure Facebook provides to connect to new audiences."[24]

However, these far-right racist groups tend to use the Internet in very different ways. On the one hand, many white supremacists rely precisely on the relative secrecy of some platforms to communicate anonymously and circulate conspiracy theories, while remaining subject to little if any moderation. Using fake accounts and bots to hide their identities, a small number of individuals can spread a message of hate to a vast global audience:

> White supremacists and other extremists tend to use anonymous message boards to plan manipulation campaigns. These places traffic in racist, sexist, and transphobic content and link to obscure podcasts and blogs. Moderation is rare and tends to occur only when too much attention is drawn to a certain post. In some forums, posts self-delete and leave few traces behind.[25]

One former white supremacist named Christian Picciolini described the Internet today as a kind of "twenty-four hour hate buffet." In the darker corners of the web, such as the largely unregulated message board 8chan, the most extreme ideologies are on offer constantly and freely for those who seek them out, or even for those who simply stumble upon them, as Picciolini claims he did: "What's happening now is people are going to this buffet, and they can feast all night long on message forums."[26]

On the other hand, social media platforms can be used in the opposite sense—not to conceal their activities but to promote and amplify them in a way that exaggerates their power and numbers.[27] Through the global scale of social media platforms, otherwise fringe and obscure movements can not only reach millions of readers but also manufacture the illusion that they are, in Mauss's words, "significant powers, even terrifying ones." As Donovon notes,

> Social media has fundamentally changed who controls the volume on certain social issues. Facebook, Google, and other platform companies want to believe they have created a circumvention technology that connects people directly to one another without any gates, walls, or barriers. Yet

this connectivity has also allowed some of the worst people in this world to find one another, get organized, and use these same platforms to harass and silence others.[28]

One of the most explicit and horrific uses of social media to amplify and "advertise" a violent white supremacist message was the series of attacks on mosques in Christchurch, New Zealand, in March 2019. In two consecutive shootings that killed fifty-one people, an Australian white supremacist attacked two Islamic centers; the first of these he posted online and live-streamed on Facebook Live. Shortly before the attacks, he wrote, "Well lads, it's time to stop shitposting and time to make a real life effort post," and then beseeched his readers to forward this post virally to others: "Please do your part by spreading my message, making memes and shitposting as you usually do."[29] Apparently, his request found an eager audience of white supremacists, Islamophobes, and other sympathizers across the globe, as some 1.5 million copies of the video were uploaded to Facebook within twenty-four hours. YouTube later reported that the mass uploading was "unprecedented both in scale and speed—at times as fast as a new upload every second."[30]

Immediately before the attacks, the shooter also emailed a large, intensely Islamophobic, and virulently racist manifesto to over thirty recipients, including New Zealand's prime minister and numerous media outlets, while also circulating it on Twitter. Among other things, the manifesto praised President Donald Trump as a "symbol of renewed white identity and common purpose" (though not, apparently, as a "policy maker and leader"),[31] linking the attacks explicitly with similar white supremacist movements now spreading across the US and Europe.

Meanwhile, President Trump has not only failed repeatedly to condemn white supremacists but has even retweeted many of the memes circulating in these extremist networks, creating a weird sort of feedback loop between the White House and those on the far-right fringe.[32] As the political scientist Peter W. Singer notes, "White supremacy has moved [from anonymous message boards] into broader Internet culture and American politics. . . . The things being voiced on these anonymous message boards have also been voiced by the President of the U.S., who is simultaneously the most powerful social media figure in the world."[33]

In the Christchurch attacks, we can clearly see the power of concealment and disclosure operating simultaneously, as the underground ideology of white supremacist terror is circulated in real time to a massive global audience. This is perhaps one of the most striking illustrations of

Guy Debord's key insight into the weird logic of late capitalist consumer society, in which the power of secrecy as domination goes hand in hand with the dominating power of the spectacle. Secrecy and the spectacle are ironically intertwined in the contemporary world, as two sides of the same coin, the invisible and visible aspects of power, as the covert operations of underground networks are often just the invisible underbelly of overt displays of spectacular violence: "Generalised secrecy stands behind the spectacle, as the decisive complement of all it displays and, in the last analysis, as its most vital operation."[34] This is also a disturbing example of what Don DeLillo called the link between "Fame and secrecy" as "the high and low ends of the same fascination, the static crackle of some libidinous thing in the world"[35]—that is, the complex connection between highly secretive terrorist groups and their obvious thirst for global attention and recognition, which we see everywhere from the Silent Brotherhood to Aum Shinrikyo, ISIS, and more recent groups such as Atomwaffen, among myriad others.[36]

Total Information Awareness:
Secrecy, Surveillance, and the Modern State of Exception

If the power of secrecy now wielded by religious extremists is alarming, the powers of surveillance now wielded by modern states in the name of combating terrorism is surely at least if not far more disturbing. In the wake of 9/11 and similar attacks in the UK, France, and elsewhere, many nations have adopted increasingly invasive new forms of surveillance, data mining, and curtailing of civil liberties that might have seemed not only shocking but unimaginable just a decade before. At the same time, as perhaps the ironic inverse of the increased transparency of the public, many government agencies have become increasingly opaque, with ever more secrecy and ever less public scrutiny of the workings of political power.

None of this current obsession with secrecy is entirely new, of course. As Foucault points out, the "problem of the secret" has been central to the development of the modern state since at least the sixteenth and seventeenth centuries, as the *arcana imperii* (imperial secrets) became integral to the *raison d'État* (reason of the state): "the knowledge that the state must develop of itself ... would be in danger of losing some of its effects and not having its expected consequences if everyone were to know what was going on. In particular, the state's enemies and rivals must not know the real resources available in terms of men, wealth, and so on, hence the need for secrecy."[37] In many ways, one might even argue that "secrecy lies at the core of modern political thought,"[38] insofar as the control of knowledge has become one of the most important resources of all modern nation-states, one of the primary means by which one political formation defines itself against another, and so also one of the most intensely sought commodities in rivalries between competing geopolitical powers. Just as the modern state is based on a claim to the "monopoly on violence," it is also typically based on a claim to the "monopoly on secrecy" or control over the flow and restriction of valued information.[39]

In short, if secrecy lies close to the heart of religion, it lies in no less intimate proximity to the heart of the modern state—and perhaps for good historical reasons. In 1922, the German political philosopher, Carl Schmitt, made the now-famous observation that the modern state is underpinned in many ways by older theological ideas. The theological concept of an all-powerful, divine being, he argued, was largely secularized and transferred to the ideal of an all-powerful lawgiver or sovereign. At the same time, the theological concept of the miracle—as a temporary suspension of natural law—was transferred to the modern political idea of the *exception*, as a temporary suspension of secular law:

> All significant concepts of the modern state are secularized theological concepts not only because of their historical development—in which they were transferred from theology to the theory of the state, whereby, for example, the omnipotent god became the omnipotent lawgiver—but also because of their systematic structure.... The exception in jurisprudence is analogous to the miracle in theology. Only by awareness of this analogy can we appreciate the manner in which the philosophical ideas of the state developed in the last centuries.[40]

The political sovereign, for Schmitt, is precisely the one who has the power to decide on a "state of exception" or a necessary suspension of normal law and order, in the same way that, in a theological understanding, the divine being is precisely the one who can suspend the normal laws of the universe.

Many have noted that Schmitt's idea of the "state of exception" seems particularly relevant in the wake of 9/11 and other terrorist attacks across the globe.[41] As Shoshana Zuboff suggests in *The Age of Surveillance Capitalism*, the events of 9/11 were used to claim a quite radical state of exception that justified both a seemingly endless "war on terror" and a rapid acceleration of surveillance technologies that quickly exceeded most previous legal and constitutional limits:

The 9/11 terrorist attacks thrust the intelligence community into an unfamiliar demand curve that insisted on exponential increases in velocity. ... [T]he agencies sought methods of deployment that could rapidly bypass legal and bureaucratic restrictions. In this environment of trauma and anxiety, a "state of exception" was invoked to legitimate a new imperative: speed at any cost.[42]

Other scholars such as David Lyon describe this state of exception in even starker terms, as something that is more reminiscent of Orwell than of most ideals of democratic society: "What 9/11 did was to produce socially negative consequences that hitherto were the stuff of repressive regimes and dystopian novels.... The suspension of normal conditions is justified with reference to the 'war on terrorism.'"[43]

If Schmitt is correct that modern theories of the state are in many ways secularized theological concepts, then it stands to reason that many aspects of secrecy and surveillance in the modern state might also have implicit theological underpinnings. Taking Schmitt a step further, we might say that "conceptions of the modern surveillance state are secularized theological concepts" and perhaps even that "the omniscient god has become the omniscient power of government surveillance."

At first, this might seem like a sort of hyperbolic or simply rhetorical assertion, were it not that US intelligence agencies have often claimed such omniscient power, in some cases imagined in almost godlike terms. Perhaps the most astonishing assertion of the divine power of surveillance in the post–9/11 era was the creation of the program called Total Information Awareness (TIA) under the Defense Advanced Research Projects Agency (DARPA) in 2002. The ambitious goal of the program was to integrate components from a wide range of both existing and newly created intelligence-gathering programs (such Genoa, Genoa II, Genisys, SSNA, EELD, WAE, TIDES, and others), combined with new data-mining technologies from the private sector, to create a vastly more powerful system of global surveillance. According to historian James Bamford, the TIA program "would permit intelligence analysts and law enforcement officials to mount a vast dragnet through electronic transaction data ranging from credit card information to veterinary records, in the United States and internationally."[44] Even apart from its Big-Brotherly scale and power, the TIA generated public outrage with its official seal—a truly remarkable image that featured the eye in the pyramid from the back of the dollar bill casting its godlike gaze over the entire planet, accompanied by the Latin phrase *Scientia est potentia* (fig. 7.2). Indeed, many wondered if those at DARPA had not perhaps been reading Foucault and putting

FIGURE 7.2. Information Awareness Office logo, Defense Advanced Research Project Agency.

some of his ideas of the panopticon rather unironically into practice. The Masonic origins of the eye in the pyramid were also not lost on many viewers, and it seemed to even the most sober legal scholars that the all-seeing eye of God on the back of the dollar bill had been transferred fairly seamlessly to the "all-seeing technological eye" of the state.[45]

This image and the vast scope of the program were so shocking that TIA was defunded by Congress in 2003 and ostensibly ended. However, according to analysts such as Bamford, the data-mining project was not so much dismantled as simply farmed out to other entities and continued in less offensive guises.[46] Many believe that the core architecture of the program has continued under more modest titles such as "Basketball" and "Topsail," while the legacy of TIA is quietly thriving at the NSA.[47]

This seemingly divine power of surveillance wielded by the NSA and other agencies has been the subject both of academic discussion and— perhaps more effectively—of satire, most famously in an episode of the American animated series *South Park* in 2013.[48] In *South Park*'s merciless yet incisive narrative, the power of the NSA has become so pervasive that the character Butters actually begins to see it as evidence of modern divinity. Not only does he pray to the government before bed, but he even confesses his sins to a clerk at the Department of Motor Vehicles, effectively fashioning a new kind of religion around the ideal of an omnipotent and omniscient bureaucracy. Finally, during a tour of the NSA headquarters, Butters is given unique insight into the secret of the agency's awesome powers of surveillance: it is the all-knowing gaze of Santa Claus, now attached to massive servers. As Matthew Patolsky aptly summarizes the *South Park* episode and its insight into modern surveillance, "Nothing but the divine, it would seem, the absolute subject from whom no human quality is concealed, whether naughty or nice, can adequately capture the work of secrecy in the age of big data."[49]

South Park's image of the godlike Surveillance State may be satirical and driven to the point of absurdity, but the issues it raises are very real ones that have been taken up by more serious scholars, as well. As Simon Chesterman observes in his study of surveillance in modern America, the phrase "under God" was first added to the "one Nation" in the US Pledge of Allegiance in 1954, and was clearly part of a Cold War context in which God-fearing Americans sought to distinguish themselves from the atheist Soviets. Today, long after the end of the Cold War, but now in the context of a seemingly endless war on terrorism, we have been perhaps transformed into "One Nation Under Surveillance," in which the liberty promised in the pledge has been increasingly replaced by the demands of national security: "The Cold War era motto of the US Air Force's 9th Reconnaissance Wing was 'In God we trust, all others we monitor.' That dictum might now be applied to the [intelligence] agencies themselves."[50]

While government entities such as Total Information Awareness have claimed a kind of godlike power of omniscience and all-seeing surveillance, it is becoming increasingly clear that perhaps an even more insidious power of surveillance lies in the private sector. Rather than a singular, monolithic, governmental Big Brother wielding the power of the panopticon, we now live in a far more decentralized information economy, in which surveillance is wielded as much by Facebook and Google as by the NSA or DARPA, and our activities are tracked less as potential terrorists than as potential consumers and ad revenue. As David Lyon argues in *Surveillance Society*, the larger process of privatization initiated during the Reagan era also led to surveillance technologies being turned over to the private sector and transformed into hugely lucrative businesses:

> Until the 1990s—consistently with *Nineteen Eighty-Four*—it was still assumed that the greatest dangers of computerized surveillance lay in the

augmented power of the nation state, with the capitalist corporation as a decidedly secondary source of risk. But it was also a period in which the policies of Reagan and Thatcher became dominant. Many state functions and utilities were sold off to become big businesses in the private sector. ... It also meant that personal data moved between sectors as some services previously offered by national or state governments were devolved to commercial interests. At the same time, database marketing encouraged a mushrooming of trade in personal data.[51]

Today, private commercial and advertising services track much of our daily activities—"what we read, listen to, and look at; where we travel to, shop and dine; and with whom we speak or associate"[52]—and they do so for the most part with our willing consent. "The idolatrous dream of omniperception embodied in the panopticon is present in contemporary surveillance," Lyon concludes;[53] but today, "no one agency is behind this focused attention on our daily lives. Modernist centralized panoptic control is not so much in question as polycentric networks of surveillance, within which personal data flow fairly freely."[54] These networks are also enormously profitable, as Facebook and others now find their primary revenue stream in commodifying and selling the private data of their users. Hence, some describe the current system as a form of "surveillance capitalism," in which human experience itself becomes the primary resource to be mined, packaged, and traded.[55]

However, these seemingly "private" and for-profit entities such as Facebook, Google, and others are themselves not disentangled from the complex web of surveillance that it is the modern military-industrial-information complex. Particularly in the wake of 9/11 and the "state of exception" created by the global war on terror, agencies such as the NSA and CIA began to seek active cooperation with the big corporations, many of which had more sophisticated technologies of surveillance than the government itself: "Google and other businesses stepped into this state of exception with new methods of data-accumulation," as Zuboff notes; and, at the same time, government agencies began to actively imitate and adopt the methods of the multinational technology giants: "In the decade that followed 9/11 surveillance exceptionalism was also expressed in the flattery of imitation, as the NSA tried to become more like Google, emulating and internalizing Google's capabilities."[56] Today, for-profit search engines and social media platforms do not operate independently of the government's all-seeing eye but are also deeply intertwined with the military-industrial complex, often serving as some of the most powerful lenses in the all-seeing eye in the pyramid, through which DARPA, the NSA, and other entities keep watch over all of us today. As Yasha Levine argues in his study of this interlocking government-corporate symbiosis, a company such as Google is now practically

> a full-fledged military contractor, selling versions of consumer data mining and analysis technology to police departments, city governments, and just about every major US intelligence and military agency. Over the years, it had supplied mapping technology used by the US Army in Iraq, hosted data for the Central Intelligence Agency, indexed the National Security Agency's vast intelligence databases, built military robots, co-launched a spy satellite with the Pentagon, and leased its cloud computing platform to help police departments predict crime. And Google is not alone. From Amazon to eBay to Facebook—most of the Internet companies we use every day have also grown into powerful corporations that track and profile their users while pursuing partnerships and business relationships with major US military and intelligence agencies. Some parts of these companies are so thoroughly intertwined with America's security services that it is hard to tell where they end and the US government begins.[57]

If the Total Information Awareness network were still to "officially" exist today, its logo would need to be significantly redesigned. Rather than a singular eye gazing in panopticon fashion over the earth, it might look more like a vast, decentralized network of tiny eyes peering through every laptop and smartphone around the globe, working in most cases with the active participation of the consumers holding them—and thereby perhaps coming much closer to "the idolatrous dream of omniperception."

"Privacy Is Dead, Get over It," but Secrecy Is Alive and Well

The growing power of surveillance in the twenty-first century raises profound questions not simply about religious freedom, terrorism, and security but also about basic issues of privacy. How far, exactly, can state and corporate surveillance penetrate into our daily lives and activities? Are some religious groups in need of even *greater* surveillance because of possible links to extremism (as the NYPD has argued in its surveillance of mosques in New York City, and as many have argued in the case of far-right white supremacist groups in the US)? Or, conversely, are some groups in need of much greater *protection* from surveillance, which could arguably interfere with their rights to free exercise of religion?[58] As sociologist Tahseen Shams argues, the intense surveillance of Muslim Americans after 9/11 has not only affected their ability to practice their faith but also fundamentally altered these communities:

> The post–9/11 terror-panic climate has irrevocably transformed Muslims from a relatively invisible minority in America to hypervisible suspects of terrorism.... [T]he U.S. government has run heightened surveillance programs specifically targeting Muslim immigrants.... [F]rom 2001 to 2013, the New York Police Department and the Central Intelligence Agency — both state agencies with a history of aggressively spying on domestic political dissidents — maintained a secret surveillance program on Muslim communities in New York that monitored and analyzed their everyday lives.... The increased surveillance of Muslims has helped create a climate of insecurity, fear, and suspicion that still organizes Muslim Americans' community life in many ways.[59]

Like secrecy, privacy is by no means a simple, static, or singular thing. On the contrary, as Sarah E. Igo has shown in her thorough genealogy of privacy in modern America, this is an extremely fluid and shifting concept that has been transformed and redefined continuously over the last two hundred years.[60] While privacy and secrecy have each been defined in various ways, perhaps one of the most useful distinctions is suggested by Carol Warren and Barbara Laslett, who argue that "Privacy is consensual where secrecy is not."[61] Privacy is generally understood to refer to information and acts that are considered to be morally and legally neutral (e.g., consensual sex with one's married partner or attendance of a "mainstream" religious organization), whereas secrecy refers to information or acts that are perceived to be morally or legally suspect (e.g., engagement in sexual acts that are criminalized in a given society or affiliation with a group labeled a "terrorist" organization). Moreover, secrecy tends to be surrounded with sanctions for the disclosure of valued information (e.g, Edward Snowden's leaking of classified intelligence from the NSA, including global surveillance programs).

In the age of surveillance capitalism and the complex intertwining of the NSA, the CIA, Google, and Facebook, privacy seems to be an increasingly endangered species. As Scott McNealy, CEO of Sun Microsystems, infamously put it, "Privacy is dead. Get over it."[62] Beneath the all-seeing gaze of government agencies and the even more insidious tracking of social media and search engines — much of which consumers happily and/ or unknowingly accept — it seems to many that the very idea of privacy is at best a naïve anachronism. As Igo summarizes this pervasive attitude,

By the early twenty-first century, privacy was finished, many said. . . . Experts in a wide range of fields, including technology, business, law, media, and behavioral science, subscribed to this view. Privacy was quaint, outmoded, or dead, the victim of a relentlessly knowing society's practices of governing, selling, reporting, and discovering—coupled with the citizenry's willingness to go along.[63]

Of course, sweeping pronouncements that "privacy is dead" are probably somewhat premature. Some would even argue that demands for privacy have become more vocal than ever in the twenty-first century, as many of the same technologies that enable mass surveillance also provide new means of evasion of scrutiny through data encryption, hidden or onion services, and other measures.[64] As Foucault famously observed, "Silence and secrecy are a shelter for power, anchoring its prohibitions; but they also loosen its holds and provide for relatively obscure areas of tolerance."[65] Nonetheless, it seems clear that more and more of our private lives are subject to the widening gaze of both governmental and corporate entities, for a complex mix of both security and commercial interests.

While privacy may be severely weakened, even if not quite yet deceased, *secrecy* is a different matter altogether, especially for governments and large corporations. More than one critic has observed that there seems to be almost an inverse relation between individual privacy and government and corporate secrecy. Even as the former grows smaller, the latter has expanded exponentially, to the point where some wonder whether the ideals of individual privacy and governmental transparency have not been inverted entirely. As legal scholar David Cole pointedly comments, "In 1956, at the height of McCarthyism in the U.S., sociologist Edward Shils wrote that liberal democracy demands confidentiality for its citizens and transparency for government. Today, it is the citizenry that is increasingly transparent while government operations are shrouded in secrecy."[66] Particularly in the US after 9/11, a number of increasingly invasive laws were enacted that seem to many critics to fundamentally undermine the ideals of citizen's privacy and government transparency. Among the most controversial of these was the ironically titled USA PATRIOT Act, which was hurriedly passed into law after 9/11. Among other things, the PATRIOT Act gave the attorney general unprecedented power to detain noncitizens indefinitely; it allowed the FBI to search citizens' homes or offices and conduct electronic surveillance of phone and Internet use, without proving probable cause; and it gave government agencies the authority to conduct so-called sneak-and-peek searches, that is, to search our homes or offices without even letting us know they've been there (though this last provision was ruled unconstitutional by a federal judge in Oregon in 2007).[67] As Elaine Scarry argues, this and other legislation profoundly invert the idea that the state should be transparent and our lives be protected from unwarranted surveillance:

> The double requirement — that people's lives be private and government actions be public — is turned inside out by the Patriot Act. The inner lives of people are made involuntarily transparent by provisions that increase the ability of federal officers of the executive branch to enter and search a person's house (section 213), to survey private medical records, business records, library records, and educational records (sections 203, 215, 218, 219, 358, 507, 508), and to monitor telephone, e-mail, and Internet use (section 216). Simultaneously, the Patriot Act obscures executive-branch actions, hiding those actions from the population and from the legislative and judicial branches, and doing so before, during, and after the executive actions are carried out.[68]

The USA PATRIOT Act is, of course, only one example of the rapid expansion of government surveillance and the erosion of privacy within the US. Other, often far more alarming new forms of surveillance have included the NSA's program of warrantless wiretapping between 2002 and 2007 and the massive global surveillance of millions of phone, email, and social media accounts revealed by Edward Snowden and others.[69] In the words of Glenn Greenwald, the journalist who first met with and reported on Snowden, "The archive of documents Edward Snowden had assembled was stunning in both size and scope. Even as someone who had spent years writing about the dangers of secret US surveillance, I found the sheer vastness of the spying systems genuinely shocking, all the more so because it had been implemented with virtually no accountability, no transparency, and no limits. The thousands of discrete surveillance programs described by the archive were never intended . . . to become public knowledge."[70] Similar expansions of secrecy and surveillance have occurred in the UK, Canada, Australia, most EU nations, and around the world — often coordinated closely with the US and often working hand in hand with the private sector.[71]

When Canetti wrote in 1960 that "it is only today that we fully realize how dangerous secrecy can become," he was referring primarily to the secrets of nuclear weapons in the context of the Cold War. Today, the dangers of secrecy are less immediately apocalyptic but in some ways more pervasive, insidious, and intransigent. These include not only the dangers of white supremacists organizing secretly on 8-chan to plot physical violence, but governmental and corporate entities that reduce the very idea of privacy to a naïve anachronism while expanding the powers of secrecy to levels never dreamed of even by the most esoteric religious order.

The task of the critical history of religions in the twenty-first century is therefore at least twofold. Not only is our challenge to critically examine religion itself—to scrutinize, in Bruce Lincoln's words, "the temporal, contextual, situated, interested, human, and material dimensions of those discourses, practices, and institutions that characteristically represent themselves as eternal, transcendent, spiritual, and divine."[72] At the same time, and perhaps no less important, it is also to examine the state (and now also corporate) entities that surveil, regulate, censor, and in some cases criminalize religious groups, particularly those that stray outside the margins of "legitimate" religiosity (particularly Muslims, people of color, new or alternative religious movements, and those who express dissident political views). This task becomes even more urgent once we acknowledge that state and corporate powers of surveillance are expanding exponentially, even as citizens' and religious groups' claims to privacy appear to be dwindling rapidly, almost to the point of nonexistence or at least of inconsequentiality.[73]

If Bourdieu is correct that "there is no science but of the hidden," then there remains a great deal of work to be done.

Acknowledgments

There are a great many friends and colleagues who deserve thanks in helping me finally finish this text. These include my former mentors, Wendy Doniger and Bruce Lincoln; interlocutors and friendly critics such as Egil Asprem, Daniel Barbu, Michael Barkun, Damon Berry, Henrik Bogdan, David Brakke, Paul Courtright, April DeConick, Gordon Djurdjevic, Cathy Gutierrez, Glen Hayes, Greg Johnson, Jason Josephson-Storm, Paul C. Johnson, Sarah Iles Johnston, Eliza Kent, Jeffrey Kripal, Wouter Hanegraaff, Nick Meylan, Rebecca Moore, Marco Pasi, Matthew Potolsky, Greg Spinner, Kocku von Stuckrad, Bruce Sullivan, Arthur Versluis, Steven Wasserstrom, and Catherine Wessinger; and my editors at the University of Chicago Press, Alan Thomas and Kyle Wagner.

Last and by no means least, I would like to thank my soulmate and life partner, Nancy; my amazing and endlessly surprising daughter, Maya; and my best friend (canine or otherwise), Shiva; who have all exhibited remarkable patience as I have undertaken yet another annoying academic book.

Notes

Preface

1. William Blake, "A Divine Image," in *The Poetical Works of William Blake*, ed. John Sampson (New York: Oxford University Press, 1913), 106.

2. The main publications in which I have addressed the problem of religious secrecy include "The Torment of Secrecy: Ethical and Epistemological Problems in the Study of Esoteric Traditions," *History of Religions* 37, no. 3 (1998): 209–48; "Elitism and Esotericism: Strategies of Secrecy and Power in South Indian Tantra and French Freemasonry," *Numen* 44 (1997): 1–38; *Tantra: Sex, Secrecy, Politics and Power in the Study of Religion* (Berkeley: University of California Press, 2003); *Magia Sexualis: Sex, Magic and Liberation in Modern Western Esotericism* (Berkeley: University of California Press, 2005); "Fair Game: Secrecy, Security and the Church of Scientology in Cold War America," *Journal of the American Academy of Religion* 74, no. 2 (2006): 356–89; *The Secrets of the Kingdom: Religion and Concealment in the Bush Administration* (Lanham, MD: Rowman and Littlefield, 2006); "Secrecy in New Religious Movements: Concealment, Surveillance, and Privacy in a New Age of Information," *Religion Compass* 2, no. 1 (2008): 66–83; *The Church of Scientology: A History of a New Religion* (Princeton, NJ: Princeton University Press, 2010); "Disclosure," in *Vocabulary for the Study of Religion*, ed. Kocku von Stuckrad (Leiden: Brill, 2016); "Esotericism Socialized: Esoteric Communities," in *Secret Religion: Gnosticism, Esotericism, and Mysticism*, ed. April DeConick (New York: Macmillan, 2016).

Introduction

1. Sisella Bok, *Secrets: On the Ethics of Concealment and Revelation* (New York: Pantheon, 1983), 6.

2. Guy Debord, *Comments on the Society of the Spectacle* (London: Verso, 1990), 60.

3. There is a now a large body of literature on the issues of secrecy, privacy, surveillance, and national security. See David Lyon, *Surveillance after September 11* (Cambridge: Polity, 2003); David Cole and James X. Dempsey, *Terrorism and the Constitution: Sacrificing Civil Liberties in the Name of National Security* (New York: New Press, 2006); David Cole and Federico Fabrinni, eds., *Secrecy, National Security and the Vindication of Constitutional Law* (Cheltenham, UK: Edward Elgar, 2013); Ronald Gold-

farb, ed., *After Snowden: Privacy, Secrecy and Security in the Information Age* (New York: Thomas Dunne, 2015); Shoshana Zuboff, *The Age of Surveillance Capitalism: The Fight for a Human Future at the New Frontier of Power* (Cambridge: Polity, 2019); Simon Chesterman, *One Nation under Surveillance: A New Social Contract to Defend Freedom without Sacrificing Liberty* (New York: Oxford University Press, 2013).

4. Gilbert Herdt, *Secrecy and Cultural Reality: Utopian Ideologies of the New Guinea Men's House* (Ann Arbor: University of Michigan Press, 2003), xiii.

5. James Bamford, *The Shadow Factory: The NSA from 9/11 to the Eavesdropping on America* (New York: Anchor, 2009), 100, 244, 324–25, 377. See also James Bamford, *Body of Secrets: Anatomy of the Ultra Secrecy National Security Agency* (New York: Anchor, 2002).

6. See Michael D. Shear, Steve Eder, and Patricia Cohen, "Donald Trump's Taxes: What We Know and Don't Know," *New York Times*, March 15, 2017, https://www.nytimes.com/interactive/2016/us/politics/donald-trump-taxes-explained.html; Matthew Rosenberg, Nicholas Confessore, and Carole Cadwalladr, "How Trump Consultants Exploited the Facebook Data of Millions," *New York Times*, March 17, 2018, https://www.nytimes.com/2018/03/17/us/politics/cambridge-analytica-trump-campaign.html; Editorial Board, "Trump Administration Unfurls a Veil of Secrecy," *USA Today*, March 9, 2018, https://www.usatoday.com/story/opinion/2018/03/09/trump-administration-unfurls-veil-secrecy-sunshine-week/407900002/.

7. Debord, *Comments*, 12. See Eric Alterman, *When Presidents Lie: A History of Official Deception and Its Consequences* (New York: Viking, 2004), 294; Urban, *Secrets of the Kingdom*.

8. Charles Barbour, *Derrida's Secret: Perjury, Testimony, Oath* (Edinburgh: Edinburgh University Press, 2017), back cover.

9. Rudolph Otto, *The Idea of the Holy* (New York: Oxford University Press, 1958), 13. See Bok, *Secrets*, 6.

10. Michael Taussig, "Transgression," in *Critical Terms for Religious Studies*, ed. Mark C. Taylor (Chicago: University of Chicago Press, 1998), 356. See also Jeffrey J. Kripal, *Roads of Excess, Palaces of Wisdom: Reflexivity and Eroticism in the Study of Mysticism* (Chicago: University of Chicago Press, 2001), xi–xiii.

11. Paul C. Johnson, *Secrets, Gossip and Gods: The Transformation of Brazilian Candomblé* (New York: Oxford University Press, 2005), 3. See Kripal, *Roads of Excess*, xii.

12. See Georg Simmel, "The Sociology of Secrecy and Secret Societies," *Journal of American Sociology* 11, no. 4 (1906): 441–98, reprinted in *The Sociology of Georg Simmel*, ed. Kurt Wolff (New York: Free Press, 1950); Stanton Tefft, ed., *Secrecy: A Cross-Cultural Perspective* (New York: Human Sciences Press, 1980); Stanton Tefft, *The Dialectics of Secret Society Power in States* (Atlantic Highlands, NJ: Humanities Press, 1992).

13. Beryl Bellman, *The Language of Secrecy: Symbols and Metaphors in Poro Ritual* (New Brunswick, NJ: Rutgers University Press, 1984); Herdt, *Secrecy and Cultural Reality*; Johnson, *Secrets, Gossip and Gods*; Ian Keen, *Knowledge and Secrecy in an Aboriginal Religion* (New York: Oxford University Press, 1998).

14. Antoine Faivre, *Access to Western Esotericism* (Albany: SUNY Press, 1994); Nicholas Goodrick-Clarke, *The Western Esoteric Traditions: A Historical Introduction* (New York: Oxford University Press, 2008); Wouter Hanegraaff, *New Age Religion and Western Culture: Esotericism in the Mirror of Secular Thought* (Albany: SUNY Press, 1997); Urban, *Magia Sexualis*.

NOTES TO PAGES 3–6 211

15. The better, more critical studies of secrecy include Johnson, *Secrets, Gossip and Gods*; Kripal, *Roads of Excess*; Urban, "Torment of Secrecy"; Hans G. Kippenberg and Guy G. Stroumsa, eds., *Secrecy and Concealment: Studies in the History of Mediterranean and Near Eastern Religions* (Leiden: Brill, 1995); Elliot R. Wolfson, ed., *Rending the Veil: Concealment and Secrecy in the History of Religions* (New York: Seven Bridges Press, 1999); Albert de Jong, "Secrets and Secrecy in the Study of Religion: Comparative Views from the Ancient World," in *The Culture of Secrecy in Japanese Religions*, ed. Bernard Scheid and Mark Teeuwen (London: Routledge, 2006), 17–59; Clark Chilson, *Secrecy's Power: Covert Shin Buddhists in Japan and Contradictions of Concealment* (Honolulu: University of Hawai'i Press, 2014); April D. DeConick, ed., *Secret Religion* (New York: Macmillan, 2016).

16. Kees Bolle, ed., *Secrecy in Religions* (New York: Brill, 1987), 2–3.

17. There are, of course, many ways of defining "religion," none of which is perfect or complete. In this book, I largely follow Bruce Lincoln's more flexible and polythetic definition, which has four basic parts: "1) *A discourse whose concerns transcend the human, temporal, and contingent, and that claims for itself a similarly transcendent status.* . . . 2) *A set of practices whose goal is to produce a proper world and/or proper human subjects.* . . . 3) *A community whose members construct their identity with reference to a religious discourse.* . . . 4) *An institution that regulates discourses, practices and community, reproducing them over time and modifying them as necessary.*" See Bruce Lincoln, *Holy Terrors: Thinking about Religion after September 11* (Chicago: University of Chicago Press, 2006), 5–7.

18. On the concept of genealogy as a historical method, see Michel Foucault, "Nietzsche, Genealogy, History," in *Language, Counter-memory, Practice*, ed. Donald F. Bouchard (Ithaca, NY: Cornell University Press, 1977), 139–64; Talal Asad, *Genealogies of Religion: Discipline and Reasons of Power in Christianity and Islam* (Baltimore: Johns Hopkins University Press, 1993).

19. See Goodrick-Clarke, *Western Esoteric Traditions*; Urban, *Magia Sexualis*; Christopher Partridge, *The Re-enchantment of the West*, vol. 1, *Alternative Spiritualities, Sacralization, Popular Culture and Occulture* (London: T & T Clark, 2005).

20. Bruce Lincoln, "Theses on Method," *Method and Theory in the Study of Religion* 8 (1996): 225–27.

21. Daniel Jütte, *The Age of Secrecy: Jews, Christians, and the Economy of Secrets, 1400–1800* (New Haven, CT: Yale University Press, 2015), vii–viii: "No other period in European history, neither before nor since, has shown so profound a fascination with secrecy and secret sciences. Arcane knowledge was widely considered positive knowledge, and this notion of 'good secrecy' extended across all fields of life."

22. Jütte, *Age of Secrecy*, 252.

23. Jason A. Josephson-Storm, *The Myth of Disenchantment: Magic, Morality, and the Birth of the Human Sciences* (Chicago: University of Chicago Press, 2017), 37. See also Partridge, *Re-enchantment of the West*; Jeffrey Kripal, *Authors of the Impossible: The Paranormal and the Sacred* (Chicago: University of Chicago Press, 2011), 16; Egil Asprem, *The Problem of Disenchantment: Scientific Naturalism and Esoteric Discourse, 1900–1939* (Albany: SUNY Press, 2018).

24. Wouter Hanegraaff, *Esotericism and the Academy: Rejected Knowledge in Western Culture* (New York: Columbia University Press, 2014), 219. See also Joshua Gunn, *Modern Occult Rhetoric: Mass Media and the Drama of Secrecy in the Twentieth Century* (Tuscaloosa: University of Alabama Press, 2011).

25. Tessel M. Bauduin, Victoria Ferentinou, and Daniel Zamani, eds., *Surrealism, Occultism and Politics: In Search of the Marvellous* (London: Routledge, 2018), 3. See Alex Owen, *The Place of Enchantment: British Occultism and the Culture of the Modern* (Chicago: University of Chicago Press, 2004).

26. R. Lawrence Moore, *Selling God: American Religion in the Marketplace of Culture* (New York: Oxford University Press, 1994), 6. Many other historians and sociologists have made similar arguments about the links between American religions and the marketplace; see Charles Grier Sellers, *The Market Revolution: Jacksonian American, 1815–1846* (New York: Oxford University Press, 1991); Roger Finke, "Supply Side Explanations for Religious Change," in *Rational Choice Theory and Religion: Summary and Assessment*, ed. Lawrence A. Young (New York: Routledge, 1997); Mark A. Noll, *God and Mammon: Protestants, Money and the Market, 1790–1860* (New York: Oxford University Press, 2001); Stewart Davenport, *Friends of Unrighteous Mammon: Northern Christians and Market Capitalism, 1815–1860* (Chicago: University of Chicago Press, 2008); Jan Stievermann, Daniel Silliman, and Philip Goff, eds., *Religion and the Marketplace in the United States* (New York: Oxford University Press, 2015).

27. Kenneth Ames, "The Lure of the Spectacular," in *Theatre of the Fraternity: Staging the Ritual Space of the Scottish Rite Freemasonry, 1896–1929*, ed. C. Lance Brockman (Jackson: University Press of Mississippi, 1996), 19.

28. Charles Heckethorn, *The Secret Societies of all Ages and Countries* (London: Richard Bentley and Son, 1875), 1:xvii; see Giovanni De Castro, *Il Mondo Secreto* (Milano: G. Daelli, 1864). The specific phrase "secret society" seems to have first appeared in the English language in Sir Walter Scott's novel, *Anne of Geierstein, or The Maiden of the Mist* (Edinburgh: Cadell, 1829), 3:80.

29. See Partridge, *Re-enchantment of the West*; Urban, "Esotericism Socialized."

30. Angus Mackenzie, *Secrets: The CIA's War at Home* (Berkeley: University of California Press, 1997), 201. See also Richard O. Curry, ed., *Freedom at Risk: Secrecy, Censorship and Repression in the 1980s* (Philadelphia: Temple University Press, 1988), 8; Athan G. Theoharis, ed., *A Culture of Secrecy: The Government vs. The People's Right to Know* (Lawrence: University Press of Kansas, 1998).

31. See Urban, *Secrets of the Kingdom*, 12–15; Matthew Potolsky, *The National Security Sublime: On the Aesthetics of Government Secrecy* (New York: Routledge, 2015), 2. See also Sarah E. Igo, *The Known Citizen: A History of Privacy in Modern America* (Cambridge, MA: Harvard University Press, 2018), 100: "The 'culture of secrecy' that developed on both sides of the superpower divide altered the relationship of the U.S. government to its own people. Although the state kept more secrets in this era than in the past—cloaking a range of national security actions . . .—it increasingly distrusted them in its citizens."

32. Philip H. Melanson, *Secrecy Wars: National Security, Privacy and the Public's Right to Know* (Washington, DC: Brassey's, 2001), 2–3.

33. See Zuboff, *Surveillance Capitalism*, 115. See Giorgio Agamben, *State of Exception* (Chicago: University of Chicago Press, 2005).

34. See Barbour, *Derrida's Secret*; Zuboff, *Surveillance Capitalism*; Chesterman, *One Nation under Surveillance*.

35. David Cole, "Preserving Privacy in a Digital Age: Lessons of Comparative Constitutionalism," in *Surveillance, Counter-Terrorism and Comparative Constitutionalism*, ed. Fergal Davis, Nicola McGarrity, and George Williams (London: Routledge, 2014), 97.

NOTES TO PAGES 8–9   213

36. On privacy vs. secrecy, see this book's conclusion and Carol Warren and Barbara Laslett, "Privacy and Secrecy: A Conceptual Comparison," *Journal of Social Issues* 33, no. 3 (1977): 43–51. On the history of privacy in the US, see Igo, *Known Citizen*.

37. In his study of Japanese Buddhism, Chilson outlines a somewhat similar typology, which distinguishes between "mystery," "esotericism," and "social secrecy" (*Secrecy's Power*, 46).

38. For useful genealogies of the term "mysticism," see Richard King, *Orientalism and Religion: Post-Colonial Theory, India, and the "Mystic East"* (New York: Routledge, 1999); Grace Jantzen, *Gender, Power, and Christian Mysticism* (Cambridge: Cambridge University Press, 1996). For other good discussions of the category of mysticism, see Bernard McGinn, *The Foundations of Mysticism: Origins to the Fifth Century* (New York: Herder and Herder, 2004), xv–xvii.

39. Louis Dupré, "Mysticism," in *Encyclopedia of Religion*, ed. Lindsay Jones (New York: Macmillan, 2005), 9:6341. See also Peter Moore, "Mysticism (Further Considerations)," in *Encyclopedia of Religion*, 9:6355: "the term mysticism relates to traditions affirming direct knowledge of or communion with the source or ground of ultimate reality, as variously experienced in visionary, ecstatic, contemplative, or unitive states of consciousness. . . . The profound transcendental experiences that empower mystics . . . are typically characterized by paradox: they are personal yet self-transcending, noetic while in some sense ineffable."

40. Michael Barkun, "Religion and Secrecy After 9/11," *Journal of the American Academy of Religion* 74, no. 2 (2006): 278. See also Michael Sells, *Mystical Languages of Unsaying* (Chicago: University of Chicago Press, 1994); McGinn, *Foundations*, xvii; Chilson, *Secrecy's Power*, 5: "In a mystical experience, a mystery may be revealed in part, but what is learned is ineffable and the mystics can never adequately convey to others a mystery revealed to them by the divine."

41. See Wouter J. Hanegraaff, *Western Esotericism: A Guide for the Perplexed* (New York: Bloomsbury, 2013), 3. The term *Esoterik* was first used in German in 1792, and *ésoterisme* was first used in French in 1828 by Jacques Matter in his *Histoire du Gnosticisme*. There is a great deal of literature now on Western Esotericism. See Antoine Faivre, *Access to Western Esotericism* (Albany: SUNY Press 1994); Wouter J. Hanegraaff, *Esotericism and the Academy: Rejected Knowledge in Western Culture* (Cambridge: Cambridge University Press, 2012); Nicholas Goodrick-Clarke, *The Western Esoteric Tradition: A Historical Introduction* (New York: Oxford University Press, 2008); Kocku von Stuckrad, *Western Esotericism: A Brief History of Secret Knowledge* (Durham: Acumen, 2005).

42. Hanegraaff, *Western Esotericism*, 15–16. See also Antoine Faivre, "Esotericism," in *Encyclopedia of Religion*, 4:2845. Faivre identifies four aspects of Western esotericism, namely: the idea of correspondences or hidden connections between all parts of the cosmos; a doctrine of living nature, in which the cosmos is seen as pervaded by a spiritual presence; the role of imagination and mediations or the use of symbols to interact with intermediary spiritual beings; and the experience of transmutation or the transformation of the self through illuminated knowledge.

There is some debate as to whether esotericism is essentially a Western phenomenon or whether there are also Eastern esoteric traditions, or whether the whole East-West binary is itself problematic. See Kennet Granholm, "Locating the West: Problematizing the *Western* in Western Esotericism," in *Occultism in a Global Perspective*, ed. Henrik Bogdan and Gordan Djurdjevic (New York: Routledge, 2014), 17–36; Gordan

Djurdjevic, *India and the Occult: The Influence of South Asian Spirituality on Modern Western Occultism* (New York: Palgrave Macmillan, 2014).

43. See Wouter J. Hanegraaff, "Occult/ Occultism," in *Dictionary of Gnosis and Western Esotericism*, ed. Wouter J. Hanegraaff (Leiden: Brill, 2006), 888. See also Christopher Partridge, ed., *The Occult World* (New York: Routledge, 2016). See, for example, the works of occultists such as Éliphas Lévi, *Transcendental Magic: Its Doctrine and Ritual* (New York: Cambridge University Press, 2011), 13: "Occult philosophy" is none other than "the nurse or god-mother of all intellectual forces, the key of all divine obscurities," which has long lain hidden "behind the veil of all the hieratic and mystical allegories of ancient doctrine, behind the shadows and the strange ordeals of all initiations, under the seal of all sacred writings."

44. Antoine Faivre, "What is Occultism?" in *Hidden Truths: Magic, Alchemy and the Occult*, ed. Lawrence Sullivan (New York: Macmillan, 1989), 7. See also Hanegraaff, *New Age Religion*, 423; Partridge, *Occult World*; Cathy Gutierrez, ed., *The Occult in Nineteenth Century America* (Aurora, CO: Davies Group, 2005).

45. Kippenberg and Stroumsa, *Secrecy and Concealment*, xiv; Chilson, *Secrecy's Power*, 5.

46. Bellman, *Language of Secrecy*, 144. See also Wolfson, *Rending the Veil*, 4.

47. Jacques Derrida, "How to Avoid Speaking: Denials," in *Languages of the Unsayable: The Play of Negativity in Literature and Literary Theory*, ed. Sanford Budick and Wolfgang Iser (New York: Columbia University Press, 1989), 25–26.

48. On mysticism, power, and authority, see King, *Orientalism*; Jantzen, *Power*.

49. See Michel Foucault, *Power/Knowledge: Selected Interviews and Other Writings, 1972–1977* (New York: Vintage, 1980); Michel Foucault, *The History of Sexuality*, vol. 1, *An Introduction* (New York: Vintage, 1990).

50. On this point, see Urban, *Economics of Ecstasy*; Sue Curry Jansen, *Censorship: The Knot that Binds Power and Knowledge* (New York: Oxford University Press, 1991).

51. On religious authority, see especially Bruce Lincoln, *Authority: Construction and Corrosion* (Chicago: University of Chicago Press, 1995), 112: "[R]eligious claims are the means by which certain objects, places, speakers and speech-acts are invested with an authority, the source of which lies *outside the human*. That is, these claims create the appearance that their authorization comes from a realm beyond history, society, and politics, beyond the terrain in which interested and situated actors struggle over scarce resources."

52. Pierre Bourdieu, *Language and Symbolic Power* (Cambridge, MA: Harvard University Press, 1984), 192. "Symbolic power—as a power of constituting the given through utterances, of making people see and believe, of confirming or transforming the vision of the world . . . an almost magical power which enables one to obtain the equivalent of what is obtained through force (whether physical or economic) . . .—is a power that can be exercised only if it is *recognized*, that is, misrecognized as arbitrary" (164). See also Pierre Bourdieu and Jean-Claude Passeron, *Reproduction in Education and Society* (London: Sage, 1977), 4; Hugh B. Urban, "Sacred Capital: Pierre Bourdieu and the Study of Religion," *Method and Theory in the Study of Religion* 15 (2003): 354–89.

53. Simmel, *Sociology of Georg Simmel*, 337.

54. Johnson, *Secrets, Gossip and Gods*, 3. Chilson similarly uses the term "secretizing" to describe "the presentation of something as secret whether or not something is actually concealed" (*Secrecy's Power*, 8).

NOTES TO PAGES 11–15   215

55. Johnson, *Secrets, Gossip and Gods*, 9.

56. Pierre Bourdieu, "Structures, Habitus, Power," in *Culture/Power/History*, ed. Nicholas B. Dirks, Geoff Eley, and Sherry B. Ortner (Princeton, NJ: Princeton University Press, 1994), 173.

57. Randall Johnson, introduction to Pierre Bourdieu, *The Field of Cultural Production* (New York: Columbia University Press, 1994), 7. See Pierre Bourdieu, "The Forms of Capital," in *Handbook of Theory and Research for the Sociology of Education*, ed. John G. Richardson (New York: Greenwood, 1986), 241–58.

58. David Swartz, *Culture and Power: The Sociology of Pierre Bourdieu* (Chicago: University of Chicago Press, 1997), 43.

59. Tanya Luhrmann, "The Magic of Secrecy," *Ethos* 17, no. 2 (1989): 161, 137.

60. See Urban, *Economics of Ecstasy* and "Torment of Secrecy." As Jütte puts it, "The economy of secrets is one part of a knowledge economy. It also reflects the commercial character of the trade in secrets. Secrets can become a commodity.... 'Economy of secrets,' then, refers to all activities that involve trading, offering, negotiating, delivering exchanging, and buying secrets" (*Age of Secrecy*, 2).

61. Lamont Lindstrom, *Knowledge and Power in a South Pacific Society* (Washington, DC: Smithsonian Institute, 1990), 119. See Keen, *Knowledge and Secrecy*.

62. Lindstrom, *Knowledge and Power*, xii–xiii.

63. See Timothy D. Lytton, *Holding Bishops Accountable: How Lawsuits Helped the Catholic Church Confront Clerical Sexual Abuse* (Cambridge, MA: Harvard University Press, 2008); Frédéric Martel, *In the Closet of the Vatican: Power, Homosexuality, Hypocrisy* (New York: Bloomsbury Continuum, 2019).

64. See Urban, *Church of Scientology*; Janet Reitman, *Inside Scientology: The Story of America's Most Secretive Religion* (New York: Houghton Mifflin Harcourt, 2011); Staff of the Tampa Bay Times, *The Truth Rundown: Stories of Violence, Intimidation and Control in the World of Scientology* (Tampa Bay, FL: Times, 2011).

65. Elias Canetti, *Crowds and Power* (New York: Farrar, Straus, and Giroux, 1984), 290.

66. Sun Tzu, *The Art of War: The New Illustrated Edition*, trans. Samuel B. Griffith (Toronto: Duncan Baird, 2012), 20.

67. See Lincoln, *Holy Terrors*, 8–16; Mark Juergesmeyer, *Terror in the Mind of God: The Global Rise of Religious Violence* (Berkeley: University of California Press, 2003).

68. Lincoln, *Holy Terrors*, 16–17.

69. See chapter 5. See also Damon T. Berry, *Blood and Faith: Christianity in American White Nationalism* (Syracuse, NY: Syracuse University Press, 2017), 119–25.

70. See Urban, "Torment of Secrecy."

71. Johnson, *Secrets, Gossip and Gods*, 19.

72. Umberto Eco, *Interpretation and Overinterpretation* (Cambridge: Cambridge University Press, 1992), 32.

73. See Urban, "Torment of Secrecy." On secrecy and intellectual property, see Urban, *Church of Scientology*, chap. 6.

74. Marcel Griaule's work on the Dogon is perhaps the most infamous and astonishing example of this imperialist attitude toward secret knowledge. See James Clifford's brilliant analysis in *The Predicament of Culture: 20th Century Ethnography, Literature, and Art* (Cambridge, MA: Harvard University Press, 1988), 67.

75. On this issue, see George Marcus and Michael Fischer, *Anthropology as Cultural Critique: An Experimental Moment in the Human Sciences* (Chicago: Univer-

sity of Chicago Press, 1986), 7–10; James Clifford and George Marcus, *Writing Culture: The Poetics and Politics of Ethnography* (Berkeley: University of California Press, 1986); Hugh B. Urban, *The Power of Tantra: Religion, Sexuality, and the Politics of South Asian Studies* (London: IB Tauris, 2010), 187–96.

76. Jonathan Z. Smith, *Imagining Religion: From Babylon to Jonestown* (Chicago: University of Chicago Press, 1988), xi. See also Hugh B. Urban, "Poétique et politique de la comparaison : suicide révolutionnaire ou meurtre collectif?" *Asdiwal* 13 (2018): 61–68.

77. Loïc J. D. Wacquant, "Toward a Reflexive Sociology: A Workshop with Pierre Bourdieu," *Sociological Theory* 7, no. 1 (1989): 55. See also Swartz, *Culture and Power*, 11; Urban, "Sacred Capital."

78. Michel Foucault, *The Use of Pleasure* (New York: Vintage, 1990), 6.

79. Foucault, *History of Sexuality*, 1:103.

80. See Urban, "Torment of Secrecy." Chilson identifies three related strategies of concealment: limiting visibility, dissimulation, and silence (*Secrecy's Power*, 10–11).

81. See Hugh B. Urban, "Elitism and Esotericism: Strategies of Secrecy and Power in South Indian Tantra and French Freemasonry," *Numen* 44, no. 1 (1997): 1–38.

82. Leo Strauss, *Persecution and the Art of Writing* (Glencoe, IL: Free Press, 1952). On "double coding," see Lincoln, *Holy Terrors*, 20–21, 32.

83. See Robert Thurman, "Vajra Hermeneutics," in *Buddhist Hermeneutics*, ed. Donald Lopez (Honolulu: University of Hawai'i Press, 1986); see Urban, "Torment of Secrecy"; Keen, *Knowledge and Secrecy*.

84. Georges Bataille, *Erotism: Death and Sensuality* (San Francisco: City Lights, 1986). See Elliot Wolfson, *Language, Eros, Being: Kabbalistic Hermeneutics and Poetic Imagination* (New York: Fordham University Press, 2005), 2, 263.

85. See chapters 1 and 3. On esoteric views of the body, see Geoffrey Samuel and Jay Johnston, eds., *Religion and the Subtle Body in Asia and the West* (New York: Routledge, 2013); John L. Crow, "Occult Bodies: The Corporeal Construction of the Theosophical Society, 1875–1935" (PhD diss., Florida State University, 2017). On esoteric views of gender and sexuality, see Urban, *Magia Sexualis*; Jeffrey J. Kripal and Wouter J. Hanegraaff, eds., *Hidden Intercourse: Eros and Sexuality in the History of Western Esotericism* (New York: Fordham University Press, 2011).

86. The most infamous case of this sort of infiltration of government agencies by an esoteric group was the Church of Scientology's infiltration of the IRS and other offices during the 1970s. See Hugh B. Urban, "Fair Game: Secrecy, Security, and the Church of Scientology in Cold War America," *Journal of the American Academy of Religion* 74, no. 2 (2006): 356–89.

87. See Aaron Hughes, *Comparison: A Critical Primer* (London: Equinox, 2017); Bruce Lincoln, "Theses on Comparison," in *Gods and Demons, Priests and Scholars* (Chicago: University of Chicago Press, 2012); Jonathan Z. Smith, *Drudgery Divine: On the Comparison of Early Christianities and Religions of Late Antiquity* (Chicago: University of Chicago Press, 1994); Urban, "Poétique et politique."

88. Bruce Lincoln, *Apples and Oranges: Explorations in, on and with Comparison* (Chicago: University of Chicago Press, 2018), 11.

89. Lincoln, *Apples and Oranges*, 27.

90. Wendy Doniger, *The Implied Spider: Politics and Theology in Myth* (New York: Columbia University Press, 1998), 66: "The great universalist theories were constructed from the top down: that is, they assumed certain continuities about broad

concepts such as sacrifice, or a High God, or an Oedipal complex. . . . The method that I am advocating is, by contrast, constructed from the bottom up. It assumes certain continuities not about overarching human universals but about particular narrative details concerning the body, sexual desire, procreation, parenting and death."

91. Smith, *Drudgery Divine*, 52. See Urban, "Poétique et politique."

92. Chesterman, *One Nation under Surveillance*. See also Zuboff, *Surveillance Capitalism*; Lyon, *Surveillance after September 11*; Cole and Fabrinni, *Secrecy*.

Chapter 1

1. Albert Pike, *Morals and Dogma of the Ancient and Accepted Scottish Rite of Freemasonry* (Charleston, SC: Supreme Council of the Ancient and Accepted Scottish Rite, 1871), 109.

2. Simmel, *Sociology of Georg Simmel*, 338.

3. On Pike's life, see Walter L. Brown, *A Life of Albert Pike* (Fayetteville: University of Arkansas Press, 1997); William Fox, *Lodge of the Double-Headed Eagle: Two Centuries of Freemasonry in America's Southern Jurisdiction* (Fayetteville: University of Arkansas Press, 1999); Frederick W. Allsopp, *The Life Story of Albert Pike* (Little Rock, AK: Parke-Harper News Service, 1920); Mark C. Carnes, *Secret Ritual and Manhood in Victorian America* (New Haven, CT: Yale University Press, 1989).

4. As a modern esoteric tradition, Freemasonry emerged out of medieval stonemasonry in England and Scotland, beginning perhaps as early as the fourteenth century and clearly by the late sixteenth and seventeenth centuries. See Jan A. M. Snoek and Henrik Bogdan, "Freemasonry," in *The Occult World*, ed. Christopher Partridge (New York: Routledge, 2015), 157–59; John Hamill, *The Craft: A History of English Freemasonry* (Wellingborough: Crucible, 1986); Jan A. M. Snoek, "Researching Freemasonry: Where Are We Now?" *Journal for Research into Freemasonry and Fraternalism* 1, no. 2 (2010): 227–48.

5. On American Freemasonry generally, see Steven C. Bullock, *Revolutionary Brotherhood: Freemasonry and the Transformation of the American Social Order 1730–1840* (Chapel Hill: University of North Carolina Press, 1996); David G. Hackett, *That Religion in Which All Men Agree: Freemasonry in American Culture* (Berkeley: University of California Press, 2014); Mary Ann Clawson, *Constructing Brotherhood: Class, Gender and Fraternalism* (Princeton, NJ: Princeton University Press, 1989); Lynn Dumenil, *Freemasonry and American Culture, 1880–1930* (Princeton, NJ: Princeton University Press, 2014); Mark A. Tabbert, *American Freemasons: Three Centuries of Building Communities* (New York: New York University Press, 2005).

6. The Scottish Rite emerged in France in the mid-eighteenth century and spread to the New World in the 1760s and 1770s. The modern system of thirty-three degrees was established in 1801 in Charleston, South Carolina. See Arturo De Huyos, "Development of the Scottish Rite Rituals," in *Scottish Rite Ritual, Monitor, and Guide* (Washington, DC: Supreme Council, 33, S.J., 2009), 109–19; Samuel Harrison Baynard, *History of the Supreme Council, 33, Ancient and Accepted Scottish Rite of Freemasonry* (Boston: Supreme Council of Sovereign Grand Inspectors General, 1938); Henry W. Coil, "Scottish Rite Masonry," in *Coil's Masonic Encyclopedia* (Richmond, VA: Macoy, 1961), 614; Ames, "Lure of the Spectacular"; Paul Naudon, *Histoire et Rituels des Hauts Grades Maçonniques* (Paris: Devry-Livres, 1966); Albert Lantoine, *Le Rite Écossais Ancien et Accepté* (Paris: E. Nourry, 1930).

7. See Mark J. R. Dennis, "The Material Culture of Freemasonry," in *Handbook of Freemasonry*, ed. Henrik Bogdan and Jan A. M. Snoek (Leiden: Brill, 2014), 606–23; Victoria Scott Dennis, *Discovering Friendly and Fraternal Organisations: Their Badges and Regalia* (Oxford: Shire, 2005); John D. Hamilton, *Material Culture of the American Freemasons* (Hanover, NH: University Press of New England, 1994).

8. On material religion, see Colleen McDannell, *Material Christianity: Religion and Popular Culture in America* (New Haven, CT: Yale University Press, 1995); S. Brent Plate, ed., *Key Terms in Material Religion* (New York: Bloomsbury Academic, 2015).

9. See Mary H. Nooter, *Secrecy: African Art that Conceals and Reveals* (New York: Museum for African Art, 1993).

10. Clawson, *Constructing Brotherhood*, 111. See Ames, "Lure of the Spectacular," 19: "[B]etween 1885 and 1900 Americans formed more than 150 new fraternal organizations. By 1920, thirty million Americans—half the country's adult population— belonged to one or more of the 800 secret orders then part of American life."

11. Dumenil, *Freemasonry*, 32–42. See also Brian Greenberg, *Worker and Community: Responses to Industrialization in the Nineteenth Century American City* (Albany: SUNY Press, 1985), 89–100.

12. Clawson, *Constructing Brotherhood*.

13. Carnes, *Secret Ritual*.

14. See Bullock, *Revolutionary Brotherhood*; Hackett, *That Religion*.

15. On this point, see Bullock, *Revolutionary Brotherhood*, 4: "As both an honorable society, aiming to provide its brothers with high standing and public reputation, and a brotherhood, suggesting equality in a nonpaternalistic family, Masonry simultaneously emphasized exclusiveness and inclusion." See also Hackett, *That Religion*, 128–30; Brockman, *Theatre*, 4.

16. See Hackett, *That Religion*, 128: "[M]ainstream American Fraternalism consistently excluded African Americans. Racial segregation was accomplished on the basis of not only appearance but also formal stipulations that all members must be white."

17. Brown, *A Life*, 417; Fox, *Lodge*, 89.

18. Carnes, *Secret Ritual*, 136.

19. Carnes, *Secret Ritual*, 138.

20. Brown, *A Life*, 443 ff.

21. See Wyn Craig Wade, *The Fiery Cross: The KKK in America* (New York: Simon and Schuster, 1987), 58.

22. Walter Lee Brown, "Albert Pike, 1809–1891" (PhD diss., University of Texas, 1955), 783.

23. Albert Pike, "Letter III," in *Letters to the People of the Northern States* (Washington, DC: Gideon, 1856), 19: "The negro in Africa *could* not civilize himself. God had so ordered it; He had so constituted him. . . . He chose to make the white man the instrument to bring about that civilization, by such slow process as He pleases to use. *We* would impatiently civilize the African at once. *He* [God] chooses to do it by means of the toil and hardships of slavery, each generation advancing a little beyond its predecessor."

24. Albert Pike, *Memphis Daily Appeal*, February 26, 1868.

25. Albert Pike, *Memphis Daily Appeal*, February 22, 1867: "We all perfectly know well that . . . the negro race is not and never will be any more fit to be entrusted with the power of voting than a stark maniac is to be entrusted with a razor. . . . If the right of suffrage is given them, does not every sane man know that the struggle for politi-

NOTES TO PAGES 28–31 219

cal power between the race will breed a war of races. . . . There is no community, North or South, in which the white man will submit to legislated and governed by the negro" (ibid).

26. Albert Pike, *Memphis Daily Appeal*, July 12, 1868.

27. Albert Pike, *Lectures on the Arya* (Whitefish, MT: Kessinger, 1998), 1.

28. Albert Pike, *Memphis Daily Appeal*, April 16, 1868.

29. Pike, *Memphis Daily Appeal*, April 16, 1868. See Brown, *A Life*, 439–40.

30. Carnes, *Secret Ritual*, 137. See also Pike, *Lectures on the Arya*; Albert Pike, *Indo-Aryan Deities and Worship as Contained in the Rig Veda* (Louisville, KY: Standard, 1930); Albert Pike, *Indian-Aryan Theosophy and Doctrine as Contained in the Zend-Avesta* (Louisville, KY: Standard, 1924); Albert Pike, *Hymns to the Gods and Other Poems* (Little Rock, AK: F. W. Allsopp, 1916).

31. Éliphas Lévi, *Dogme et Rituel de la Haute Magie* (Cambridge: Cambridge University Press, 2011).

32. James Richardson, *Centennial Address* (Washington, DC: Pearson Printing Office, 1910), 26. See Joseph Newton, *Address on Albert Pike, 33rd Degree* (Cedar Rapids, IA: Torch Press, 1909), 3. Besides *Morals and Dogma*, Pike's other key work on Freemasonry is *Albert Pike's Esoterika: The Symbolism of the Blue Grades* (Washington, DC: Scottish Rite Research Society, 2005).

33. Clawson, *Constructing Brotherhood*, 6–7. See Robert Wiebe, *The Search for Order, 1877–1920* (New York: Hill and Wang, 1967), 1–75.

34. Henry Highton, "The Function of Freemasonry in Modern Society" (1883), quoted in Dumenil, *Freemasonry*, 93. "Ancient and changeless, [Freemasonry] is the very type of immutable law. . . . It insists upon order and subordination, because without them, the world would be Pandemonium" (ibid).

35. See Ames, "Lure of the Spectacular," 23: "[T]he home, the arts, the church, and the theater were all feminized to varying degrees. . . . [M]any men were reacting to this far-reaching feminization of former male strongholds. The growth of fraternal lodges and the creation of males-only Scottish Rite theatre can be seen as part of that reaction."

36. See Dumenil, *Freemasonry*, 109: "Masons themselves offered the reason for this appeal: a rapidly changing world apparently dominated by conflict, commercialism, freed, and financial insecurity. An increasingly heterogeneous society, it was a world characterized by political and social clashes. . . . Masonry offered a spiritual oasis, a retreat from this world."

37. Ames, "Lure of the Spectacular," 23. See Clawson, *Constructing Brotherhood*, 179; Hackett, *That Religion*, 5.

38. Dumenil, *Freemasonry*, 88.

39. Pike, *Morals and Dogma*, 62–105.

40. "Masonry had a tangible appeal rooted in the order's ability to confer respectability. Far from being suspect as a cabal of . . . libertines, Masonry was a prestigious organization" (Dumenil, *Freemasonry*, 30).

41. Pike, *Morals and Dogma*, 837, 67–68, 83, 33.

42. Pike, *Morals and Dogma*, 43.

43. See Brown, *A Life*, 439–40; Cécile Révauger, "Freemasonry and Blacks," in *Handbook of Freemasonry*, ed. Henrik Bogdan and Jan A. M. Snoek (Leiden: Brill, 2017), 429.

44. See Dumenil, *Freemasonry*, 8–9: "Masons insisted that their order was com-

mitted to the principle of *universality*, which they defined as the association of good men without regard to religion, nationality, or class. . . . Although Masonic principles technically allowed for heterogeneity, the fraternity was, in fact, predominantly a white, native, Protestant, middle-class organization. Despite its insistence on the equality of men, for example, in practice the order excluded non-whites. Not only did Masonry not admit blacks, but Grand Lodges also denied that Prince Hall Masonry . . . was an authentic part of Masonry."

45. Bullock, *Revolutionary Brotherhood*, 4. See Hackett, *That Religion*, 128–29.

46. Pike, *Morals and Dogma*, 219.

47. Margaret Jacob, *Living the Enlightenment: Freemasonry and Politics in Eighteenth Century Europe* (New York: Oxford University Press, 1991), 45.

48. Hackett, *That Religion*, 129. See Tabbert, *American Freemasons*, 143: "To receive the 29 degrees (4th–32nd) was expensive and time-consuming."

49. Carnes, *Secret Ritual*, 22–23. "[M]embership carried tangible benefits. Businessmen made contacts, cultivated credit sources, and gained access to a nationwide network of lodges. Ambitious young men could socialize with their bosses" (ibid., 2).

50. In much of the southern US, Masonic lodges remain racially segregated, and the Grand Lodges of twelve former Confederate states still refuse to even recognize Prince Hall Masons as brothers. See Jay Reeves, "Racial Traditions vs. Brotherhood: Masonic Units Struggle with Recognition," *Washington Post*, October 29, 2006. Meanwhile, the Supreme Council Southern Jurisdiction of the Scottish Rite began to recognize the legitimacy of the Prince Hall lodges only in 2013. See Fred Milliken, "Mainstream Scottish Rite Recognizes Prince Hall Rite in All States," *Freemason Information*, August 27, 2013, http://freemasoninformation.com/2013/08/mainstream-scottish-rite-recognizes-prince-hall-scottish-rite-in-all-states/. See also Chris McGreal, "Georgia Freemasons at Loggerheads over Admission of Black Man to Lodge," *Guardian*, July 3, 2009, https://www.theguardian.com/world/2009/jul/03/atlanta-georgia-freemasons-race.

51. In 1775, Prince Hall and fourteen other black men were first admitted into the Grand Lodge of Ireland, a military lodge attached to the British forces stationed in Boston. After Prince Hall's death, the African Grand Lodge was formed; however, the lodge was not recognized by the Grand Lodge of Massachusetts and so became an independent order. This was followed by the spread of other separate African American lodges, collectively known as Prince Hall masonry. On black Freemasonry, see Hackett, *That Religion*, 151–74; Peter P. Hinks and Stephen Kantrowitz, eds., *All Men Free and Brethren: Essays on the History of African American Freemasonry* (Ithaca, NY: Cornell University Press, 2013).

52. See Hackett, *Revolutionary Brotherhood*, 128; Révauger, "Freemasonry and Blacks," 429: "American white Grand lodges repeatedly excluded black Freemasons, alleging they were 'clandestine,' refusing to acknowledge the validity of their initial charter."

53. Albert Pike, *Proceedings of the Grand Lodge of the Ancient and Accepted Honorable Fraternity of Free & Accepted Masons of the State of Ohio at its Sixty-eighth Annual Grand Communication begun and held at Columbus, October A.L. 5875* (Cincinnati: Western Methodist Book Concern Press, 1875), 49–50. See Révauger, "Freemasonry and Blacks," 429.

54. Dumenil, *Freemasonry*, 147. See Brown, *A Life*, 439 ff. It is also worth noting that the Klan would in turn exploit the prestige of the Masonic Lodge to legitimize

its own racial agenda. As Miguel Hernandez argues, the KKK not only borrowed the secrecy and hierarchy of Freemasonry but also appropriated much of the symbolic power of the lodges in its efforts to appear "respectable" in late nineteenth-century America: "It was precisely this desirability and the order's historical reputation as an honorable and progressive men's order that fueled the Ku Klux Klan's drive to appear as a Masonic affiliate. By tying themselves to Freemasonry, they were imbuing their own organization with the Craft's respectability" (*The Ku Klux Klan and Freemasonry in 1920s America: Fighting Fraternities* [New York: Routledge, 2019], 17).

55. Pierre Bourdieu, *The Logic of Practice* (Stanford, CA: Stanford University Press, 1981), 114.

56. Swartz, *Culture and Power*, 203. See Bourdieu, *Logic of Practice*, 133; Paul Willis, *Learning to Labour: How Working Class Kids Get Working Class Jobs* (London: Saxon House, 1977), 128.

57. Tabbert, *American Freemasons*, 142.

58. Pike, *Morals and Dogma*, 218.

59. Pike, *Morals and Dogma*, 221.

60. Pike, *Morals and Dogma*, 104–5.

61. Norman Mackenzie, ed., *Secret Societies* (New York: Holt, Rhinehart and Winston, 1967), 176.

62. Pike, *Morals and Dogma*, 7.

63. On the first three grades, in addition to Pike's *Morals and Dogma*, see *Albert Pike's Esoterika*; Jonathan Blanchard, *Scottish Rite Masonry Illustrated* (Chicago: Ezra Cooke, 1882); Naudon, *Histoire et Rituels*, 235 f.

64. Pike, *Morals and Dogma*, 22.

65. Pike, *Morals and Dogma*, 101.

66. Pike, *Morals and Dogma*, 819 (emphasis added).

67. Blanchard, *Scottish Rite Masonry*, 438.

68. Lévi, *Great Secret*, 67–68.

69. Pike, *Morals and Dogma*, 63.

70. McDannell, *Material Christianity*, 221.

71. McDannell, *Material Christianity*, 220.

72. Dennis, "Material Culture of Freemasonry," 606.

73. Hackett, *That Religion*, 130.

74. Hernandez, *Ku Klux Klan and Freemasonry*, 17.

75. Hamilton, *Material Culture*, 96.

76. Hamilton, *Material Culture*, 98.

77. Pike, *Morals and Dogma*, 278.

78. Pike, *Morals and Dogma*, 290.

79. Arthur C. Parker, "The Double-Headed Eagle and Whence It Came," *The Builder*, 1923. Reproduced in *Masonic Dictionary*, 2019, http://www.masonicdictionary .com/doubleeagle.html.

80. Victor Turner, *The Forest of Symbols: Aspects of Ndembu Ritual* (Ithaca, NY: Cornell University Press, 1970), 50.

81. Ames, "Lure of the Spectacular," 22. "Bringing the Scottish Rite into modern times by theatricalizing its initiation rituals was a savvy marketing decision that recognized the waning appeal of the low-tech and sometimes tedious rituals of the past" (ibid., 25).

82. Simmel, *Sociology of Georg Simmel*, 343.

83. Simmel, *Sociology of Georg Simmel*, 339–40. "In the adorned body we possess more; if we have adorned the body at our disposal, we are masters over more and nobler things. . . . Bodily adornment becomes private property above all: it expands and the ego and enlarges the sphere around us" (ibid., 344).

84. Mark C. Carnes, "Scottish Rite and the Visual Semiotics of Gender," in *Theatre of the Fraternity: Staging the Ritual Space of the Scottish Rite of Freemasonry, 1896–1929*, ed. C. Lance Brockman (Jackson: University Press of Mississippi, 1996), 89–90.

85. Pike, letter of March 11, 1866, quoted in Brown, *A Life*, 423. On this point, see also Clawson, *Constructing Brotherhood*, 181: "[A] key feature of Masonic and quasi-Masonic fraternalism was its interposition of numerous layers of hierarchy into relations among members. Fraternal ritual articulated themes that are closely identified with the constitution of masculine social order: brotherhood/ manhood as an achieved identity, society as a hierarchically organized structure of subordination and deference."

86. Bruce Lincoln, *Discourse and the Construction of Society: Comparative Studies of Myth, Ritual, and Classification* (New York: Oxford University Press, 1989), 85.

87. Blanchard, *Scottish Rite Masonry*, 2:438. See also Henry Wilson Coil, *Coil's Msonic Encyclopedia* (New York: Macoy, 1961), 159; Pike, *Albert Pike's Esoterika*.

88. Blanchard, *Scottish Rite Masonry*, 2:397. See Carnes, *Secret Ritual*, 146.

89. Carnes, *Secret Ritual*, 146–47.

90. Pike, *Morals and Dogma*, 3. See Moore, "From Lodge Room to Theatre," 31.

91. Bourdieu, *Outline*, 89.

92. Lincoln, *Discourse*, 139–41.

93. Dumenil, *Freemasonry*, 14. See Clawson, "Spectatorship and Masculinity," 52.

94. Ames, "Lure of the Spectacular," 25.

95. Pike, *Morals and Dogma*, 849.

96. Carnes, *Secret Ritual*, 149–50.

97. Pike, *Morals and Dogma*, 854–55.

98. Pike, *Morals and Dogma*, 860.

99. Pike, *Morals and Dogma*, 829. "God has . . . made necessary among mankind a division of labour, intellectual and moral. He has made necessary the varied relations of society and dependence, obedience and control. . . . We have the right to live . . . by the legitimate exercise of our intellect and hire or buy the labour of the strong arms of others, to till our grounds, to dig in our mines, to toil in our manufactories" (ibid., 831–32).

100. Dumenil, *Freemasonry*, 163. On the decline of Freemasonry in the latter half of the twentieth century, see Tabbert, *American Freemasons*, 208–10.

101. Clawson, *Constructing Brotherhood*, 241: "The aggressive tactics of the leading orders produced tremendous growth throughout the late nineteenth century and up through the 1920s. Even the Masons . . . found themselves caught up in the competition for expansion, setting up contests and other incentives for lodges to increase their size. But well before the movement had reached its numerical peak, thoughtful commentators were beginning to express concern over the consequences of the hard sell."

102. Ames, "Lure of the Spectacular," 27.

103. See Tabbert, *American Freemasons*, 208–10.

104. See Reeves, "Racial Traditions vs. Brotherhood"; Associated Press, "Masons in South Struggle with Racial Separation," NBCNews.com, October 24, 2006, http://

NOTES TO PAGES 50-53 223

www.nbcnews.com/id/15405618/ns/us_news-life/t/masons-south-struggle-racial
-separation/#.XOsISNPwbVo. On race in Freemasonry, see Révauger, "Freemasonry
and Blacks."

105. See Milliken, "Mainstream Scottish Rite Recognizes Prince Hall."

Chapter 2

1. Helena Petrovna Blavatsky, *The Secret Doctrine*, vol. 1, *Cosmogenesis* (Pasadena,
CA: Theosophical University Press, 2014), xxii.

2. Johnson, *Secrets, Gossip and Gods*, 3. See also Tanya Luhrmann, "The Magic of
Secrecy," *Ethos* 17, no. 2 (1989): 161.

3. Elliot R. Wolfson, "The Occultation of the Feminine and the Body of Secrecy in
Medieval Kabbalah," in *Rending the Veil*, 118–19.

4. See Bellman, *Language of Secrecy*, 144.

5. Johnson, *Secrets, Gossip and Gods*, 3.

6. On esotericism in Mormonism, see John L. Brooke, *The Refiner's Fire: The
Making of Mormon Cosmology, 1644–1844* (Cambridge: Cambridge University Press,
1994). On neo-Gnosticism, see Hugh B. Urban, "The Knowing of Knowing: Neo-
Gnosticism, from the O.T.O. to the Church of Scientology," *Gnosis: Journal of Gnostic
Studies* 4 (2019): 99–116.

7. Moore, *Selling God*, 51. On the links between religion and the market in the nineteenth century, see Noll, *God and Mammon*; Stieverman, Stillman, and Goff, *Religion
and the Marketplace*; Davenport, *Friends of Unrighteous Mammon*; Sellers, *Market
Revolution*.

8. Gunn, *Modern Occult Rhetoric*, 26: "Modern occultism can be identified by its
commodification, particularly in terms of the wider dispersal of texts designed for
audiences much larger than a small cabal of true believers." See also Hanegraaff, *Esotericism and the Academy*, 219.

9. Jütte, *Age of Secrecy*, 2.

10. See Gunn, *Modern Occult Rhetoric*, 26; Hanegraaff, *Esotericism and the
Academy*, 219.

11. Helena Petrovna Blavatsky, *The Key to Theosophy* (London: Theosophical Publishing House, 1889), 7–8.

12. See Joscelyn Godwin, preface to K. Paul Johnson, *The Masters Revealed:
Madame Blavatsky and the Myth of the Great White Lodge* (Albany: SUNY Press,
1994), xv.

13. There is a large body of work on Blavatsky and Theosophy; see Johnson, *Masters
Revealed*; Nicholas Goodrick-Clarke, *Helena Blavatsky* (Berkeley, CA: North Atlantic Books, 2004), 2; Olav Hammer, "Theosophy," in *The Occult World*, ed. Christopher Partridge (New York: Routledge, 2015), 250–51; Olav Hammer and Mikael Roth-
stein, eds., *Handbook of the Theosophical Current* (Leiden: Brill, 2013); Olav Hammer,
Claiming Knowledge: Strategies of Epistemology from Theosophy to the New Age (Lei-
den: Brill, 2003); Joscelyn Godwin, *The Theosophical Enlightenment* (Albany: SUNY
Press, 1994); Sylvia Cranston, *HPB: The Extraordinary Life and Influence of Helena
Blavatsky, Founder of the Modern Theosophical Movement* (New York: G. P. Putnam's
Sons, 1993).

14. Gunn, *Modern Occult Rhetoric*, 26.

15. I adapt the term "habitus" mainly from Pierre Bourdieu, who in turn adapted

it from Marcel Mauss. See Pierre Bourdieu, *In Other Words: Essays Toward a Reflexive Sociology* (Stanford: Stanford University Press, 1990), 190, 167; Mauss, *Sociology and Psychology: Essays* (London: Routledge and Kegan Paul 1979), 101.

16. On Theosophy and Orientalism, see Chris Goto-Jones, *Conjuring Asia: Magic, Orientalism, and the Making of the Modern World* (Cambridge: Cambridge University Press, 2016), 4–5, 105; Donald Lopez, *Prisoners of Shangri-La: Tibetan Buddhism and the West* (Chicago: University of Chicago Press, 1998), 5; King, *Orientalism and Religion*, 32, 120, 137.

17. See Johnson, *Masters Revealed*.

18. See R. A. Gilbert, *The Golden Dawn and the Esoteric Section* (London: Theosophical History Centre, 1987).

19. Goodrick-Clarke, *Helena Blavatsky*, 2. On Blavatsky's biography, see Cranston, *HPB*; Joscelyn Godwin, "Blavatsky and the First Generation of Theosophy," in *Handbook of the Theosophical Current*, ed. Olav Hammer and Mikael Rothstein (Leiden: Brill, 2013), 15–31.

20. Robert S. Ellwood and Harry Partin, *Religious and Spiritual Groups in Modern America* (Englewood Cliffs, NJ: Prentice Hall, 1988), 61; Goodrick-Clarke, *Western Esoteric Tradition*, 213.

21. Goodrick-Clarke, *Helena Blavatsky*, 5; Hammer, "Theosophy," 251–52.

22. Goto-Jones, *Conjuring Asia*, 105. "[T]he new occultism participated in a mixture of intellectual and cultural fashions of the fin de siècle, capturing popular (and scholarly) discontent with materialism . . . but also entering into the discourse of Orientalism. . . . Drawn by the popular accounts of anthropologists and the new class of travel writers, who seemed to locate 'real' magic outside the modernity of the West, leading members of the Theosophical Society, including . . . Blavatsky herself, told countless stories of their journeys of discovery around India, China and Tibet, where they apparently studied secret, esoteric and occult arts of magic with gurus, adepts and mahatmas. . . . Theosophy became synonymous with 'Oriental Philosophy' and found a natural place in the Orientalism of the turn of the nineteenth and early twentieth centuries" (ibid., 29–30).

23. Sinnett, *Esoteric Buddhism* (London: Chapman and Hall, 1885), 181–82.

24. Lopez, *Prisoners of Shangri-La*, 5, 50–51.

25. See Ann Braude, *Radical Spirits: Spiritualism and Women's Rights in Nineteenth Century America* (Bloomington: Indiana University Press, 2001).

26. Letter to Prof. Hiram Corson, February 16, 1875, in Helena Petrovna Blavatsky, *Collected Writings*, vol. 1, *1874–1878* (Wheaton, IL: Theosophical Publishing House, 1966), lv.

27. Ellwood and Partin, *Religious and Spiritual Groups*, 60. See Emily Sellon and Renée Weber, "Theosophy and the Theosophical Society," in *Modern Esoteric Spirituality*, ed. Antoine Faivre and Jacob Needleman (New York: Crossroad, 1992), 312.

28. Holt, quoted in John Symonds, *The Lady with the Magic Eyes: Madame Blavatsky, Medium and Mystic* (New York: Thomas Yoseloff, 1960), 31–33. See Holt, "A Reminiscence of H. P. Blavatsky in 1873," *Theosophist* 53 (1931): 260.

29. Henry Steel Olcott, *Old Diary Leaves: The True Story of the Theosophical Society* (New York: G. P. Putnam's Sons, 1895), 4.

30. Olcott, quoted in Symonds, *The Lady*, 29.

31. *Daily Graphic*, quoted in Symonds, *The Lady*, 42.

32. Goodrick-Clarke, *Helena Blavatsky*, 10–11.

NOTES TO PAGES 58–63   225

33. Ellwood and Partin, *Religious and Spiritual Groups*, 62.

34. Goodrick-Clarke, *Western Esoteric Tradition*, 213. See Hammer, *Claiming Knowledge*, 380–82.

35. See Ellwood and Partin, *Religious and Spiritual Groups*, 78–79: "The developed Hierarchy found a place for adepts of all national lines, symbolizing thereby the syncretism. The personal 'God' is the Solar Logos ruler of the solar system. At the terrestrial summit is Sanat Kumara, Lord of the World, the supreme guide of earthly evolution of mind who came from Venus some eighteen million years ago. He presides in Shambhala, a mysterious paradise in the Gobi desert. Under him the Buddha is spiritual head. . . . There is under the Buddha the Bodhisattva, or future Buddha, and under Sanat Kumara the Manu, the archetypal man and future world Lord."

36. Helena Petrovna Blavatsky, *Isis Unveiled: A Master Key to the Mysteries of Ancient and Modern Science and Theology*, 2 vols. (Point Loma, CA: Theosophical University Press, 1936), 2:306–8.

37. Bulwer-Lytton, *Zanoni* (London: G. Routledge, 1856), xv.

38. Godwin, *Theosophical Enlightenment*, 126.

39. See Goodrick-Clarke, *Western Esoteric Tradition*, 192–96.

40. Peter Washington, *Madame Blavatsky's Baboon: A History of the Mystics, Mediums, and Misfits Who Brought Spiritualism to America* (New York: Schocken, 1996), 36.

41. Blavatsky, *Isis Unveiled*, 1:1.

42. Godwin, *Theosophical Enlightenment*, 189. See Symonds, *The Lady*, 66.

43. Godwin, *Theosophical Enlightenment*, 291.

44. Godwin, foreword, to Johnson, *Masters Revealed*, xviii; see Johnson, *Masters Revealed*, 208.

45. Johnson, *Masters Revealed*, 175. "Her Theosophy was a brilliant synthesis of elements from dozens of unrelated sources. But she mythologized her search for the Masters in such a way that her real quest remained secret. Due to her adolescent fascination with the mysterious world of occult Masonry, in which hidden Masters sent unquestioned orders from unknown Oriental locations, she presented her experiences according to an elaborate hierarchical model. In truth, her Masters constituted not a stable hierarchy but an ever evolving network" (ibid., 8).

46. Robert S. Ellwood, *Alternative Altars: Unconventional and Eastern Spirtuality in America* (Chicago: University of Chicago Press, 1979), 119–20.

47. Olcott, *Old Diary Leaves*, 208–9. "[E]ach change in the HPB manuscript would be preceded, either by her leaving the room for a moment or two, or by her going off into the trance or abstracted state, when her lifeless eyes would be looking beyond me into space, as it were and returning to the normal waking state almost immediately. And there would also be a distinct change of personality . . . in gait, vocal expression, vivacity of manner and all in all temper" (ibid., 211–12).

48. See Gunn, *Modern Occult Rhetoric*.

49. Blavatsky, *Isis Unveiled*, 1:xliv.

50. Goodrick-Clarke, *Helena Blavatsky*, 9; see Blavatsky, *Isis Unveiled*, 1:511, 613.

51. Blavatsky, "Death and Immortality," in *The Complete Works of H. P. Blavatsky*, vol. 4, *1882–1883* (Point Loma, CA: Theosophical University Press, 1936), 113.

52. David and Nancy Reigle, *Blavatsky's Secret Books: Twenty-Years' Research* (San Diego: Wizards Bookshelf, 1999).

53. Goodrick-Clarke, *Helena Blavatsky*, 15.

226 NOTES TO PAGES 64–70

54. Blavatsky, *The Secret Doctrine: The Synthesis of Race, Religion and Theosophy*, 2 vols. (Pasadena, CA: Theosophical University Press, 1988), 1:31.

55. Blavatskty, *Secret Doctrine*, 1:23.

56. Blavatsky, *Isis Unveiled*, 1:1; Goodrick-Clarke, *Helena Blavatsky*, 76.

57. Blavatsky, *Secret Doctrine*, 1:xliii.

58. Blavatsky, *Secret Doctrine*, 1:299.

59. Blavatsky, *Secret Doctrine*, 1:xix–xx.

60. Blavatsky, *Secrecy Doctrine*, 1:1. See Blavatsky, "Esoteric Buddhism," in *Complete Works*, 4:329.

61. Blavatsky, *Secret Doctrine*, 1:1.

62. Blavatsky, *Secret Doctrine*, 1:164–65.

63. Helena Petrovna Blavatsky, *Studies in Occultism* (Whitefish, MT: Kessinger, 1997), 42–43.

64. Simmel, *Sociology of Georg Simmel*, 333–34.

65. See Rev. George Patterson, "The Collapse of Koot Hoomi," *Madras Christian College Magazine* (September 1884): 199–215. On the Coulomb affair, see also Cranston, *HPB*, 269; Godwin, "Blavatsky."

66. Richard Hodgson, "Report of the Committee Appointed to Investigate Phenomena Connected with the Theosophical Society," *Proceedings of the Society for Psychical Research* 3 (1885): 207.

67. Franz Boas, "Religion in the Kwakiutl Indians," in *Kwakiutl Ethnography*, ed. Helen Codere (Chicago: University of Chicago Press, 1966), 121.

68. Taussig, "Transgression," 356–57.

69. Daniel H. Caldwell, *The Esoteric Papers of Madame Blavatsky* (Tuscon: Daniel H. Caldwell, 2004), 3.

70. Caldwell, *Esoteric Papers*, 3–4; see Olcott, "The Esoteric Section of the Theosophical Society," *Lucifer* 3, no. 14 (October 1888): 176; Crow, "Occult Bodies," 144.

71. See William Q. Judge, "Eastern School of Theosophy: Suggestions and Aids," in *Echoes of the Orient: Collected Writings of William Q. Judge*, 4 vols. (Point Loma, CA: Theosophical University Press, 2010), 3:273–82.

72. Blavatsky, memorandum of December 14, 1888, in Caldwell, *Esoteric Papers*, 11.

73. Caldwell, *Esoteric Papers*, 27, 43, 227–31. See Helena Petrovna Blavatsky, "EI: Instruction No. III," in *H. P. Blavatsky Collected Writings*, vol. 12, *1889–1890* (Wheaton, IL: Theosophical Publishing House, 1980), 600. The Esoteric Instructions for the section are also explicit about the reasons for the need for such intense secrecy, suggesting that: "a) The whole truth is too sacred to be given out promiscuously; b) The knowledge of all the details and missing links in the exoteric teaching is dangerous in the wrong hands" (ibid).

74. Caldwell, *Esoteric Papers*, 5–7. See also "The Meaning of a Pledge" first published in *Lucifer* (September 1888): 63–67, and reproduced in Caldwell, *Esoteric Papers*, 13–15. According to Rule number 8 of the E.S., "No member shall, under any circumstances, bring any charge of whatever nature against another member, whether to H. P. B., William Q. Judge, or any other member of the section" ("EI: Esoteric Instruction No. III," 495).

75. Caldwell, *Esoteric Papers*, 28–29.

76. Blavatsky, letter dated September 14, 1888, in Caldwell, *Esoteric Papers*, 18. In her "Preliminary Memorandum" for the Esoteric Instructions, Blavatsky also notes that the Theosophical Society had been "almost extinguished" due to "conspiracies

NOTES TO PAGES 70-73   227

of its enemies openly" ("Esoteric Instructions," *H. P. Blavatsky Collected Writings*, 12:490).

77. Blavatsky, letter of August 1890, in Caldwell, *Esoteric Papers*, 233. In the same letter, Blavatsky makes it clear that the E.S. is for those who do not doubt the legitimacy of her contact with the Masters: "Either I have stated the truth as I know it about the Masters and teach what I have been taught by them, or I have invented both them and the Esoteric Philosophy" (232).

78. "A Declaration," *Lucifer* (May 1891): 247.

79. Blavatsky, "Esoteric Instructions," in *H. P. Blavatsky Collected Writings*, 12:489.

80. Blavatsky, "Esoteric Instructions," 496.

81. Gilbert, *Golden Dawn*, 1–7. See also R. A. Gilbert, *Revelations of the Golden Dawn: The Rise and Fall of a Magical Order* (London: Quantum, 1997); and R. A. Gilbert, "The Hermetic Order of the Golden Dawn," in *The Occult World*, ed. Christopher Partridge (New York: Routledge, 2015), 241.

82. See Trevor Hamilton, "F. W. H. Meyers, William James and Spiritualism," in *The Spiritualist Movement: Speaking with the Dead in America and Around the World*, ed. Christopher Moreman (Santa Barbara, CA: Praeger, 2013), 103: "Blavatsky retained a tight hold on her Mahatmas and in a sense, we can see the Secret Chiefs as an attempt by the founders of the Golden Dawn, particularly Mathers . . . to find their own Western Mahatmas."

83. Gilbert, *Golden Dawn*, 1–4.

84. On Yeats's involvement with the Theosophical Society, Esoteric Section, and Golden Dawn, see Alex Owen, *The Place of Enchantment: British Occultism and the Culture of the Modern* (Chicago: University of Chicago Press, 2004), 60. On Crowley, see Henrik Bogdan and Martin P. Starr, eds., *Aleister Crowley and Western Esotericism* (New York: Oxford University Press, 2012).

85. Gilbert, *Golden Dawn*, 6–7. See Hamilton, "F. W. H. Meyers," 109: "Blavatsky instituted the Esoteric Section of the Theosophical Society in 1888 to counter competition from the new Golden Dawn and forbade her members to join it. . . . The rules and pledge form of the Esoteric Section swore members to obey Blavatsky, observe absolute secrecy, promote Theosophy and give freely of their time, work and money."

86. Gilbert, *Golden Dawn*, 7–9.

87. Gilbert, *Golden Dawn*, 15.

88. See Annie Besant, "Notice," to E.S. Instruction No. IV (July 1891), in Caldwell, *Esoteric Papers*, 235. See Helena Petrovna Blavatsky, *The Inner Group Teachings of H. P. Blavatsky: To Her Personal Pupils (1890–91)*, ed. Henk J. Spierenburg (San Diego: Point Loma, 1995).

89. Alice Leighton Cleather, *H. P. Blavatsky as I Knew Her* (Calcutta: Thacker and Spink, 1923), 24.

90. "The Inner Group Teachings," August 20, 1890, in Caldwell, *Esoteric Papers*, 479.

91. Blavatsky, letter dated March 24, 1890, in Caldwell, *Esoteric Teachings*, 554.

92. C. Jinarajadasa, *The Theosophist* (April 1932): 20–21n. See Blavatsky, letter of March 24, 1890, in Caldwell, *Esoteric Papers*, 554; Alice Leighton Cleather, *H. P. Blavatsky: A Great Betrayal* (Calcutta: Thacker and Spink, 1922), 84n.

93. Crow, "Occult Bodies," 144. See "The Inner Group Teachings," August 20, 1980, in Caldwell, *Esoteric Papers*, 479–85.

94. Blavatsky, "Esoteric Instructions,"488. Required reading for E.S. included, in

addition to theosophical texts such as the *Secret Doctrine*, classic works on Hinduism and yoga such as "Patanjali's Yoga Philosophy" and "The Bhagavad Gita" ("Esoteric Instructions," 497).

95. On the concept of the subtle body, see Crow, "Occult Bodies"; Geoffrey Samuel and Jay Johnston, eds., *Religion and the Subtle Body in Asia and the West* (New York: Routledge, 2013), 2; Jeffrey J. Kripal, *Secret Body: Erotic and Esoteric Currents in the History of Religions* (Chicago: University of Chicago Press, 2017); Julie Hall, "The Saptaparna: The Meaning and Origins of the Septenary Construction of Man," *Theosophical History* 13, no. 4 (2007): 5–38.

96. Crow, "Occult Bodies," 10. See Helena Petrovna Blavatsky, "Esoteric Instructions: Instruction No. III," in *H. P. Blavatsky Collected Writings*, vol. 12, *1889–1890* (Wheaton, IL: Theosophical Publishing House, 1980), 628–29, 645; Goodrick-Clarke, *Western Esoteric Tradition*, 220–21.

97. Crow, "Occult Bodies," 147. See Helena Petrovna Blavatsky, *The Key to Theosophy* (London: Theosophical Publishing Society, 1890).

98. For a discussion of the development and diversity of the chakras in Indian thought, see David Gordon White, *Kiss of the Yogini: Tantric Sex in its South Asian Contexts* (Chicago: University of Chicago Press, 2002), 221–24. For the most famous system of seven chakras, see Arthur Avalon, *The Serpent Power: The Secrets of Tantric and Shaktic Yoga* (London: Dover, 1974).

99. Blavatsky, "EI: Instruction No. III," 616.

100. Blavatsky, "EI: Instruction No. III," 616.

101. Blavatsky, "EI: Instruction No. III," 619.

102. Blavatsky, "EI: Instruction No. I," in *H. P. Blavatsky Collected Writings*, 12:524.

103. On the inscription of the body, see Bourdieu, *In Other Words*, 190; Hugh B. Urban, "Sacred Capital: Pierre Bourdieu and the Study of Religion," *Method and Theory in the Study of Religion* 15 (2003): 354–89.

104. Blavatsky, "EI: Instruction No. III," 620.

105. See Hanegraaff, *New Age*, 23–41, 448–50; Hammer, *Constructing Authority*; Olav Hammer, "Theosophical Elements in the New Age," in *Handbook of the Theosophical Current*, ed. Olav Hammer and Mikael Rothstein (Leiden: Brill, 2013), 237–58; Urban, *New Age*, 220–41.

106. On Knight and her following, see Hanegraaff, *New Age Religion*, 23–41; Urban, *New Age*, 220–41; J. Gordon Melton, *Finding Enlightenment: Ramtha's School of Ancient Wisdom* (New York: Atria Books, 1998).

107. See Hugh B. Urban, "The Medium is the Message in the Spacious Present: Channeling, Television and the New Age," in *Handbook of Spiritualism and Channeling*, ed. Cathy Gutierrez (Leiden: Brill, 2015), 317–39.

108. Helena Petrovna Blavatsky, "A Few Questions to Hiraf***," in *H. P. Blavatsky Collected Writings*, vol. 1, *1874–1878* (Wheaton, IL: Theosophical Publishing House, 1966), 101.

Chapter 3

1. Elliot R. Wolfson, "Occultation of the Feminine and the Body of Secrecy in Medieval Kabbalah," in *Rending the Veil*, 118.

2. Maria de Naglowska, "Une Vision Polaire," *La Flèche: Organe d'Action Magique* 5 (15 Février 1931): 3.

3. Don DeLillo, *Underworld* (New York: Scribner, 2007), 17.

4. Wolfson, "Occultation," 119. See also Hanegraaff and Kripal, *Hidden Intercourse*, xiv; Kripal, *Roads of Excess*.

5. Georges Bataille, *Erotism: Death and Sensuality* (San Francisco: City Lights, 1986), 276. "[E]verywhere—and doubtless from the earliest times—our sexual activity is sworn to secrecy, and everywhere, though to a variable degree, it appears contrary to our dignity so that the essence of eroticism is to be found in the inextricable confusion of sexual pleasure and taboo. In human terms, the taboo never makes an appearance without suggesting sexual pleasure, nor does the pleasure without evoking the taboo" (ibid., 108). See also Hugh B. Urban, "The Power of the Impure: Transgression, Violence and Secrecy in Bengali Tantra and Modern Western Magic," *Numen* 15, no. 4 (2003): 269–308.

6. See Urban, *Magia Sexualis*; Kripal and Hanegraaff, *Hidden Intercourse*; Arthur Versluis, *The Secret History of Western Sexual Mysticism: Sacred Practices and Spiritual Marriage* (Rochester, VT: Destiny Books, 2008).

7. Urban, *Magia Sexualis*, 55–80.

8. Foucault, *History of Sexuality*, 1:35. "What is peculiar to modern societies, in fact, is not that they consigned sex to a shadow existence, but that they dedicated themselves to speaking of it *ad infinitum* while exploiting it as *the* secret."

9. See R. von Krafft-Ebing, *Psychopathia Sexualis: With Especial Reference to Contrary Sexual Instinct: A Medico-Legal Study* (London: F. A. Davis, 1892), 24: "[S]exual feeling is the basis upon which social advancement is developed. . . . Sexual feeling is the root of all ethics and no doubt of aestheticism and religion. The sublimest virtues . . . spring from sexual life, which, however on account of its sensual power, may easily degenerate into the lowest passion and basest vice. Love unbridled is a volcano that burns down and lays waste to all around it; it is an abyss that devours all—honor, substance and health."

10. Aleister Crowley, *The Confessions of Aleister Crowley: An Autohagiography*, ed. John Symonds (New York: Hill and Wang, 1989), 767. On Crowley and sexual magic, see Urban, *Magia Sexualis*, 1–20; Henrik Bogdan and Martin P. Starr, eds., *Aleister Crowley and Western Esotericism* (New York: Oxford University Press, 2015); Henrik Bogdan, "The Babalon Working 1946: L. Ron Hubbard, John Whiteside Parsons, and the Practice of Enochian Magic," *Numen* 63, no. 1 (2016): 12–32.

11. See Tessel M. Bauduin, Victoria Ferentinou, and Daniel Zamani, eds. *Surrealism, Occultism and Politics: In Search of the Marvellous* (London: Routledge, 2018), 9; Alan Riding, "How Surrealists Made a Movement Out of Love and Sex," *New York Times*, October 21 2001, https://www.nytimes.com/2001/10/21/arts/art -architecture-how-surrealists-made-a-movement-of-love-and-sex.html.

12. Donald Traxler, "Introduction: The Reconciliation of Light and Dark Forces," in *The Light of Sex: Initiation, Magic and Sacrament*, by Maria de Naglowska (Rochester, VT: Inner Traditions, 2011), 1–2. On Evola and sexual magic, see his key work *Eros and the Mysteries of Love: The Metaphysics of Sex* (Rochester, VT: Inner Traditions, 1983); Urban, *Magia Sexualis*, 140–61.

13. On Naglowska and her work, see Marc Pluquet, *La Sophiale: Maria de Naglowska, Sa Vie, Son Oeuvre* (Paris: Ordo Templi Orientis, 1993); Sarane Alexandrian, *Les Libérateurs de l'amour* (Paris: Éditions du Seuil, 1977), 185–206; Michele Olzi, "The Devil's Popess: The French Reception of Maria de Naglowska (1883–1936) in Early Thirties in France," https://www.uni-erfurt.de/max-weber-kolleg/archiv/oeffentliche

-vortraege-ab-ws201213/esswe6/programmeesswe6/session-4/abstract-olzi/; Massimo Introvigne, *Satanism: A Social History* (Leiden: Brill, 2016); Hans Thomas Hakl, "Foreward: Maria de Naglowska: A Protagonist of Sexual Magic in the Early Twentieth Century," in *The Light of Sex: Initiation, Magic and Sacrament*, by Maria de Naglowska (Rochester, VT: Inner Traditions, 2011), ix–xiv; Hans Thomas Hakl, "The Theory and Practice of Sexual Magic, Exemplified by Four Magical Groups in the Early Twentieth Century," in Hanegraaff and Kripal, *Hidden Intercourse*, 445–79; Traxler, "Introduction," 1–8.

14. See Nadia Choucha, *Surrealism and the Occult* (Oxford: Mandrake, 1991); Robert Ziegler, *Magic and Mysticism in Fin-de-siècle France* (New York: Palgrave Macmillan, 2012).

15. See Hugh B. Urban, "Desire, Blood, and Power: Georges Bataille and the Study of Hindu Tantra in Northeast India," in *Negative Ecstasies: Georges Bataille and the Study of Religion*, ed. Jeremy Biles and Kent Brintnall (New York: Fordham University Press, 2015), 68–80. For feminist critiques of Bataille's rather masculine idea of sexuality, see Ladelle McWhorter, "Is There Sexual Difference in the Work of Georges Bataille?" *International Studies in Philosophy* 27, no. 1 (1995): 33–41.

16. On Satanism in the nineteenth century, see Ziegler, *Satanism*; Introvigne, *Satanism*; Gareth Medway, *The Lure of the Sinister: The Unnatural History of Satanism* (New York: New York University Press, 2001).

17. Naglowska referred to herself as a "Satanic woman." See Traxler, "Introduction," 4.

18. See Frater U. D., *The Secrets of Western Sex Magic* (Woodbury, MN: Llewellyn, 2002); Margot Ananda, *The Art of Sexual Ecstasy* (New York: G. P. Putnam Sons, 1995).

19. Pluquet, *La Sophiale*. For an overview of the existing historical materials, see Donald Traxler, "Eyewitness Accounts," in *The Light of Sex: Initiation, Magic and Sacrament*, by Maria de Naglowska (Rochester, VT: Inner Traditions, 2011). Other early accounts of Naglowska include René Thimmy, *La Magie à Paris* (Paris, 1934); Pierre Geyraud, *Les Petites Églises de Paris* (Paris: Éditions Émile-Paul, 1937).

20. Hakl, "Foreword," xi.

21. Traxler, "Introduction."

22. According to Michele Olzi, Naglowska's political views during this period (1909–19) combined elements of anarchism, socialism, and nationalism along with the philosophy of Henri Bergson and his concept of *élan vital*. However, the reason for her expulsion from Geneva was her 1918 lecture, "La paix et son principale obstacle," with its attack on both Russian and German politics (personal communication, June 21, 2018).

23. Hakl, "Foreword," xi; Mark Sedgwick, *Against the Modern World: Traditionalism and the Secret Intellectual History of the Twentieth Century* (New York: Oxford University Press, 2009), 103. See H. T. Hansen, "Die 'magische' Gruppe von Ur in ihrem historischen und esoterischen Umfeld," in *Schritte zur Initiation: Magie als Wissenschaft vom Ich*, by Julius Evola/Gruppe von UR (Interlaken, Switzerland: Ansata, 1997), 2:7–27.

24. Julius Evola, *Metafisica del sesso*, translated as *Eros and the Mysteries of Love: The Metaphysics of Sex* (Rochester, VT: Inner Traditions, 1991), 262–63.

25. Traxler, "Introduction," 1–2.

26. Hakl, "Foreward," xi.

NOTES TO PAGES 84-89   231

27. Auguste Apôtre, "Notre Thèse Sociale," *La Flèche: Organe d'Action Magique* 1 (15 Octobre 1930): 2-3.

28. Apôtre, "Notre Thèse Sociale," 2-3.

29. See Ziegler, *Satanism*.

30. Breton, *Manifestoes of Surrealism* (Ann Arbor: University of Michigan Press, 1969), 174-75.

31. Choucha, *Surrealism and the Occult*, 9.

32. Jeffrey Burton Russell, *The Prince of Darkness: Radical Evil and the Power of Good in History* (Ithaca, NY: Cornell University Press, 1992), 235. See Baudelaire, *The Flowers of Evil* (New York: Oxford, 2008), 269-76.

33. Robert Ziegler, *Satanism, Magic and Mysticism in Fin-de-siècle France* (New York: Palgrave Macmillan, 2012). See Huysmans, *Là-bas (Down There)* (New York: Dover, 2011).

34. Ziegler, *Satanism*, 15. See Docteur Bataille (aka Léo Taxil), *Le Diable au XIX siècle* (Paris: Delhomme, 1896).

35. Naglowska, "Preview of the Hanging Ritual," in *Light of Sex*, 110.

36. *La Flèche: Organe d'Action Magique* 1 (15 Octobre 1930): 1. See also "Vérités pharaoniques et phalliques chez Randolph," *La Flèche: Organe d'Action Magique* 8 (15 Décembre 1931): 1: "la vérité phallique est à la base de tous les rituels des sociétés secrètes, et l'art sacré et les écritures saintes de toutes les nations en disent le mystère à ceux qui savent les lire."

37. See Ioan Coulianu, *Eros and Magic in the Renaissance* (Chicago: University of Chicago Press, 1987). See Urban, *Magia Sexualis*; Versluis, *Secret History*; Kripal and Hanegraaff, *Hidden Intercourse*.

38. See Foucault, *History of Sexuality*, vol. 1.

39. Paschal Beverly Randolph, *The Immortality of Love: Unveiling the Secret Arcanum of Affectional Alchemy* (Quakertown, PA: Beverly Hall Corp., 1978), 48. See also Paschal Beverly Randolph, *Eulis! The History of Love: A History of Its Magic, Chemistry, Rules, Laws, Moods, Modes and Rationale* (Toledo, OH: Randolph, 1874).

40. John Patrick Deveney, *Paschal Beverly Randolph: A Nineteenth Century Black American Spiritualist, Rosicrucian and Sex Magician* (Albany: SUNY Press, 1996), 211.

41. Paschal Beverly Randolph, "The Mysteries of Eulis," manuscript reproduced in Deveney, *Paschal Beverly Randolph*, 339-40.

42. Randolph, "Mysteries of Eulis," 337.

43. See Urban, *Magia Sexualis*, chap. 2.

44. See Hakl, "Theory and Practice," 470; Introvigne, *Satanism*, 277.

45. Advertisement for *Magia Sexualis* in *La Flèche: Organe d'Action Magique* 1 (13 Octobre 1930): 7.

46. See, for example, *La Flèche: Organe d'Action Magique* 16 (15 Mars 1933): 1, which contains the following advertisement for Naglowska's book, *La Lumière du sexe*: "Our metaphysical teaching, as well as the Satanic rite of purification necessary to the transition from the Second to the Third Era, is definitively revealed in the volume entitled *The Light of Sex*."

47. *La Flèche: Organe d'Action Magique* 14 (15 Octobre 1932).

48. Hakl, "Theory and Practice," 470. See Maria de Naglowska, *Le Rite sacré de l'amour magique* (Paris: Ordo Temple Orientis, 1993), translated by Donald Traxler as *The Sacred Rite of Magical Love: A Ceremony of Word and Flesh* (Rochester, VT: Inner Traditions, 2012).

232 NOTES TO PAGES 89-92

49. Naglowska, *Sacred Rite*, 74.

50. Naglowska, *Sacred Rite*, 86.

51. Naglowska, *Sacred Rite*, 83.

52. Naglowska, *Sacred Rite*, 88.

53. Pluquet, *La Sophiale*, 23.

54. Introvigne, *Satanism*, 273.

55. Introvigne, *Satanism*, 275.

56. Maria de Naglowska, *Le Mystère de la pendaison: Initiation satanique selon de la doctrine du troisième terme de la Trinité* (Paris: Éditions de la Flèche, 1934), 96, translated by Donald Traxler as *Advanced Sex Magic: The Hanging Mystery Initiation* (Rochester, VT: Inner Traditions, 2011), 63–64.

57. "Nous ouvrons le Livre de la vie pour dévoiler la raison occulte de l'attrait sexuel," *La Flèche: Organe d'Action Magique* 1 (15 Octobre 1930): 1–2. See Pluquet, *La Sophiale*, 41: "la transformation et la stabilisation de notre société vers l'équilibre qui assurera sa survie s'accompliraient par la femme. . . . [L]a survie de notre civilisation mécanicienne se ferait par une ère matriarcale, conséquence de la 'remontée du Triangle Temporel.'"

58. *La Flèche: Organe d'Action Magique* 1 (15 Octobre, 1930): 1. See Pluquet, *La Sophiale*, 41–43.

59. "La Doctrine du Troisième Terme de la Trinité," *La Flèche Organe d'Action magique* 14 (15 Octobre 1932): 1.

60. Advertisement for *La Lumière du sexe*, *La Flèche: Organe d'Action magique* 14 (15 Octobre 1932): 1. See Auguste Apôtre, "Erotisme Initiatique," *La Fleche: Organe d'Action magique* 20 (15 Janvier 1935): 1: "[N]o one will share in the joys and equilibrium of the Third Term of the Trinity, unless he resolutely engages in the path of Initiatory Eroticism."

61. Maria de Naglowska, *La Lumière du sexe: ritual d'initiation satanique selon la doctrine du troisième terme de la Trinité* (Paris: Ordo Templi Orientis, 1993), 57, translated by Donald Traxler as *The Light of Sex: Initiation, Magic and Sacrament* (Rochester, VT: Inner Traditions, 2011), 41: "In the beginning, the two Hearts—that of the Man and that of the Woman—being in perfect Balance, and sex not yet having spoken, only the heart of Eve opposed the head of Adam. . . . In that brief paradisiacal period, on the Second Morning of the Divine Triangle, Satan was vanquished and God (=Life) triumphed. But after the sin, the voluptuous Fall of Adam and Eve, the struggle of the Day and the Night recommenced. Since that time this struggle has been within the human couple. The head of the Man belongs to Satan (−), the head of the Woman to God (+), the sex of the Woman to Satan (−), the sex of the Man to God (+)."

62. Naglowska, *La Lumière du sexe*, 58; *Light of Sex*, 43: "But the very thing that was a fault can become, must become, a redemption. . . . The Woman who will vanquish Satan within her womb, that one will regenerate the world, for 'just as Death entered into everyone and everything through one who was following the Woman, it will be withdrawn from everyone and everything thanks to the Victory of One, through the Woman.'"

63. Evola, *Eros*, 262.

64. On Spiritualism and women, see Ann Braude, *Radical Spirits: Spiritualism and Women's Rights in Nineteenth Century America* (Bloomington: Indiana University

NOTES TO PAGES 93–98 233

Press, 2001). On neopaganism and Wicca, see Ronald Hutton, *Triumph of the Moon: A History of Modern Pagan Witchcraft* (New York: Oxford University Press, 2001).

65. Michele Olzi, personal communication, June 21, 2018. See Michele Olzi, "Il Diavolo al Femminile: rappresentazione e ruolo della donna nell'occultimso di Maria de Naglowska," *La Rosa di Paracelso* 2 (2017), http://www.larosadiparacelso.com/in dex.php/rosa/article/view/32.

66. "Dogme," *La Flèche: Organe d'Action magique* 15 (15 Février 1933): 1. See Pluquet, *La Sophiale*, 48: "Le couple humain, comme tout couple de forces, constitue un système fonctionnant d'autant mieux qu'il fermé sur lui-même et que chaque signe est de force égale et de polarité contraire. Chez la femme le pôle positif (qui veut LA VIE) se situe dans sa tête. Le pôle négatif (qui s'oppose à LA VIE) se trouve dans son sexe. . . . Chez l'homme, le pôle positif est dans son sexe qui, instinctivement, est prêt à projeter sa semence et essaimer LA VIE sans restriction. Le pôle négatif est dans la tête."

67. Maria de Naglowska, "La Colère et la Patience de Dieu," *La Flèche: Organe d'Action magique* 17 (15 Avril 1933): 31.

68. Naglowska, "La Colère," 32.

69. "Lettre ouverte à Pie XI," *La Flèche: Organe d'Action magique* 19 (15 Mars 1933): 1.

70. "Avant la Guerre de 1936," *La Flèche: Organe d'Action magique* 20 (15 Janvier 1935): 3.

71. Traxler, "Note on the Translation," xv.

72. Introvigne, *Satanism*, 271.

73. Evola, *Eros*, 261.

74. Paul Ricoeur, *A Ricoeur Reader: Reflection and Imagination* (Toronto: University of Toronto Press, 1991), 32. See Paul Ricoeur, "The Metaphorical Process as Cognition, Imagination, and Feeling," in *On Metaphor*, ed. S. Sacks (Chicago: University of Chicago Press, 1978); Richard Kearney, *Poetics of Imagining: From Husserl to Lyotard* (London: HarperCollins, 1991), 152.

75. Urban, "Torment of Secrecy," 239.

76. Ziegler, *Satanism*, 12.

77. Hakl, "Theory and Practice," 468–69. See Naglowska, *La Lumière du sexe*, 50; *Light of Sex*, 36: "From the struggle between God (= Will to Live) and Satan (= Will to Die) the Son, the Second Hypostasis (hypothesis of immobility)—who confirms Life (= God)—in his visible manifestation called the Creation is eternally born."

78. See Pluquet, *La Sophiale*, 69: "Pendant le Troisième Terme de le Trinité, l'ère de l'esprit sain, la nouvelle Ethique détermine une ère de paix, car même Satan (la négation), se reconciliera momentanément avec DIEU."

79. Naglowska, *Sacred Rite of Magical Love*, 95–96. See Pluquet, *La Sophiale*, 20ff; Introvinge, *Satanism*, 274.

80. Naglowska, *Advanced Sex Magic*, 3–4; Naglowska, *La Mystère de la pendaison*, 11.

81. Ziegler, *Satanism*, 12.

82. Russell, *Prince of Darkness*, 224: "For Blake, no goods or evils are absolute. 'All deities reside in the human breast,' and no element of the psyche is wholly good or evil. True evil arises from the lack of integration of psychic elements; true good form the balance, union, and integration of opposites. For the title page of *The Marriage*, Blake drew an angel and a demon embracing. Reason and energy, love and hatred,

passive and active, apparent good and evil, must all merge in a transcendent, integrated whole" (224). See William Blake, *Marriage of Heaven and Hell: A Facsimile in Full Color* (New York: Dover, 1994).

83. Naglowska, *Light of Sex*, 103–4.

84. Naglowska, "Masculine Satanism, Feminine Satanism," in *Light of Sex*, 106.

85. Hakl, "Theory and Practice," 469; see Naglowska, *La Lumière du sexe*; Introvigne, *Satanism*, 272.

86. *La Flèche: Organe d'Action magique* 20 (15 Janvier 1935): 4.

87. Naglowska, "Preview of the Hanging Mystery," in *Light of Sex*, 110–11. See Naglowska, *Le Mystère de la pendaison*, 103–21.

88. Hakl, "Theory and Practice," 473. See Naglowska, "Preview of the Hanging Mystery," 111; Naglowska, *Le Mystère de la pendaison*, 103–21.

89. See Donald C. Traxler, "Maria de Naglowska: A Herald of the New Era," *New Dawn Magazine* 135 (2012), https://www.newdawnmagazine.com/articles/maria-de -naglowska-a-herald-of-the-new-era. On Bataille's work, see also Kent Brintnall and Jeremy Biles, eds., *Negative Ecstasies: Georges Bataille and the Study of Religion* (New York: Fordham University Press, 2015). On Bataille's secret society "Acéphale," see Marina Galletti, "Communautés Morales, Communautés Politiques," *Les Temps Modernes* 54 (Janvier-Février 1999): 153–67; Marina Galletti, "The Secret and the Sacred in Leiris and Bataille," in "The Collège de Sociologie and French Social Thought," Special Issue, *Economy and Society* 32, no. 1 (2003): 9–100; Frank Pearce, "The Collège de Sociologie and Acéphale," *Encyclopedia of Social Theory*, ed. George Ritzer (London: Sage, 2004), 118–22; Alastair Brotchie, introduction to *Encyclopedia Acephalica*, ed. Georges Bataille (London: Atlas Press, 1995), 14–15.

90. Bataille, *Erotism*, 11. "Eroticism opens the way to death. Death opens the way to the denial of our individual lives" (ibid., 24).

91. Georges Bataille, *The Accursed Shared*, vols. 2 and 3, *The History of Erotism* and *Sovereignty* (New York: Zone Books, 1993), 119. See Bataille, *Erotism*, 20–21: "If the union of two lovers comes about through love, it involves the idea of death, murder or suicide. . . . Only in the violation, through death if need be, of the individual's solitariness can there appear that image of the beloved object which in the lover's eyes invests all being with significance. . . . [R]eligious or sacred eroticism [is] full and limitless being unconfined within trammels of separate personalities, continuity of being, glimpsed as a deliverance through the person of the beloved."

92. See Introvigne, *Satanism*, 276.

93. On the genealogy of modern sexual magic, see Urban, *Magia Sexualis*. Popular works include Christopher S. Hyatt and Lon Milo Duquette, *Sex Magic, Tantra and Tarot: The Way of the Secret Lover* (Tempe, AZ: New Falcon, 1991); Christopher S. Hyatt, *Secrets of Western Tantra: The Sexuality of the Middle Path* (Tempe, AZ: Original Falcon Press, 2017); and Nikolas Schreck and Zeena Schreck, *Demons of the Flesh: The Complete Guide to Left-Hand Path Sex Magick* (London: Creation Books, 2002).

94. See Wolfson, "Occultation of the Feminine;" Bataille, *Erotism*, 17: "The whole business of eroticism is to destroy the self-contained character of the participators as they are in their normal lives. Stripping naked is the decisive action. Nakedness offers a contrast to self-possession, to discontinuous existence. . . . It is a state of communication revealing a quest for possible continuance of being beyond the confines of the self."

Chapter 4

1. God Supreme Allah, *Supreme Lessons of the Gods and Earths* (God Supreme Knowledge 1993), 6.

2. Wu Tang Clan, "Wu Revolution," *Wu Tang Forever*, Loud/RCA Records, 1997.

3. Scott, *Domination*, 138–39.

4. The RZA, *Wu Tang Manual* (New York: Riverhead Books, 2004).

5. On Nation of Islam, see Edward E. Curtis IV, *Black Muslim Religion in the Nation of Islam, 1960–1975* (Chapel Hill: University of North Carolina Press, 2006); Martha F. Lee, *The Nation of Islam: A Black Millenarian Movement* (Syracuse, NY: Syracuse University Press, 1996); Mattias Gardell, *In the Name of Allah: Louis Farrakhan and the Nation of Islam* (Durham, NC: Duke University Press, 1996).

6. On the Five Percenters or NGE, see Felicia Miyakawa, *Five Percenter Rap: God Hop's Music, Message, and Black Muslim Mission* (Bloomington: University of Indiana Press, 2005); Michael Muhammad Knight, *The Five Percenters: Islam, Hip-Hop, and the Gods of New York* (London: Oneworld, 2008); Su'ad Adbul Khabeer, *Muslim Cool: Race, Religion and Hip-Hop in the United States* (New York: New York University Press, 2016).

7. See Stephen Finley, Margarita Guillory and Hugh Page Jr., eds., *Esotericism in African American Religious Experience* (Leiden: Brill, 2014); Peter Lamborn Wilson, *Sacred Drift: Essays on the Margins of Islam* (San Francisco: City Lights Books, 1993), 26; Adib Rashad, *Elijah Muhammad and the Ideological Foundation of the Nation of Islam* (Hampton, VA: U.B. & US Communications Systems, 1994), 6; Ted Swedenburg, "Islam in the Mix: Lessons of the Five Percent," paper presented at the Anthropology Colloquium, University of Arkansas, February 19, 1997, https://sites.la.utexas.edu/mhc/files/2009/10/swedenburg_us.pdf.

8. See Yusuf Nuruddin, "The Five Percenters: A Teenage Nation of Gods and Earths," in *Muslim Communities in North America*, ed. Yvonne Yazbeck Haddad and Jane Idleman Smith (Albany: SUNY Press, 1994), 103–33.

9. Juan M. Floyd-Thomas, "A Jihad of Words: The Evolution of African American Islam and Contemporary Hip Hop," in *Noise and Spirit: The Religious and Spiritual Sensibilities of Rap Music*, ed. Anthony B. Pinn (New York: New York University Press, 2003), 56.

10. Simmel, *Sociology of Georg Simmel*, 347.

11. Scott, *Domination*, 138–39; see Paul C. Johnson, "Secretism and the Apotheosis of Papa Doc Duvalier," *Journal of the American Academy of Religion* 74, no. 2 (2006): 425.

12. See Monica R. Miller, "Real Recognize Real: Aporetic Flows and the Presence of New Black Godz in Hip Hop," in *Religion in Hip Hop*, ed. Monica R. Miller, Anthony B. Pinn, and Bernard "Bun B" Freedom (London: Bloomsbury, 2015), 203.

13. On black market symbolic capital, see Urban, *Economics of Ecstasy*, 12, 19–26.

14. See Miller, "Real Recognize Real;" Miyakawa, *Five Percent Rap*; Khabeer, *Muslim Cool*; Tricia Rose, *Black Noise: Rap Music and Black Culture in Contemporary America* (Middletown, CT: Wesleyan University Press, 1994); Anthony Pinn, "Rap Music and its Message: On Interpreting the Contact between Religion and Popular Culture," in *Religion and Popular Culture in America*, ed. Bruce David Forbes and Jeffrey H. Mahan (Berkeley: University of California Press, 2000), 263.

15. See Swedenburg, "Islam in the Mix."

16. There are many conflicting sources for Drew's biography. See Judith Weisenfeld, *New World A-Coming: Black Religion and Racial Identity during the Great Migration* (New York: New York University Press, 2016), 46–48; Fathie Abdat, "Before the Fez-Life and Times of Drew Ali," *Journal of Race Ethnicity and Religion* 5, no. 8 (2014); Miyakawa, *Five Percent Rap*, 9; Wilson, *Sacred Drift*, 16; Gardell, *In the Name of Allah*, 37–41.

17. Abdat, "Before the Fez."

18. Wilson, *Sacred Drift*, 16. See Abdat, "Before the Fez"; Clifton Marsh, *From Black Muslims to Muslims: The Resurrection, Transformation and Change of the Lost-Found Nation of Islam in America: 1930–1995* (Lanham, MD: Scarecrow Press, 1996), 29, 36.

19. Abdat, "Before the Fez."

20. Noble Drew Ali, *The Holy Koran of the Moorish Science Temple of America* (Hunlock Creek, PA: E. World, n.d. [1927]).

21. Wilson, *Sacred Drift*, 2.

22. Levi H. Dowling, *The Aquarian Gospel of Jesus the Christ* (Los Angeles: E. S. Dowling, 1911); Nicolas Notovich, *Le Vie Inconnue de Jésus-Christ* (Paris: Paul Olendorff, 1894). See Wilson, *Sacred Drift*, 19.

23. Sri Ramatherio, *Unto Thee I Grant: The Economy of Life* (San Jose, CA: Supreme Grand Lodge of the Ancient and Mystical Order Rosae Crucis, 1948). See Wilson, *Sacred Drift*, 21.

24. See Wilson, *Sacred Drift*, 25.

25. Ali, *Holy Koran*, prologue.

26. Ali, *Holy Koran*, X.20–24.

27. See Abdat, "Before the Fez"; Wilson, *Sacred Drift*, 26; Gardell, *In the Name of Allah*, 42.

28. Wilson, *Sacred Drift*, 26.

29. Wilson, *Sacred Drift*, 26–28.

30. Wilson, *Sacred Drift*, 20.

31. Ali, *Holy Koran*, V.14–15. See Gardell, *In the Name of Allah*, 41.

32. Knight, *Five Percenters*, 19. See Wilson, *Sacred Drift*, 28.

33. H. Carr, *An Examination of the Early Masonic Catechisms* (Leicester: Bros. Johnson, Wykes and Paine, 1946), 10.

34. Koran Questions for Moorish Americans, quoted in Knight, *Five Percenters*, 19.

35. See Gardell, *In the Name of Allah*, 51.

36. On Fard's possible connection with Moorish Science, see Arna Bontemps and Jack Conroy, *"Beloved and Scattered Millions": They Seek a City* (New York: Doubleday, Doran, 1945); E. U. Essien-Udom, *Black Nationalism: The Search for an Identity* (Chicago: University of Chicago Press, 1995); Marsh, *From Black Muslims*.

37. See Curtis, *Black Muslim Religion*, 60–61; Urban, *New Age*, 94–111.

38. See Justine M. Bakker, "On the Knowledge of Self and Others: Secrecy, Concealment, and Revelation in Elijah Muhammad's Nation of Islam," in *Esotericism in African American Religious Experience*, ed. Stephen Finley, Margarita Guillory, and Hugh Page Jr. (Leiden: Brill, 2014), 138–51.

39. Knight, *Five Percenters*, 25.

40. Floyd-Thomas, "Jihad of Words," 68n. See Swedenborg, "Islam in the Mix."

41. Amir Fatir, quoted in Knight, *Five Percenters*, 35. See Prince-A-Cuba, "Black Gods of the Inner City," *Gnosis Magazine* (1992): 56–63.

NOTES TO PAGES 112–121   237

42. Master Fard Muhammad, *The Supreme Wisdom Lessons by Master Fard Muhammad to His Servant the Most Honorable Elijah Muhamad for the Lost-Found Nation of Islam in North America* (Detroit: Department of Supreme Wisdom, n.d.), 14–15.

43. Elijah Muhammad, *Message to the Black Man in America* (Phoenix: Secretarius MEMPS, 2006), 116.

44. Muhammad, *Supreme Wisdom Lessons*, 26–27.

45. Swedenburg, "Islam in the Mix."

46. Knight, *Five Percenters*, 78; Khabeer, *Muslim Cool*, 25.

47. See George Breitman, ed., *Malcolm X Speaks: Selected Speeches and Statements* (New York: Grove Press, 1994), 9.

48. Wakeel Allah, *In the Name of Allah: A History of Clarence X and the Five Percenters*, 2 vols. (Atlanta: A Team, 2009), 2:13.

49. Knight, *Five Percenters*, 35.

50. Floyd-Thomas, "Jihad of Words," 55.

51. Miyakawa, *Five Percent Rap*, 16.

52. Floyd-Thomas, "Jihad of Words," 56. See Allah, *In the Name of Allah*, 1:134.

53. Clarence 13X, quoted in Allah, *In the Name of Allah*, 1:114.

54. Rose, *Black Noise*, 27.

55. Rose, *Black Noise*, 34.

56. "Harlem Hit by Five Percenters" *New York Amsterdam News*, October 16, 1965, 1. See Miyakawa, *Five Percent Rap*, 16.

57. Knight, *Five Percenters*, 78–79.

58. Allah, *In the Name of Allah*, 1:153; Knight, *Five Percenters*, 78–80.

59. Allah, *In the Name of Allah*, 1:167.

60. See Rose, *Black Noise*, 27–34.

61. See Biko Mandela Gray, "Show and Prove: Five Percenters and the Study of African American Esotericism," in *Esotericism in African American Religious Experience*, ed. Stephen Finley, Margarita Guillory and Hugh Page Jr. (Leiden: Brill, 2014), 177–97.

62. Floyd-Thomas, "Jihad of Words," 57.

63. Floyd Thomas, "Jihad of Words," 68n.

64. Floyd-Thomas, "Jihad of Words," 56.

65. Knight, *Five Percenters*, 52.

66. Floyd-Thomas, "Jihad of Words," 57. See Gardell, *In the Name of Allah*, 225–225.

67. God Supreme Allah, *Supreme Lessons*, n.p.

68. Knight, *Five Percenters*, 53. See Allah, *In the Name of Allah*, 1:116–21.

69. Knight, *Five Percenters*, 54.

70. Miyakawa, *Five Percent Rap*, 29. See Swedenburg, "Islam in the Mix."

71. See Miller, *Religion and Hip-Hop*, 61.

72. On "black market symbolic capital," see Urban, *Economics of Ecstasy*.

73. Dick Hebdige, *Subculture: The Meaning of Style* (London: Metheun, 1979), 104; Umberto Eco, "Towards a Semiotic Enquiry into the Television Message (1966)," trans. Paola Splendore, *Working Papers in Cultural Studies* 3 (1972): 103–21.

74. Hebdige, *Subculture*, 104.

75. John Clarke, "Style," in *Resistance through Rituals: Youth Subcultures in Postwar Britain* (London: Routledge, 2006), 149.

76. Nuruddin, "Teenage Nation," 118.

77. Rose, *Black Noise*, 38.

78. Allah, *In the Name of Allah*, 1:204.

79. Rose, *Black Noise*, 27–38.

80. RZA, *Wu Tang Manual*, 43.

81. Russell Simmons, *Life and Def: Sex, Drugs, Money + God* (New York: Three Rivers Press, 2002), 38–39.

82. Simmons, *Life and Def*, 39.

83. Nas, "No Idea's Original," *Stillmatic*, Columbia Records, 2001.

84. Simmons, *Life and Def*, 39.

85. "The GODS of Hip-Hop: A Reflection on the Five Percenter Influence on Rap Music and Culture," *HipHopWired*, March 24, 2010, https://hiphopwired.com/32991/the-gods-of-hip-hop-a-reflection-on-the-five-percenter-influence-on-rap-music-culture/.

86. RZA, *Wu Tang Manual*.

87. "GODS of Hip-Hop."

88. Eric B. and Rakim, "Move the Crowd," *Paid in Full*, Power Play, 1987.

89. Lakim Shabazz, "Lost Tribe of Shabazz," *Lost Tribe of Shabazz*, Tuff City, 1990.

90. Gravediggaz, *The Pick, the Sickle, and the Shovel*, BMG Records, 1997. See Miyakawa, *Five Percent Rap*.

91. Wu Tang Clan, "Wu Revolution." See also Brand Nubian's "Meaning of the 5%," on *In God We Trust* (1993), which plays a sermon by Louis Farrakhan over a hip-hop beat: "[T]he Honorable Elijah Muhammad said to us that there is 5% who are the Poor Righteous Teachers, who don't believe the teaching of lies of the 10%. But this 5% are all wise and know who the true and living God is, and they teach that the true and living God is the Son of Man, the Supreme Being, the Blackman of Asia. . . . Here is a small percentage of people who know God."

92. Lord Jamar, "Mathematics," *The Five Percent Album*, Babygrande Records, 2006.

93. RZA, *Wu Tang Manual*, 158. See "Triumph," *Wu Revolution*.

94. Floyd-Thomas, "Jihad of Words," 58. See also Rose, *Black Noise*, 184.

95. Simmel, "Sociology," 471–72.

96. Pinn, "Rap Music," 269.

97. Public Enemy, "Party for Your Right to Fight," *It Takes a Nation of Millions to Hold us Back*, Def Jam, 1988.

98. Miller, "Real Recognize Real," 203. See Khabeer, *Muslim Cool*, 5.

99. RZA, *Wu Tang Manual*, 41.

100. See Urban, *Economics of Ecstasy*.

101. On women in hip-hop generally, see Rose, *Black Noise*, 146–82.

102. Nuruddin, "Five Percenters," 128.

103. Floyd-Thomas, "Jihad of Words," 60.

104. Swedenburg, "Islam in the Mix."

105. Brand Nubian, "Love Me or Leave Me Alone," *In God We Trust*.

106. Lord Jamar, "Same Ole Woman," *Five Percent Album*.

107. Poor Righteous Teachers, "Can I Start This?" *Holy Intellect*, Profile/Arista Records, 1990.

108. Derrida, "How to Avoid Speaking," 25–26.

109. Keith Negus, "The Business of Rap: Between the Street and the Executive Suite," in *That's the Joint: The Hip-Hop Studies Reader*, ed. Murray Forman and Mark

Anthony Neal (New York: Routledge, 2012), 656–57. See S. Craig Watkins, "Black Youth and the Ironies of Capitalism," in Forman and Neal, *That's the Joint*, 691–713; Eric K. Watts, "An Exploration of Spectacular Consumption: Gangsta Rap as Cultural Commodity," in Forman and Neal, *That's the Joint*, 715–31; Andre Craddock-Willis, "Rap Music and the Black Musical Tradition: A Critical Assessment," in *Popular Music*, vol. 4, *Cultures and Subcultures of Popular Music*, ed. Chris Rojek (London: Sage, 2011).

110. On neoliberalism, see David Harvey, *A Brief History of Neoliberalism* (New York: Oxford, 2007).

111. "GODS of Hip-Hop." For a similar critique, see Brooke Daniel, "The Commodification of Hip Hop," DaInnocent, YouTube, 2006, https://www.youtube.com/watch?v=LiCo_uUD2SY.

112. Christopher John Farley, "Hip Hop Nation," *Time*, February 8, 1999, http://content.time.com/time/magazine/article/0,9171,19134,00.html.

113. Becky Blanchard, "The Social Significance of Rap & Hip Hop," *Edge: Ethics of Development in a Global Environment*, 1999, https://web.stanford.edu/class/e297c/poverty_prejudice/mediarace/socialsignificance.htm.

114. Nas, "Life's a Bitch" (featuring AZ), *Illmatic*, Columbia Records, 1994.

Chapter 5

1. Michael Barkun, *Religion and the Racist Right: The Origins of the Christian Identity Movement* (Chapel Hill: University of North Carolina Press, 1994), 229–30. See Kevin Flynn and Gary Gerhardt, *The Silent Brotherhood: Inside America's Racist Underground* (New York: Free Press, 1989), 81, 93, 140, 194; "An Oath to Read and Ponder," *From the Mountain*, September–October 1987, 10.

2. Macaba, *The Road Back: A Plan for the Restoration of Freedom When Our Country Has Been Taken Over by Its Enemies* (Torrance, CA: Noontide Press, 1973), 17–18.

3. Marcel Mauss, *Manual of Ethnography* (New York: Berghahn Books, 2007), 119.

4. Canetti, *Crowds and Power*, 290.

5. On the Jugantar movement, see Urban, *Tantra*, 73–205.

6. Jonathan Masters, "Militant Extremists in the U.S.," *Council on Foreign Relations*, February 7, 2011, https://www.cfr.org/backgrounder/militant-extremists-united-states: "Since September 11, the threat of internationally based Islamic extremist networks has dominated concerns of Homeland Security officials. And while authorities say the threats posed by homegrown Islamic extremism is growing, the FBI has reported that roughly two-thirds of terrorism in the United States was conducted by non-Islamic American extremists from 1980–2001; and from 2002–2005, it went up to 95 percent. . . . The most recent swell of extremist violence began to emerge from right-wing militants in the late 1980s and 1990s. According to a 2005 FBI report on terrorism, these groups, which are 'primarily in the form of domestic militias and conservative special interest causes, began to overtake left-wing extremism as the most dangerous . . . domestic terrorist threat to the country.'"

7. Southern Poverty Law Center, "Hate Groups Increase for Second Consecutive Year as Trump Electrifies Radical Right," February 15, 2017, https://www.splcenter.org/news/2017/02/15/hate-groups-increase-second-consecutive-year-trump-electrifies-radical-right. See also Damon T. Berry, *Blood & Faith: Christianity in*

White Nationalism (Syracuse, NY: Syracuse University Press, 2017), 199–208; Kathleen Belew, *Bring the War Home: The White Power Movement and Paramilitary America* (Cambridge. MA: Harvard University Press, 2018), 238–39.

8. "Hate Groups Increase."

9. For good discussions of the *Brüder Schweigen*, see James A. Aho, *The Politics of Righteousness: Idaho Christian Patriotism* (Seattle: University of Washington Press, 1995), 61–66; Evelyn A. Schlatter, *Aryan Cowboys: White Supremacists and the Search for a New Frontier* (Austin: University of Texas Press, 2006); Barkun, *Religion and the Racist Right*; Belew, *Bring the War Home*.

10. Flynn and Gerhardt, *Silent Brotherhood*, 20: "Over fifteen months it became the most dangerous right-wing underground group since the Ku Klux Klan. . . . His was a white underground with an ambitious plan: funding the far right's victory through robberies, battling its enemies with assassinations, and establishing its presence through a guerilla force bent on domestic terrorism and sabotage. Its aim: a separate white nation on U.S. soil."

11. Mark S. Hamm, *Terrorism as Crime: From Oklahoma City to Al-Qaeda and Beyond* (New York: New York University Press, 2007), 144. See Belew, *Bring the War Home*, 111.

12. Taussig, "Transgression," 356.

13. Abby Ferber, *White Man Falling: Race, Gender and White Supremacy* (Lanham, MD: Rowman and Littlefield, 1998).

14. Simmel, *Sociology of Georg Simmel*, 365.

15. Belew, *Bring the War Home*, 1–2. "Narratives of betrayal and crisis cemented this alliance. . . . [T]his movement did not seek to defend the American nation, even when it celebrated some elements of U.S. history and identity. Instead white power activists increasingly saw the state as their enemy. Many pursued the idea of an all-white, racial nation, one that transcended national borders" (ibid.).

16. See Nicholas Goodrick-Clarke, *Black Sun: Aryan Cults, Esoteric Nazism, and the Politics of Identity* (New York: New York University Press, 2001), chaps. 1 and 12; Frederick J. Simonelli, *American Fuehrer: George Lincoln Rockwell and the American Nazi Party* (Urbana: University of Illinois Press, 1999).

17. Southern Poverty Law Center, "William Pierce," 2018, https://www.splcenter.org/fighting-hate/extremist-files/individual/william-pierce. See also Berry, *Blood & Faith*, 45–56.

18. Mattias Gardell, *Gods of the Blood: The Pagan Revival and White Separatism* (Durham, NC: Duke University Press, 2003), 244.

19. Robert S. Griffin, *The Fame of a Dead Man's Deeds: An Up-Close Portrait of White Nationalist William Pierce* (Bloomington, IN: 1st Book Library, 2001), 29.

20. William Pierce, *Lincoln Rockwell: A Nationalist Life* (Arlington, VA: NS, 1967).

21. Berry, *Blood & Faith*, 49.

22. Anti-Defamation League, "Explosion of Hate: The Growing Danger of the National Alliance," 2012, https://www.adl.org/sites/default/files/documents/assets/pdf/combating-hate/Explosion-of-Hate.pdf.

23. Griffin, *Fame*, 166–67. See also Barkun, *Religion and the Racist Right*.

24. Griffin, *Fame*, 344.

25. William Pierce, *The Path* (Arlington, VA: Cosmotheist Community, 1977), 9–10.

26. William Pierce, "The Cosmotheism Trilogy," https://www.scribd.com/docu ment/348950906/cosmotheism-trilogy-william-luther-pierce-pdf. See also Berry, *Blood & Faith*, 55–56: "All of life is understood as rightly organized in nature accord- ing to the Creator's will, and thus 'races' are understood as natural manifestations of the Creator's will . . . [M]an best serves the Creator's purpose through a union of 'awakened consciousness' and 'true reason' that Pierce calls 'Divine Consciousness.' The ultimate purpose of the white man is therefore to realize this truth and to enact in his life in order to realize the 'Urge' which will advance man . . . to the 'higher man, who then must advance toward 'Godhood.'"

27. Griffin, *Fame*, 180.

28. Southern Poverty Law Center, "William Pierce."

29. Southern Poverty Law Center, "William Pierce."

30. See Belew, *Bring the War Home*, 111.

31. Andrew Macdonald (pseud.), *The Turner Diaries* (Hillsboro, WV: National Vanguard Books, 1999), 80.

32. Macdonald, *Turner Diaries*, 1–4.

33. Macdonald, *Turner Diaries*, 13, 6–7.

34. Macdonald, *Turner Diaries*, 70.

35. Macdonald, *Turner Diaries*, 73.

36. Macdonald, *Turner Diaries*, 73–74.

37. Griffin, *Fame*, 153.

38. For the Aryan Nations oath of initiation, see James Ridgeway, *Blood in the Face: The Ku Klux Klan, Aryan Nations, Nazi Skinheads, and the Rise of a New White Culture* (New York: Thunder's Mouth Press, 1995).

39. Heinz Höhne, *The Order of the Death's Head: The History of Hitler's S.S.* (New York: Coward-McCann, 1970), 147: "Himmler followed the Jesuits: just as the Jesuit novice has to undergo two years of severe tests and exercises before taking the three vows of poverty, chastity and obedience and entering the ranks of the scholastics, so the SS candidate had to undergo manifold tests before he was allowed to swear the 'kith and kin oath' and call himself an SS man."

40. Macdonald, *Turner Diaries*, 91–92.

41. Macdonald, *Turner Diaries*, 92: "A public 'show trial' was planned for me, pre- sumably in the Adolf Eichmann manner. . . . *Note to the reader:* Adolf Eichmann was a middle-level German official during World War II. Fifteen years after the war . . . he was kidnapped in South America by Jews, flown to Israel, and made the central figure in an elaborately staged, two-year propaganda campaign to evoke sympathy from the non-Jewish world for Israel."

42. Macdonald, *Turner Diaries*, 203–4.

43. Macdonald, *Turner Diaries*, 204.

44. Macdonald, *Turner Diaries*, 211.

45. Macdonald, *Turner Diaries*, 197.

46. Macdonald, *Turner Diaries*, 209.

47. Macdonald, *Turner Diaries*, 210.

48. Mark Hamm, *Apocalypse in Oklahoma: Waco and Ruby Ridge Revenged* (Bos- ton: Northwestern University Press, 1997), 198.

49. Southern Poverty Law Center, "William Pierce." Later, Pierce was asked whether the Oklahoma City bombing was directly inspired by the *Turner Diaries*, to

which he responded: "[T]he fact of the matter is that we are engaged in a war for the survival of our people. In a war, people jump the gun, it's not unusual. Often a war is preceded by border incidents, and something like Oklahoma City could be a border incident" (Griffin, *Fame*, 166–67).

50. See Flynn, *Silent Brotherhood*, 140; Barkun, *Religion*, 229; Aho, *Politics*, 62–63.

51. Aho, *Politics*, 63: "[T]here is little doubt that the *Turner Diaries* profoundly affected Robert Mathews."

52. Schlatter, *Aryan Cowboys*, 188, n87.

53. los341, "Re: The road back by macaba noontide press 1973," Stormfront forum, February 25, 2009, https://www.stormfront.org/forum/t453221/.

54. Macaba, *Road Back: A Plan for the Restoration of Freedom When Our Country Has Been Taken Over by Its Enemies* (Newport Beach, CA: Noontide Press, 1973), 1-1.

55. Macaba, *Road Back*, 1-1, 17-8.

56. Macaba, *Road Back*, 2-1, 2-2.

57. Macaba, *Road Back*, 18-3.

58. Macaba, *Road Back*, 18-4.

59. Macaba, *Road Back*, 18-6.

60. Macaba, *Road Back*, dedication.

61. Macaba, *Road Back*, figs. 1a and 1b.

62. Barkun, *Religion*, 228.

63. Mattias Gardell, "Robert J. Mathews," in *Encyclopedia of White Power: A Sourcebook on the Radical Racist Right* (New York: Rowman and Littlefield, 2000), 200.

64. William Pierce, "Commentary on Robert J. Mathews Speech" (1983), BitChute, https://www.bitchute.com/video/CKbKENbWJJLi/.

65. Flynn, *Silent Brotherhood*, 235.

66. Pierce, "Commentary on Robert J. Mathews Speech."

67. Pierce, "Commentary on Robert J. Mathews Speech."

68. Barkun, *Religion*, 218.

69. See Robert Jay Mathews, "Call to Aryan Warriors, 1983," BitChute, https://www.bitchute.com/video/CKbKENbWJJLi/.

70. Mathews, "Call to Aryan Warriors."

71. Mathews, "Call to Aryan Warriors."

72. Flynn and Gerhardt, *Silent Brotherhood*, 294–95.

73. Aho, *Politics*, 65; see Barkun, *Religion*, 230.

74. Martinez, *Brotherhood of Murder*, 25.

75. Flynn and Gerhardt, *Silent Brotherhood*, 96.

76. According to Schlatter, the child was Ken Loff's six-week-old daughter, Jamie Ann (*Aryan Cowboys*, 188n).

77. The Order's oath is almost identical to the Aryan Nations oath reproduced in Ridgeway's *Blood in the Face*. See also Schlatter, *Aryan Cowboys*, 188n.

78. Barkun, *Religion*, 229–30; see Flynn and Gerhardt, *Silent Brotherhood*, 81, 93, 140, 194.

79. Mircea Eliade, *Rites and Symbols of Initiation: The Mysteries of Birth and Rebirth* (New York: Harper and Row, 1958, xi. See also Bruce Lincoln, *Emerging from the Chrysalis: Rituals of Women's Initiation* (New York: Oxford University Press, 1991).

80. Belew, *Bring the War Home*, 118.

81. Belew, *Bring the War Home*, 116.

NOTES TO PAGES 155–162   243

82. Belew, *Bring the War Home*, 118.

83. Barkun, *Religion*, 228. Apparently, Berg was a last-minute substitute for the original assassination target, Morris Dees, founder of the Southern Poverty Law Center.

84. Robert Jay Mathews, "Letter to the Editor," in *Encyclopedia of White Power*, 527.

85. Flynn and Gerhardt, *Silent Brotherhood*, 7; see Aho, *Politics*, 61.

86. George Michael, "David Lane and the Fourteen Words," *Totalitarian Movements and Political Religions* 10 (2009): 43–61.

87. Gardell, "Robert J. Mathews," 200.

88. Mattias Gardell, "David Lane," in *Encyclopedia of White Power*, 168.

89. Mattias Gardell, "Ron McVan," in *Encyclopedia of White Power*, 202.

90. Berry, *Blood & Faith*, 119. See Ron McVan, *Creed of Iron: Wotansvolk Wisdom* (Saint Marie, ID: Fourteen Words Press, 1997), 17.

91. David Lane, *Victory or Valhalla: The Final Compilation of Writings by David Lane* (CreateSpace, 2010), 224, 225–26.

92. Lane, *Victory*, 368–69. See also David Lane, *Deceived, Damned & Defiant: The Revolutionary Writings of David Lane* (Saint Marie, ID: Fourteen Words Press, 1999), 310–11.

93. Lane, *Victory*, 226.

94. Lane, *Victory*, 226.

95. Gardell, *Gods of the Blood*, 217. See Michael, "David Lane," 43–61; Berry, *Blood & Faith*, 120–21.

96. Masters, "Militant Extremists in the U.S."

97. Others claim that the tern "alt-right" originated in the writings of Paul Gottfried, a Jewish intellectual who also invented the term "paleoconservative" in the 1980s, to refer to a new alternative within the establishment right (Berry, *Blood & Faith*, 200). On the alt-right as a movement, see George Hawley, *Making Sense of the Alt-Right* (New York: Columbia University Press, 2017); David Neiwhart, *Alt-America: The Rise of the Radical Right in the Age of Trump* (London: Verso, 2017).

98. Potok, "The Year in Hate and Extremism," Southern Poverty Law Center, 2017, https://www.splcenter.org/fighting-hate/intelligence-report/2017/year-hate-and -extremism.

99. Hugh B. Urban, "The Theology of Stephen K. Bannon," *Religion & Politics*, April 4, 2017, http://religionandpolitics.org/2017/04/17/the-theology-of-stephen-k -bannon/.

100. Allum Bokhari and Milo Yiannopoulos, "An Establishment Conservative's Guide to the Alt-Right," Breitbart, March 29, 2016, https://www.breitbart.com/tech /2016/03/29/an-establishment-conservatives-guide-to-the-alt-right/.

101. Stephen Piggot, "White Nationalists Rejoice at Trump's Appointment of Breitbart's Stephen Bannon," Southern Poverty Law Center, November 14, 2016, https://www.splcenter.org/hatewatch/2016/11/14/white-nationalists-rejoice-tru mps-appointment-breitbarts-stephen-bannon.

102. Mark Potok, "The Year in Hate and Extremism," Southern Poverty Law Center, February 15, 2017, https://www.splcenter.org/fighting-hate/intelligence-report /2017/year-hate-and-extremism.

103. Potok, "Year in Hate and Extremism."

104. Stephen Piggot, "Donald Trump to Mainstream White Nationalist Memes," Southern Poverty Law Center, August 4, 2016, https://www.splcenter.org/hatewatch /2016/04/04/donald-trump-continues-mainstream-white-nationalist-memes.

105. Glenn Thrush and Maggie Haberman, "Trump Gives White Supremacists an Unequivocal Boost," *New York Times*, August 15, 2017, https://www.nytimes.com /2017/08/15/us/politics/trump-charlottesville-white-nationalists.html?mcubz=0.

106. "Andew Anglin," Southern Poverty Law Center, accessed March 24, 2020, https://www.splcenter.org/fighting-hate/extremist-files/individual/andrew-anglin. As Belew notes, "the self-proclaimed 'alt-right'" rose up from the websites and forums founded by white power activists and then exploded "into mainstream politics during the presidential campaign and election of Donald Trump"; meanwhile, "[h]ate crimes proliferated into the wake of the election" (*Bring the War Home*, 238).

107. "Hate Map," Southern Poverty Law Center, 2017, https://www.splcenter.org /hate-map.

108. Anna North, "The Scope of Hate in 2017," *New York Times*, June 2, 2017, https://www.nytimes.com/2017/06/01/opinion/hate-crime-lebron-james-college -park-murder.html.

109. See "Anders Behring Breivik's Complete Manifesto, 2083: A European Declaration of Independence," *Public Intelligence*, July 28, 2011, https://publicintelligence .net/anders-behring-breiviks-complete-manifesto-2083-a-european-declaration-of -independence/; Val Burris, Emery Smith, and Ann Strahm," White Supremacist Networks on the Internet," *Sociological Focus* 33, no. 2 (2000): 215–35.

110. See "The Great Replacement: The Manifesto of the New Zealand Mosque Shooter," *European Freedom*, March 16, 2019, https://www.europeanfreedom.com /2019/03/16/the-great-replacement-the-manifesto-of-brenton-tarrant-the-new -zealand-mosque-shooter/.

Chapter 6

1. "OT VIII: Truth Revealed," *Advance!* 155 (2001): 27.

2. Taussig, "Transgression," 349–64.

3. See Mark Teeuwen, "Introduction," in Scheid and Teeuwen, *Culture of Secrecy*, 6: "Secrecy practices and even the concept of secrecy itself are subject to regional variation and historical development. A comparative study of secrecy is most valuable if it can identify clear differences between conceptions of secrecy in different periods and places." See also Johnson, *Secrets, Gossip and Gods*.

4. On this point, see Urban, *Economics of Ecstasy*.

5. Janet Reitman, *Inside Scientology: The Story of America's Most Secretive Religion* (New York: Houghton Mifflin, 2011); "The Secrets of Scientology," *BBC Panorama*, October 7, 2010.

6. Exceptions include Mikael Rothstein, "His Name Was Xenu: He Used Renegades ... Aspects of Scientology's Founding Myth," in *Scientology*, ed. James R. Lewis (New York: Oxford University Press, 2009), 365–88; Hugh B. Urban, "The Secrets of Scientology: Concealment, Information Control and Espionage in a Controversial New Religion," in *Contemporary Esotericism*, ed. Egil Asprem and Kennet Granholm (Sheffield: Equinox, 2013), 181–99; Hugh B. Urban, "Fair Game: Secrecy, Security and the Church of Scientology in Cold War America," *Journal of the American Academy of Religion* 74, no. 2 (2006): 356–89; Susan Raine, "Surveillance in a New

Religious Movement: Scientology as a Test Case," *Religious Studies and Theology* 28, no. 1 (2009): 63–94.

7. See Urban, "Secrets of Scientology;" Hugh B. Urban, "The Church of Scientology," in Revisionism and Diversification in New Religious Movements, ed. Eileen Barker (London: Ashgate, 2013).

8. Raine, "Surveillance."

9. Urban, "Fair Game;" Urban, *Church of Scientology*.

10. Rothstein, "His Name was Xenu;" see Susan Raine, "Astounding History: L. Ron Hubbard's Scientology Space Opera," *Religion* 45, no. 1 (2015): 66–88.

11. Urban, *Church of Scientology*, 89–117.

12. "OT VIII: Truth Revealed," 27.

13. Rothstein, "His Name was Xenu;" see Joel Sappell and Robert W. Welkos, "Defining the Theology," *Los Angeles Times*, June 24, 1990; *South Park*, "Trapped in the Closet," Comedy Central, November 16, 2005.

14. Urban, "Torment of Secrecy," 209–48.

15. Urban, "Torment of Secrecy." See Scheid and Teeuwen, *Culture of Secrecy*, 4–5.

16. Raine, "Astounding History." See also Harriet Whitehead, "Reasonably Fantastic: Some Perspectives on Scientology, Science Fiction, and Occultism," in *Religious Movements in Contemporary America*, ed. I. I. Zaretsky (Princeton, NJ: Princeton University Press, 1974).

17. Raine, "Astounding History"; Hugh B. Urban, "Typewriter in the Sky: L. Ron Hubbard's Fiction and the Birth of the Thetan," in *Scientology and Popular Culture*, ed. Stephen Kent and Susan Raine (Westport, CT: Praeger, 2017), 33–52.

18. Urban, "Typewriter in the Sky." For different views of Hubbard's early magical interests, see Hugh B. Urban, "The Occult Roots of Scientology? L. Ron Hubbard, Aleister Crowley and the Origins of a Controversial New Religion," *Nova Religio* 15, no. 3 (2012): 91–116; Massimo Introvigne, "The Gnostic L. Ron Hubbard: Was He Influenced by Aleister Crowley?" *Journal of CESNUR* 3, no. 3 (2019): 53–81.

19. See Urban, "Occult Roots"; Introvigne, "Gnostic L. Ron Hubbard"; Henrik Bogdan, "The Babalon Working 1946: L. Ron Hubbard, John Whiteside Parsons, and the Practice of Enochian Magic," *Numen* 63, no. 1 (2016): 12–32; George Pendle, *Strange Angel: The Otherworldly Life of John Whiteside Parsons* (Orlando: Harcourt, 2005), 253–54.

On Crowley's work and influence, see Henrik Bogdan and Martin P. Starr, eds., *Aleister Crowley and Western Esotericism* (New York: Oxford University Press, 2015); Marco Pasi, *Aleister Crowley and the Temptation of Politics* (New York: Routledge, 2014); Gordan Djurdjevic, *India and the Occult: The Influence of South Asian Spirituality on Modern Western Occultism* (New York: Palgrave Macmillan, 2014).

20. Pendle, *Strange Angel*, 253–54; Lawrence Sutin, *Do What Thou Wilt: A Life of Aleister Crowley* (New York: St. Martin's, 2000), 414–15.

21. See Bogdan, "Babalon Working," 12–32; Urban, "Occult Roots;" Pendle, *Strange Angel*; Introvigne, "Gnostic L. Ron Hubbard."

22. Sutin, *Do What Thou Wilt*, 412–15; Urban, "Occult Roots;" Introvigne, "Gnostic L. Ron Hubbard."

23. Church of Scientology, letter to the *Sunday Times*, December 28, 1969.

24. Urban, "Occult Roots." See also Jon Atack, *A Piece of Blue Sky: Scientology, Dianetics, and L. Ron Hubbard Exposed* (New York: Carol, 1990); George M. Witek, *Lucifer's Bridge: Scientology's Lost Paradise* (self-pub., 2015).

25. L. Ron Hubbard, "Dianetics: The Evolution of a Science," *Astounding Science Fiction* 45, no. 3 (1950): 43–87; L. Ron Hubbard, *Dianetics: The Modern Science of Mental Health* (Los Angeles: Bridge, 2007).

26. Urban, *Church of Scientology*, 60–68; see also Roy Wallis, *The Road to Total Freedom: A Sociological Analysis of Scientology* (New York: Columbia University Press, 1976), 34–68.

27. See L. Ron Hubbard, *The E-Meter Essentials* (Phoenix: Hubbard College of Scientology, 1967).

28. Hubbard, *Dianetics*, 113.

29. Wallis, *Road to Total Freedom*, 125; Harriet Whitehead, *Renunciation and Reformulation: A Study of Conversion in an American Sect* (Ithaca, NY: Cornell University Press, 1987), 185.

30. "Success Beyond Man's Wildest Dreams. *Advance!* 7 (1969): 3; "OT Phenomena Success," *Advance!* 17 (1973): 14–17. See Urban, *Church of Scientology*, 77–82.

31. *Advance!* 1 (1969): 13.

32. Flag Service Organization, "Donation and Registration Rates" (Clearwater, FL, 2009); Urban, *Church of Scientology*, 130–38.

33. Richard Behar, "The Thriving Cult of Greed and Power," *Time*, May 6, 1991, 50–57.

34. Bridge Publications, *Dianetics and Scientology Catalog* (Los Angeles: Bridge, 2009).

35. L. Ron Hubbard, *Have You Lived Before This Life?* (Los Angeles: Bridge, 1990), 307. See also L. Ron Hubbard, *Ron's Journal 67* (Los Angeles: Golden Era, 1983).

36. See Rothstein, "His Name Was Xenu"; Raine, "Astounding History."

37. The document is contained in the record for *Church of Scientology International v. Fishman and Geertz*, Case No. CV 91-6426 HLH (Tx) (C.D. Cal. 1993). See also Karen Spaink, "The Fishman Affidavit," 1995, https://kspaink.home.xs4all.nl /fishman/index2.html. See Urban, *Church of Scientology*, 186–88.

38. Alan Prendergast, "Stalking the Net," *Westword*, October 4, 1995, http://www .westword.com/news/stalking-the-net-5055577.

39. In one advertisement from 1973, Hubbard indicates there are even more levels beyond OT XV: "there are 15 levels above OT VII just waiting for more people to fully obtain OT VI and VII" (*Advance!* 20 [1973]:1).

40. L. Ron Hubbard, *Hymn of Asia* (Los Angeles: Golden Era, 2009).

41. This point was brought to my attention by Catherine Wessinger. Under the leadership of Annie Besant, the Theosophical Society promoted the young Indian Jiddu Krishnamurti as Maitreya. See Catherine Wessinger, "The Second Generation Leaders of the Theosophical Society," in *The Brill Handbook of the Theosophical Current*, ed. Olav Hammer and Mikael Rothstein (Leiden: Brill, 2013), 80–96.

42. *Church of Scientology International v. Fishman and Geertz*, 1993; Spaink, "Fishman Affidavit."

43. Again, this was brought to my attention by Catherine Wessinger. Helena Petrovna Blavatsky also used the image of Lucifer as the "light-bearer" of gnosis, for example, in her London journal, *Lucifer*. See John Alegeo, "Lucifer: What's in a Name?" *Quest* 89, no. 5 (2001): 162–63.

44. *Church of Scientology International v. Fishman and Geertz*, 1993.

45. *Church of Scientology International v. Fishman and Geertz*, 1993.

NOTES TO PAGES 173–178 247

46. *Church of Scientology International v. Fishman and Geertz*, 1993.

47. Prendergast, "Stalking the Net."

48. "Church of Scientology Collection: Operating Thetan Documents," Wikileaks, March 24, 2008, https://wikileaks.org/wiki/Church_of_Scientology_collected_Op erating_Thetan_documents.

49. Witek, *Lucifer's Bridge*, 58; Tony Ortega, "Up the Bridge: We Finally Reach 'OT 8,'" *Underground Bunker*, June 25, 2014, http://tonyortega.org/2014/06/24/up -the-bridge-we-finally-reach-ot-8-but-was-its-first-version-really-a-hoax/.

50. Urban, "Occult Roots;" see Sutin, *Do What Thou Wilt*. For different views on the Crowley-Hubbard connection, see Introvigne, "Gnostic L. Ron Hubbard."

51. This is also what a high-level Scientology spokesman named John Wood told me in an email exchange (December 16, 2015–January 3, 2016).

52. Mark Rathbun, "Truth Revealed About OT VIII," *Moving Up a Little Higher*, March 16, 2011, https://markrathbun.wordpress.com/2011/03/16/truth-revealed -about-ot-viii/.

53. Urban, "Torment of Secrecy."

54. See Bellman, *Language of Secrecy*, 144; Gunn, *Modern Occult Rhetoric*; John-son, *Secrets, Gossip and Gods*.

55. Nooter, *Secrecy*, 24.

56. "OT III," *Advance!* 66 (1980): 21. This theme recurs in later issues, as we see in the ad for "The Second Wall of Fire," special issue, *Advance!* 137 (1998): 30: "Once the hidden secrets of the universe are revealed your infinite power cannot be contained."

57. Back cover advertisement, *Advance!* 50 (1978); "Now that You Know Where You're Going. . . . Let Us Help You Get There!" *Advance!* 57 (1979): 21.

58. "Regain Your Full Ability," *Advance!* 44 (1977): 29.

59. "OT Phenomena Success," *Advance!* 21 (1973): 16.

60. "OT Phenomena," *Advance!* 33 (1975): 8.

61. "OT Phenomena Success," *Advance!* 17 (1973): 14–17; "Success Beyond Man's Wildest Dreams," *Advance!* 7 (1969): 3.

62. "OT Phenomena," *Advance!* 33 (1975): 8. Other promotions for the OT levels recount being able to "exteriorize" to find the nearest McDonald's restaurant and the most convenient movie theater while visiting Los Angeles from out of town. See "OT Phenomena," *Advance!* 31 (1975): 10. On "exteriorization," see also Urban, *Church of Scientology*, chap. 2, and Urban, "Occult Roots."

63. "Ron Is Waiting for You on the Other Side of the Bridge," *Advance!* 21 (1973): 12; "Advance Course Donations," *Advance!* 53 (1978): 20.

64. "OT VIII: Truth Revealed," *Advance!* 155 (2001): 27.

65. "Life After New OT VIII," *OT VIII Newsletter* 68 (2010): n.p.

66. Georg Simmel, "The Sociology of Secrecy and Secret Societies," *Journal of American Sociology* 11, no. 4 (1906): 441–98, reprinted in *The Sociology of Georg Sim-mel*, ed. Kurt Wolff (New York: Free Press, 1950), 337.

67. Bridge Publications, *Dianetics and Scientology Catalog*; see "New OT VIII Bracelet," *New OT VIII Newsletter* 67 (2009): n.p.

68. Randall Johnson, introduction to *The Field of Cultural Production*, by Pierre Bourdieu (New York: Columbia University Press, 1994), 7.

69. Swartz, *Culture and Power*, 43; see Urban, "Torment of Secrecy."

70. Pierre Bourdieu, "The Forms of Capital," in *Handbook of Theory and Research*

of the Sociology of Education, ed. J. Richardson (New York: Greenwood, 1986), 241–58; Pierre Bourdieu, *Outline of a Theory of Practice* (Cambridge: Cambridge University Press, 1986).

71. See "Celebrity Centre Thirty-Sixth Annual Gala," *Celebrity* 369 (2005): 8–9.

72. Lawrence Wright, *Going Clear: Scientology, Hollywood, and the Prison of Belief* (New York: Vintage, 2013), 277; see Urban, *Church of Scientology*, 139–45.

73. Ann Brill and Ashley Packard, "Silencing Scientology's Critics on the Net: A Mission Impossible," *Communications and the Law* 19, no. 4 (1997): 1–23; Prendergast, "Stalking the Net"; Mark Fearer, "Scientology's Secrets," in *Composing Cyberspace: Identity, Community and Knowledge in the Electronic Age*, ed. Richard Holeton (Boston: McGraw-Hill), 350–52.

74. Religious Technology Center, "Holder of the Dianetics and Scientology Trademarks," 2011, http://www.theta.com/goodman/rtc.htm. See also Urban, "Fair Game."

75. Joel Sappell and Robert Welkos, "Scientologists Block Access to Secret Documents," *Los Angeles Times*, November 15, 1985.

76. Brill and Packard, "Silencing Scientology's Critics," 5.

77. Fearer, "Scientology's Secrets"; Brill and Packard, "Silencing Scientology's Critics," 5.

78. Behar, "Thriving Cult of Greed."

79. Brill and Packard, "Silencing Scientology's Critics," 9–10.

80. Spaink, "Fishman Affidavit;" Prendergast, "Stalking the Web."

81. Urban, *Church of Scientology*, 194–96.

82. On the liability of secrecy, see also Urban, *Economics of Ecstasy*, 161–206.

83. *South Park*, "Trapped in the Closet."

84. John Cook, "Cult Friction," *Radar*, April 2008, http://www.xenu-directory .net/news/20080317-radar.html.

85. Gerry Armstrong, phone interview, August 10, 2009. Today, it is difficult to accurately gauge Scientology's numbers; the church claims to be "the world's fastest growing religion," with over eight million members worldwide, while most scholars regard this number as grossly exaggerated. As J. Gordon Melton notes, the church's numbers include "anyone who ever bought a Scientology book or took a basic course. Ninety-nine percent of them don't ever darken the door of the church again" (Elaine Jarvik, "Scientology: Church Now Claims More Than 8 Million Members," *Desert Morning News*, September 20, 2004, http://web.archive.org/web/20071212145039 /http://deseretnews.com/dn/view/0,1249,595091823,00.html. Some more critical scholars, such as Stephen Kent, believe Scientology's numbers are in steep decline. See Geoff McMaster, "Once Thriving Church of Scientology Faces Extinction, Says Cult Tracker," *Folio*, January 11, 2018, https://www.folio.ca/once-thriving-church-of -scientology-faces-extinction-says-cult-tracker/.

86. Anonymous, "Message to Scientology," YouTube, January 21, 2008, https:// www.youtube.com/watch?v=JCbKv9yiLiQ. See Urban, *Church of Scientology*, 104–96.

87. "Scientology: Questions and Answers," ABC News, October 23, 2009.

88. "What Scientologists Say about Scientology," 2019, https://www.scientology .org/what-is-scientology/what-scientologists-say-about-scientology.html. See also Church of Scientology International, *Scientology: Theology and Practice of a Contemporary Religion* (Los Angeles: Bridge, 1999).

89. Scientology Volunteer Ministers, 2016, http://www.volunteerministers.org /home.html.

NOTES TO PAGES 183–185 249

90. See, for example, "How Would You Describe the State of Operating Thetan?" Scientology.org, 2019: "As a being becomes more and more OT, they become more stable, powerful and responsible as a spiritual being."

91. See Urban, "Knowing of Knowing."

92. See Wolfson, *Eros, Language, Being*; Johnson, *Secrets, Gossip and Gods*; Gunn, *Modern Occult Rhetoric*; Carnes, *Secret Ritual*; Urban, "Secrecy in New Religious Movements"; Urban, "Elitism and Esotericism."

93. Allison Fish, "Laying Claim to Yoga: Intellectual Property, Cultural Rights, and the Digital Archive" (PhD diss., University of California, Irvine, 2010). See Andrea Jain, *Selling Yoga: From Counterculture to Pop Culture* (New York: Oxford University Press, 2014).

94. Hugh B. Urban, *Zorba the Buddha: Sex, Spirituality and Capitalism in the Global Osho Movement* (Berkeley: University of California Press, 2016), 155–78.

95. See Andrew Ventimiglia, *Copyrighting God: Ownership of the Sacred in American Religion* (Cambridge: Cambridge University Press, 2018); Mario Biagioli et al., eds., *Making and Unmaking Intellectual Property: Creative Production in Legal and Cultural Perspective* (Chicago: University of Chicago Press, 2011).

96. Bullock, *Revolutionary Brotherhood*, 318–19. See also Mark A. Tabbert, *American Freemasonry: Three Centuries of Building Communities* (New York: New York University Press, 2006), 215.

97. Michael Homer, *Joseph's Temples: The Dynamic Relationship between Freemasonry and Mormonism* (Salt Lake City: University of Utah Press, 2014). On the esoteric elements in Mormonism, see also Brooke, *Refiners' Fire*.

98. See Mircea Eliade, *The Myth of the Eternal Return: Cosmos and History* (Princeton, NJ: Princeton University Press, 2005).

99. Urban, "Fair Game."

100. Among the many recent works by ex-members making such allegations, see Marc Headley, *Blown for Good: Behind the Iron Curtain of Scientology* (Burbank, CA: BFG Books, 2010); Nancy Many, *My Billion Year Contract: Memoir of a Former Scientologist* (Bloomington, IN: Xlibris, 2009); Staff of the Tampa Bay Times, *The Truth Rundown: Stories of Violence, Intimidation, and Control in the World of Scientology* (Tampa Bay, FL: Times, 2015); Leah Remini, *Troublemaker: Surviving Hollywood and Scientology* (New York: Ballantine Books, 2015).

101. There is surprisingly little critical scholarship on the allegations of abuse in Scientology. While there are numerous accounts by ex-members and journalists, many of the academic discussions largely dismiss the allegations of abuse in the RPF and elsewhere. See J. Gordon Melton, "A Contemporary Ordered Religious Community: The Sea Organization," CESNUR Center on New Religions, 2001, http://www .cesnur.org/2001/london2001/melton.htm; Juha Pentikäinen, Jurgen F. K. Redhardt, and Michael York, "The Church of Scientology's Project Rehabilitation Force," CESNUR Center on New Religions, 2002, http://www.cesnur.org/2002/scient_rpf _01.htm. One of the few more critical accounts is Stephen Kent, "Brainwashing in Scientology's Rehabilitation Project Force," 1997, http://www.arts.ualberta.ca/~ske nt/Linkedfiles/Brainwashing%20in%20Scientology%27s%20Rehabilitation%20 Project%20Force%20%28RPF%29.htm. For a more sort of "middle-way" account, see Urban, *Church of Scientology*, chap. 4.

Conclusion

1. Pierre Bourdieu, *Sociology in Question* (London: Sage, 1993), 10.

2. Carl Schmitt, *Roman Catholicism and Political Form* (Westport, CT: Greenwood Press, 1996), 34.

3. J. William Fulbright, quoted in Victor Marchetti and John D. Marks, *The CIA and the Cult of Intelligence* (New York: Dell, 1974), 29.

4. See Joseph G. Jorgenson, *The Sun Dance Religion: Power for the Powerless* (Chicago: University of Chicago Press, 1986); Omar Stewart, *Peyote Religion: A History* (Norman: University of Oklahoma Press, 1993).

5. See Herdt, *Secrecy and Cultural Reality.* On women's initiation rites in a variety of cultures, see Lincoln, *Emerging from the Chrysalis.*

6. On secrecy in Hindu and Buddhist Tantra, see Urban, *Economics of Ecstasy*; Urban, *Tantra*; Ronald Davidson, *Indian Esoteric Buddhism: A Social History of the Tantric Movement* (New York: Columbia University Press, 2002).

7. See especially the work of Elliot R. Wolfson, such as *Language, Eros, Being.*

8. See Nooter, *Secrecy.*

9. See Ventimiglia, *Copyrighting God*; Urban, *Church of Scientology*, chap. 6; Urban, *Zorba the Buddha*, 155–78.

10. Again, I understand authority primarily in Bruce Lincoln's sense; see Lincoln, *Authority.*

11. Barbour, *Derrida's Secret*, 8.

12. See Kripal, *Road of Excess*, xi–xiii; Johnson, *Secrets, Gossip and Gods*; Taussig, "Transgression."

13. Canetti, *Crowds and Power*, 296.

14. See Cole and Fabbrini, *Surveillance*; Zuboff, *Surveillance Capitalism*; Lyon, *Surveillance Society.*

15. Bruce Lincoln, *Death, War and Sacrifice: Studies in Ideology and Practice* (Chicago: University of Chicago Press, 1991), 244. See also Urban and Johnson, *Irreverence and the Sacred*, introduction and Lincoln's afterword to the same volume.

16. Swartz, *Culture and Power*, 261. See Bourdieu, *Sociology in Question*, 9: "[Sociology] reveals things that are hidden and sometimes *repressed.*"

17. On this point, see Elaine Scarry, "Resolving to Resist," *Boston Review*, February/March 2004, bhttp://bostonreview.net/archives/BR29.1/scarry.html#7.

18. On terrorism as form of theatrical spectacle, see Mark Juergensmeyer, *Terror in the Mind of God: The Global Rise of Religious of Violence* (Berkeley: University of California Press, 2017), 149–81. See also Retort, *Afflicted Powers: Capital and Spectacle in a New Age of War* (New York: Verso, 2005), 27: "The terrorists . . . followed the logic of the spectacle to its charnel house conclusion. If, to trot out [Guy] Debord's over-famous aphorism again, 'the spectacle is capital accumulated to the power where it becomes image,' then what more adequate encapsulation of the process could there be but the World Trade Center . . . ? And what other means of defeating it . . . than have it be literally obliterated on camera?"

19. See Lincoln, *Holy Terrors*, 16.

20. Lincoln, *Holy Terrors*, 75.

21. Retort, *Afflicted Powers*, 152.

22. See Scott Gates and Sukanya Podder, "Social Media, Recruitment, Allegiance and the Islamic State," *Perspectives on Terrorism* 9, no. 4 (2015): 107–16.

NOTES TO PAGES 192–196   251

23. See Adam Taylor, "From Daniel Pearl to James Foley: The Modern Tactic of Islamist Beheadings," *Washington Post*, August 21, 2014, https://www.chicagotribune.com/nation-world/chi-foley-pearl-islamist-beheadings-20140821-story.html.

24. Joan Donovan and Brian Friedberg, "What Mark Zuckerberg Doesn't Get: Facebook Is Amplifying Hate by Letting Conspiracy Theorists Sell Their Wares," *New York Daily News*, July 20, 2018, https://www.nydailynews.com/opinion/ny-oped-what-mark-zuckerberg-doesnt-get-20180720-story.html#. See also Peter W. Singer and Emerson T. Brooking, *Like War: The Weaponization of Social Media* (New York: Houghton Mifflin Harcourt, 2018); Burris, Smith, and Strahm, "White Supremacist Networks."

25. Joan Donovan, "In Tech Platforms, White Supremacists Found Their Amplfier," *Atlantic*, March 2019, https://www.theatlantic.com/ideas/archive/2019/03/extremists-understand-what-tech-platforms-have-built/585136/.

26. "Ex-White Supremacist: 24-Hour Hate Buffet on Internet," 2019, https://www.cnn.com/videos/us/2019/03/16/former-white-supremacist-24-hour-hate-buffet-on-internet-picciolini-cpt-sot-vpx.cnn.

27. See Burris, Smith, and Strahm, "White Supremacist Networks."

28. Donovan, "In Tech Platforms."

29. Billy Perrigo, "The New Zealand Attack Exposed How White Supremacy Has Long Flourished Online," *Time*, March 20, 2019, http://time.com/5554783/white-supremacy-online-christchurch/.

30. Alex Hern, "Facebook and YouTube Defend Response to Christchurch Videos," *Guardian*, March 19, 2019, https://www.theguardian.com/world/2019/mar/19/facebook-and-youtube-defend-response-to-christchurch-videos.

31. Simon Harris, "The Great Replacement: The Manifesto of Brenton Tarrant," *European Freedom*, March 16, 2019, https://www.europeanfreedom.com/2019/03/16/the-great-replacement-the-manifesto-of-brenton-tarrant-the-new-zealand-mosque-shooter/. See "Jacinda Anderson's Office Received Manifesto from Christchurch Shooter Minutes Before Attack," ABCNews, March 17, 2019, https://www.abc.net.au/news/2019-03-17/jacinda-ardern-christchurch-shooter-manifesto-email/10909874.

32. As *Time* magazine reported in 2019, "The Trump campaign flirted with that constituency, retweeting white supremacist accounts and echoing their talking points as campaign promises, like banning Muslims from the U.S. and building a wall on the border with Mexico. Those policies . . . received a crucial boost from its prowess in online amplification" (Perrigo, "New Zealand Attack").

33. Singer, quoted in Perrigo, "New Zealand Attack." See Singer and Brooking, *Like War*.

34. Debord, *Comments*, 12. See also Guy Debord, *The Society of the Spectacle* (New York: Zone Books, 1994), 24; Juergensmeyer, *Terror in the Mind*, 149–81; Retort, *Afflicted Powers*, 27.

35. DeLillo, *Underworld*, 17.

36. On Atomwaffen and other extreme far-right groups, see "Documenting Hate: The New American Nazis," *Frontline*, PBS, November 20, 2018, https://www.pbs.org/wgbh/frontline/film/documenting-hate-new-american-nazis/.

37. Michel Foucault, *Security, Territory, Population: Lectures at the College de France, 1977–1978* (London: Picador, 2009), 275.

38. Jütte, *Age of Secrecy*, 19.

39. Barbour, *Derrida's Secret*, 261–62: "[T]he leviathan, as part of its absolute public authority, has the right . . . to keep secrets, both from external enemies and from internal subjects. . . . Only the sovereign right to secrecy ensures that its political power transcends non-political interests."

40. Carl Schmitt, *Political Theology: Four Chapters on the Concept of Sovereignty* (Chicago: University of Chicago Press, 2006), 36. See also Giorgio Agamben, *The Omnibus Homo Sacer* (Stanford, CA: Stanford University Press, 2017), 374; Robert Yelle, *Sovereignty and the Sacred: Secularism and the Political Economy of the Sacred* (Chicago: University of Chicago Press, 2018), 1–2.

41. See Giorgio Agamben, *State of Exception* (Chicago: University of Chicago Press, 2005); Barbour, *Derrida's Secret*, 10: "[I]n the wake of 11 September 2001, and with the justification of a potentially endless war on terror, [the US] exists in a permanent, if also undeclared, state of emergency. Or more precisely, the executive branch of the American government can choose, more or less at its whim, to operate as if it were in a state of emergency and thus suspend or break the law in the name of preserving or protecting it."

42. Zuboff, *Surveillance Capitalism*, 115.

43. David Lyon, *Surveillance after September 11* (London: Polity, 2003), 15.

44. James Bamford, "The Agency That Could Be Big Brother," *New York Times*, December 25, 2005, https://www.nytimes.com/2005/12/25/weekinreview/the-agency-that-could-be-big-brother.html.

45. David Cole, "Preserving Privacy: in a Digital Age: Lessons of Comparative Constitutionalism," in *Surveillance, Counter-Terrorism and Comparative Constitutionalism*, ed. Fergal Davis, Nicola McGarrity, and George Williams (London: Routledge, 2014), 115.

46. Bamford, "Agency." See Daniel Solove, "'I've Got Nothing to Hide' and Other Misunderstandings of Privacy," GW Law Scholarly Commons, 2007, https://scholarship.law.gwu.edu/cgi/viewcontent.cgi?referer=https://en.wikipedia.org/&httpsredir=1&article=1159&context=faculty_publications: "When the program came to light, a public outcry erupted, and the U.S. Senate subsequently voted to deny the program funding, ultimately leading to its demise. Nevertheless, many components of TIA continue on in various government agencies, though in a less systematic and more clandestine fashion."

47. Shane Harris, "Giving in to the Surveillance State," *New York Times*, August 22, 2012, https://www.nytimes.com/2012/08/23/opinion/whos-watching-the-nsa-watchers.html. See also Mark Williams Pontin, "The Total Information Awareness Project Lives On," *MIT Technology Review*, April 26, 2006, https://www.technologyreview.com/s/405707/the-total-information-awareness-project-lives-on/.

48. Trey Parker, "Let Go, Let Gov," *South Park*, season 17, episode 1, Comedy Central, 2013. See Matt Potolsky, "Beyond Fiction: The NSA and Representation," paper presented at the conference "The Politics and Practices of Secrecy," King's College, London, May 15, 2015.

49. Potolsky, "Beyond Fiction." See also Potolsky, *National Security Sublime*, 128–30.

50. Simon Chesterman, *One Nation Under Surveillance: A New Social Contract to Defend Freedom without Sacrificing Liberty* (New York: Oxford University Press, 2013), 259. See also Potolsky, *National Security Sublime*.

NOTES TO PAGES 200–204   253

51. Lyon, *Surveillance Society*, 143–44.

52. Cole, "Preserving Privacy," 96.

53. Lyon, *Surveillance Society*, 147.

54. Lyon, *Surveillance Society*, 146.

55. Zuboff, *Surveillance Capitalism*, 8.

56. Zuboff, *Surveillance Capitalism*, 116.

57. Yasha Levine, *Surveillance Valley: The Secret Military History of the Internet* (New York: PublicAffairs, 2018), 5.

58. See ACLU, "Fact Sheet: NYPD Mosque Surveillance Program," 2019, https://www.aclu.org/other/factsheet-nypd-muslim-surveillance-program.

59. Tahseen Shams, "Visibility as Resistance by Muslim Americans in a Surveillance and Security Atmosphere," *Sociological Forum* 33, no. 1 (2018): 73–94. See also Anny Bakalian and Mehdi Bozorgmehr, *Backlash 9/11: Middle Eastern and Muslim Immigrants Respond* (Berkeley: University of California Press, 2009); Erik Love, *Islamophobia and Racism in America* (New York: New York University Press, 2017).

60. Igo, *Known Citizen*.

61. Carol Warren and Barbara Laslett, "Privacy and Secrecy: A Conceptual Comparison," *Journal of Social Issues* 33, no. 3 (1977): 43–51. For a similar distinction, see also Chilson, *Secrecy's Power*, 7–8; Scarry, "Resolving to Resist"; Kenneth L. Karst, "Right of Privacy," in *Encyclopedia of the American Constitution* (New York: Macmillan, 1990), 1577–81.

62. Judith Rauhofer, "Privacy is Dead, Get Over it! Information Privacy and the Dream of a Risk Free Soceity," *Information and Communications Technology and Law* 17, no. 3 (2008): 185–97, https://www.tandfonline.com/doi/abs/10.1080/1360083 0802472990.

63. Igo, *Known Citizen*, 350.

64. See Igo, *Known Citizen*, 350–51; Emily Dreyfus, "Privacy isn't Dead: Its More Popular than Ever," *Wired*, July 27, 2017.

65. Foucault, *History of Sexuality*, 1:101.

66. Cole, "Preserving Privacy," 97.

67. For a thorough analysis of the PATRIOT Act and its implications, see David Cole, *Terrorism and the Constitution: Sacrificing Civil Liberties in the Name of National Security* (New York: New Press, 2006), 195–218. On the sneak-and-peak searches, see Susan Jo Keller, "Judge Rules Provisions in Patriot Act to Be Illegal," *New York Times*, September 27, 2007, https://www.nytimes.com/2007/09/27/washington/27patriot .html.

68. Scarry, "Resolving to Resist."

69. The NSA's warrantless wiretapping was first revealed in the media in 2005; see James Risen and Eric Lichtblau, "Bush Lets U.S. Spy on Callers without Warrant," *New York Times*, December 16, 2005, https://www.nytimes.com/2005/12/16 /politics/bush-lets-us-spy-on-callers-without-courts.html.

70. Glenn Greenwald, *No Place to Hide: Edward Snowden, the NSA, and the U.S. Surveillance State* (London: Picador, 2015), 90. "Snowden's files indisputably laid bare a complex web of surveillance aimed at Americans (who are explicitly beyond the NSA's mission) and non-Americans alike. The archive revealed the technical means used to intercept communications: the NSA's tapping of Internet servers, satellite, underwater fiber optic cables, local and foreign telephone systems, and personal computers" (ibid., 92).

71. See Cole, Fabbrini, and Vedaschi, *Surveillance*; Zuboff, *Surveillance Capitalism*; Lyon, *Surveillance Society*.

72. Lincoln, "Theses on Method."

73. As David Cole aptly concludes, "If the right to privacy is to survive the challenge of the all-seeing technological eye, it will be because citizens, enraged by stories of abusive and overly intrusive monitoring of their own activities, insist on it" ("Preserving Privacy," 115).

Index

adornment, 11, 19, 23–26, 35, 38–41, 122, 125, 165, 167, 175, 177–79, 183, 188, 222n

advertisement, 19–20, 39, 51–77, 88, 102, 105, 165, 167, 175–77, 183, 188, 192

alchemy, 28, 39, 46, 84–85, 90

Allah, 104, 107, 111, 115–16, 119–20, 125, 130–31

al-Qaeda, 13, 137, 191–92

alt-right, 21, 139, 160–63, 243n, 244n

androgyne, 46

Antichrist, 173–74

anti-Semitism, 140–55, 241n

Aryan Nations, 137–38, 140, 146, 152–53, 242n

Aryan race, 28, 113, 137–38, 153–54, 157–58

authority, 2, 4, 8, 10, 12–13, 16, 47, 53, 105, 189–90, 214n, 250n; religious, 4, 53, 189, 214n

Bannon, Stephen K. 161–62

Bataille, Georges, 17, 79, 81, 84, 100–102, 229n, 234n

Baudelaire, Charles, 85, 96–98

Blake, William, vii, 96–98, 233n

Blavatasky, Helena Petrovna, 20, 51–77, 107, 158, 224n, 227n, 246n

bodies, 17, 73–76, 129–30, 217n, 222n, 228n. *See also* chakras; esoteric anatomy

Bok, Sisella, 1

Bourdieu, Pierre, 10–11, 15, 22, 26, 34, 44, 178, 187, 205, 214n

Brand Nubian, 124, 127, 131–32

Breivik, Anders, 163

Breton, André, 81, 84

Brotherhood of Luxor, 58

Brüder Schweigen, 14, 21, 137–63, 195, 240n

Buddhism, 53, 58–59, 62–63, 71, 172, 184, 188, 225n

Canetti, Elias, 13, 137–38, 190, 204

capital, 11, 37, 105–6, 117–21, 134, 175, 178; black market, 105, 117–21, 128, 235n; symbolic, 11–12, 17, 37–38, 67, 105–6, 117–21, 175, 178–79, 235n

capitalism, 6, 21, 49–50, 66, 105, 135–37, 195, 200. *See also* surveillance capitalism

Carbonari, 6, 137

Catholic Church, 2–3, 13, 188, 191

Central Intelligence Agency (CIA), 7, 22, 200–202

chakras, 17, 73–76, 228n

Christian Identity, 137, 157

Christianity, 3, 25, 32, 62, 90, 94, 96–97, 129, 152–53, 157–58, 161, 173

Church of Scientology, vii, 4, 13, 21–22, 50, 165–85, 248n, 249n

Civil War, 23–25, 27, 29, 39, 140

Clarence 13X, 104–5, 114–20, 135

clothing, 38–39, 49

Cold War, vii, 1, 7, 166, 190, 199, 204

colonialism, 15, 18

comparison, 4, 18–19, 184, 189, 216–17n; as method, 18–19, 216–17n

counterespionage, 17–18
Crowley, Aleister, 71, 80, 168, 174, 229n, 245n

Debord, Guy, 1–2, 195, 250n
Derrida, Jacques, 9–10, 135
Dianetics, 169–70
disenchantment, 5–6, 66, 187, myth of, 5
Doniger, Wendy, 19, 207, 216–17n
double-coding, 17, 19, 117–22, 126, 128, 135

Eco, Umberto, 15, 120
economy of secrets, 5–6, 12, 20, 52, 135–36, 191, 215n
Eliade, Mircea, 16, 18, 155, 184, 189
eroticism, 17, 20–21, 79–80, 82, 100–102, 229n, 234n
esoteric anatomy, 17, 73–76, 228n
esotericism, 3–5, 8–9, 24–25, 38–42, 53–54, 62, 64, 70, 82, 85–86, 101–2, 106, 110, 118–19, 123, 126, 166, 178, 183, 213n, 224n; material, 25, 38–42, 126, 178
Esoteric Section, 20, 53, 69–76, 226n, 227n
espionage, 21, 166, 184
Evola, Julius, 83–84, 91, 95, 158, 161–62, 229n

Facebook, 7, 22, 193–94, 199–201
Fard, Wallace D., 110–12, 115, 118, 129
Federal Bureau of Investigation (FBI), 114–15, 117, 145, 156, 159–60, 166, 203, 239n
femininity, 30–31, 47, 82, 85, 90–95, 130–33, 142, 219n, 232n
feminism, 92–93, 98; Satanic, 98
Fishman, Steven, 171–75, 180
Five Percenters, 21, 50, 103–35, 238n
Foucault, Michel, 10, 16, 80, 195, 198, 203, 229n
fraternal orders, 6, 23–25, 28–31, 49–50, 108, 184, 218n, 219n
Freemasonry, 6, 14, 19–20, 23–50, 52, 67, 104, 106–12, 114, 118, 120, 122, 126, 128, 130–31, 135, 139, 147, 155, 158, 177, 183–84, 198, 217n

genealogy, 4, 8, 202, 211n, 234n
Gnosticism, 4, 6, 8, 28–29, 39, 52, 85–87, 104, 113, 118, 135, 158
Google, 22, 193, 199–201

Hermetic Brotherhood of Luxor, 87
Hermeticism, 8, 15, 53, 63, 158
Hermetic Order of the Golden Dawn, 4, 9, 20, 50, 53, 70–71, 135, 183, 227n
hidden transcript, 105
hierarchy, 17, 19, 37, 39, 42–48, 89, 131, 150, 159, 221n, 222n, 225n
Hinduism, 53, 57, 62–63, 71–73, 102, 141, 184, 228n
hip-hop, 22, 103–6, 118, 121–35, 238n
history of religions, 3–4; 15, 22, 184, 190, 205; defined, 4, 190
Hubbard, L. Ron, 166–74, 245n, 246n
Huysmans, J. K., 85, 96–97

initiation, 15, 17, 35–36, 39, 42–43, 47, 65, 89, 98, 106, 109, 111–12, 138, 145–46, 153–55, 221n, 242n
Inner Group, 53, 70–72, 74
inscription of the body, 17, 74–75
intellectual property, 179–80, 183, 189, 215n
ISIS/ISIL, 13, 137, 192, 195
Isis Unveiled, 53, 61–64, 76
Islam, 21, 32, 62, 104, 107–8, 114, 119, 127, 131, 137–38, 161, 191–94, 201–2, 205, 251n
Islamophobia, 194, 202, 205

Jesus Christ, 173–74
jewelry, 17, 20, 38–42, 50, 122–23, 177–78. *See also* adornment; regalia
Judaism, 94, 146, 153–54, 160, 183, 188, 241n

Kabbalah, 23, 28–29, 46–47, 51, 53, 64–65, 71, 79–80, 86, 118, 184
Koot Hoomi, 58, 60–61
Ku Klux Klan, 14, 27–28, 33, 137, 139, 146, 153, 157, 159–60, 162–63, 220–21n, 240n

INDEX 257

Lane, David, 14, 153, 157–60
Lévi, Éliphas, 29, 36–37, 52, 59, 84–85, 214n
Lincoln, Bruce, 4, 18–19, 42–44, 190, 205, 207, 211n, 214n, 250n
litigation of the secret, 21, 165, 179–80, 183, 188
Lucifer, 85, 172–73, 246n

Macaba, 137, 149–51
Magia Sexualis, 82, 88, 102
magic, 6, 20, 54, 68, 74, 80, 83–84, 93, 102, 106, 168, 174, 224n, 245n
Malcolm X, 104, 114
masculinity, 14, 21, 25, 30, 47, 130–33, 139, 142, 153–54, 158, 160, 219n, 222n
Masters, 53, 58–61, 67, 71–72, 158, 225n, 227n
material esotericism, 25, 38–42, 178
Mathews, Robert Jay, 138, 148–57, 242n
Mauss, Marcel, 137, 193
meritocracy, 31–34
modernity, 5–6
Moorish Science Temple, 104, 106–11, 114
Mormonism, 52, 184
Morya, 58, 60
Muhammad, Elijah, 111–12, 114, 116, 126, 129, 238n
mysticism, 3–4, 8–9, 34–35, 51, 82, 102, 104, 213n, 214n

Naglowska, Maria de, 20–21, 79–102, 230n
National Alliance, 138–43, 152–53, 161
National Security Agency (NSA), 2, 7, 22, 198–204, 253n
Nation of Gods and Earths, 104, 110, 114–18, 125, 130–33. *See also* Five Percenters
Nation of Islam, 4, 21, 50, 104, 111–18, 123–24, 129, 135
Nazism, 138, 141, 146, 153, 158, 161–62, 241n; occult, 141, 158
neo-Nazis, 137, 140–42, 160, 162–63
New Age, 77, 98, 101

9/11, 1–2, 7, 13–14, 137–38, 148, 195–97, 200, 202–4, 252n
Noble Drew Ali, 106–10, 236n
Norse paganism, 14, 152–53, 157–60

Obama, Barack, 139
obscurity, 17, 34
occult *habitus*, 53, 69, 76
occultism, 4–6, 8–9, 52–54, 63–64, 66, 72–73, 80, 84, 168–69, 174, 214n, 224n
occult marketplace, 6, 52–53, 76, 105
occult physiology, 73–76
occult rhetoric, 53, 61, 63, 76–77
Odinism, 14, 153–54, 157–58
Olcott, Henry Steel, 52, 56–57, 60, 62
Operating Thetan (OT), 165–67, 169–83, 246n, 247n
Order, the, 138, 145–48, 153–57. See also *Brüder Schweigen*
Ordo Templi Orientis (OTO), 4, 87, 168
Orientalism, 5, 53–55, 57–58, 61, 66, 71, 77, 224n
Orwell, George, 2, 197, 199
Otto, Rudolph, 3

Pierce, William Luther, 140–48, 152, 241–42n
Pike, Albert, 20, 23–50, 59, 158–59, 218n; racial views of, 27–28, 33, 48, 218–19n. *See also* Scottish Rite
power, 2–3, 10, 12–13, 15–16, 22, 66–69, 74, 80, 82, 102, 105, 130, 133–35, 137–40, 175–77, 182, 187–88, 190, 193, 195, 200, 203, 214n, 247n; and secrecy, 13, 15, 36, 42, 55–56, 66–69, 82, 102, 105, 133–35, 137–40, 175–77, 187–88, 190, 195, 203, 247n; symbolic, 10, 34, 36, 42, 44, 67, 79, 139, 214n, 221n
power/knowledge, 10, 16, 187–88, 197–98
Prince Hall Freemasonry, 33, 50, 108, 114, 220n
privacy, 2, 7–8, 22, 201–5, 213n, 253n, 254n; definitions of, 202, 253n
Protestantism, 25, 29–30
Public Enemy, 124, 129, 136

258　INDEX

racism, 14, 21, 26–28, 30, 33, 48, 50, 104–5, 111–14, 129–30, 135–36, 142–48, 154–63, 193–94, 218–19n, 220n. *See also* Trump, Donald J.
Randolph, Paschal Beverly, 86–88, 231n
regalia, 20, 24, 26, 32, 38–42, 44–45, 49–50, 122
religion, 2–3, 6, 12, 22, 127, 150, 165, 167, 169, 179, 184, 189–90, 196, 201–5, 209n, 211n, 214n, 234n; critical study of, 22, 167, 184–85, 190, 205; definitions of, 3, 211n; and secrecy, 3–4, 6, 12, 16, 165, 167, 179, 184, 189–90, 196, 201–5, 209n
resistance, 10, 13, 19–21, 103–35, 165, 188, 203
Road Back, The, 148–51
Rosicrucian Fraternity, 9, 59, 158
RZA, 103–4, 123, 125, 128, 130

sacred, 1, 15, 23, 51
Satan, 82–85, 95–96, 100, 232n, 233n
Satanism, 20, 82–85, 95, 102
Schmitt, Carl, 187, 196–97
Scott, James, C., 103, 105
Scottish Rite, 19–20, 23–24, 28, 31–32, 43–50, 122, 158–59, 177, 217n, 221n
secrecy, vii, 1–22, 23–26, 34–38, 51–77, 79–80, 82, 89–91, 97, 101, 105, 107–8, 116–21, 128–30, 133–35, 137–40, 143, 145–47, 149–50, 154–55, 159–60, 165–67, 173, 175–85, 187–205, 226n, 229n, 244n; as adornment, 11, 23–26, 35, 38–41, 165, 167, 175, 177–79, 188; "age of," 5, 8, 211n, 252n; definitions of, 8–14; economy of, 6; etymology of, 9; methods of study, 3–4, 14–16, 166–67, 174–75, 191, 205, 244n; and power, 13, 66, 68, 82, 102, 133–35, 137, 140, 147, 165, 175–76, 187–88, 195, 205, 214n, 215n, 252n; and religion, 3–4, 6, 12, 16, 165, 167, 175, 184, 187–95, 201–5, 209n; and resistance, 10, 13, 19, 21, 105–35, 165, 203; as strategy, 10, 16–19, 128–29, 137, 143, 149–50, 160, 167, 175, 183–84, 189; theorizing, 8–14, 17–18; as vestment, 11–12, 22
secrecy-industrial complex, 7
Secret Doctrine, 20, 53, 63–66, 761, 07

secretism, 11, 52–54, 58, 61, 63, 77
secret societies, 5–6, 17, 21, 27–28, 139, 159, 188, 211n, 212n, 231n
secret war, 155–57
security, 2, 166, 190, 212n
seduction, 79, 82, 89, 102, 188, 192
sexual abuse, 2, 13, 16, 188, 191
sexuality, 20–21, 79–80, 82, 84, 86, 91, 100–102, 217n, 229n, 231n, 232n; as *the* secret, 80, 86–87, 91, 229n, 231n
sexual magic, 20–21, 80, 83, 85–90, 97, 100–102, 168, 229n, 231n, 234n
silence, 9, 17, 19, 35, 51, 82, 103, 203, 216n; and power, 203
Simmel, Georg, 3, 9, 11, 23–24, 41, 49, 67, 105, 128–29, 139, 160, 165, 175, 222n
slavery, 27–28, 48, 104, 113, 218n
Smith, Jonathan Z., 15, 19
Snowden, Edward, 202, 204, 253n
Society for Psychical Research, 67–68
South Park, 181, 198–99
spectacle, 1–2, 191–95, 250n
Spencer, Richard, 161–63
Spiritualism, 5, 9, 52–57, 68, 86
state of exception, 7, 196–97, 200, 252n
Strauss, Leo, 17
subtle body, 73–76
Sufism, 118
Supreme Alphabet, 117–21, 125
Supreme Mathematics, 117–21, 124–25, 127–28, 132
Sun Tzu, 13
surveillance, 1–2, 7–8, 22, 145, 166, 190–91, 195–205
surveillance capitalism, 7, 196–97, 200
symbols, 35–37, 39–40, 49, 104, 110, 118–22, 128

Tantra, vii, 14, 53, 73, 80, 85, 102, 184, 188
Tarrant, Brenton Harrison, 163, 194
Templars, 28
terror, vii, 21, 137, 147, 188, 192
terrorism, 2, 13–14, 16, 21, 137–63, 165, 187–88, 190–94, 196–97, 199, 201–3, 239n, 240n, 250n, 252n
Theosophy, 5, 9, 14, 20, 50, 51–77, 104, 106–7, 113, 128, 135, 158, 172, 175, 183, 224n, 246n

INDEX 259

Thetan, 169–71, 176

Tibet, 54–55, 66, 224n

Total Information Awareness, 197–99, 252n

trade secrets, 179–80, 183

transparency, 5–8, 184, 187, 195, 203–4

Trump, Donald J., 2, 14, 21, 138–39, 161–63, 194, 251n. *See also* racism; white supremacy

Turner, Victor, 40

Turner Diaries, 138, 143–48, 152, 242n

USA PATRIOT Act, 203–4, 253n

Vedanta, 53, 73

Vedas, 23, 29

Weber, Max, 5–6

white power, 143, 155, 157

white supremacy, 14, 21, 113–14, 129–30, 137–63, 191–94, 201, 204, 240n, 251n. *See also* Trump, Donald J.

Wicca, 4, 92

Wikileaks, 7, 174

Wotansvolk, 157–61

Wu Tang Clan, 103–4, 123–24, 127, 130

Xenu, 166, 181–82

Yacob, 112–13

yoga, 17, 53, 73–76, 183, 189, 228n

YouTube, 181, 192, 194

Ingram Content Group UK Ltd.
Milton Keynes UK
UKHW020409090323
418268UK00005B/249